Integrating Excel and Access

Other Microsoft Windows resources from O'Reilly

Related titles

Excel Hacks™
Access Hacks™
Excel 2003 Programming: A Developer's Notebook™

Analyzing Business Data with Excel
Access Data Analysis Cookbook™

Windows Books Resource Center

windows.oreilly.com is a complete catalog of O'Reilly's Windows and Office books, including sample chapters and code examples.

oreillynet.com is the essential portal for developers interested in open and emerging technologies, including new platforms, programming languages, and operating systems.

Conferences

O'Reilly brings diverse innovators together to nurture the ideas that spark revolutionary industries. We specialize in documenting the latest tools and systems, translating the innovator's knowledge into useful skills for those in the trenches. Visit *conferences.oreilly.com* for our upcoming events.

Safari Bookshelf (*safari.oreilly.com*) is the premier online reference library for programmers and IT professionals. Conduct searches across more than 1,000 books. Subscribers can zero in on answers to time-critical questions in a matter of seconds. Read the books on your Bookshelf from cover to cover or simply flip to the page you need. Try it today with a free trial.

Integrating Excel and Access

Michael Schmalz

O'REILLY®

Beijing · Cambridge · Farnham · Köln · Paris · Sebastopol · Taipei · Tokyo

Integrating Excel and Access
by Michael Schmalz

Copyright © 2006 O'Reilly Media, Inc. All rights reserved.
Printed in the United States of America.

Published by O'Reilly Media, Inc., 1005 Gravenstein Highway North, Sebastopol, CA 95472.

O'Reilly books may be purchased for educational, business, or sales promotional use. Online editions are also available for most titles (*safari.oreilly.com*). For more information, contact our corporate/institutional sales department: (800) 998-9938 or *corporate@oreilly.com*.

Editor:	Simon St.Laurent
Production Editor:	Reba Libby
Cover Designer:	Karen Montgomery
Interior Designer:	David Futato

Printing History:

October 2005:   First Edition.

 This book uses RepKover™, a durable and flexible lay-flat binding.

ISBN: 0-596-00973-9
[M]   [7/06]

Table of Contents

Preface

The Microsoft Office Suite is, in my opinion, the most useful set of applications in a corporate setting. Besides being easy to use and practically perfecting the "What-You-See-Is-What-You-Get" (WYSIWYG) display, the applications in Microsoft Office can work together to share information, produce reports, etc. The problem is that while there are many references available to help users develop their skills in any of the applications, there are few references available to show how to use the applications together. I did quite a bit of integration work as both a consultant and employee at various companies, and I quickly found those skills in demand in many departments—from Human Resources to Operations to Finance. As people asked me to do things that I had never done before and I figured out how to do them, I began building a base of code and knowledge that I could use to solve problems. I kept thinking, "I wish there were a book that could show me how to…" and then, when I had figured out how to do those things, I thought, "I could write that book."

Based on my experience, Microsoft Access and Microsoft Excel allow for the most benefit from integration, so this book focuses mainly on these applications. In addition to Access and Excel, I have included a chapter on SQL Server and a chapter on integrating with other Microsoft Office applications. In each topic, I show how integrating features in different applications can solve problems. Although the examples use rather generic data, you will be able to apply the same concepts to your own data.

The difficulty in writing a book like this lies in tailoring the skill level to fit a wide audience. For example, many of the Excel GUI features might seem very basic to some readers, while they are new to others. In addition, some readers might be very comfortable with Visual Basic for Applications (VBA), and others may have anywhere from no experience with VBA to experience only using the macro recorder. As much as possible, I have tried to build from the basics to the complex when covering each topic. I hope that you will be neither bored nor overwhelmed as you go through the topics.

Who Should Read This Book

Integrating Excel and Access will be useful to people who use Microsoft Office to handle data. This book will show you how Access and Excel can work together to improve your reporting and data analysis. Along the way, it will also introduce many programming topics that will help you sharpen your skills in VBA. While you do not need to be a programming expert, this book assumes that you have basic knowledge of Excel and that you are somewhat familiar with Excel macros. Any experience with Access will be helpful; however, you do not need that experience to learn from this book. Excel power-users will find ways that Microsoft Access can be used to increase the power of their applications. Also, you may find that something that you were doing in Excel is better done in Access, or vice versa.

After reading this book, you will understand how to do the following:

- Utilize the built-in features of Access and Excel to access data
- Use VBA within Access or Excel to access data
- Build connection strings using ADO and DAO
- Access data in a corporate data warehouse, such as SQL Server
- Automate Excel reports, including formatting, functions, and page setup
- Write complex functions with VBA
- Write simple and advanced queries with the Access GUI
- Write queries with VBA
- Produce pivot tables and pivot charts with your data
- Use your data in other Office applications

After these topics have been introduced, the book ends with a project that walks you through the steps to solve a business problem. After practicing the skills this book illustrates, you will have the necessary knowledge to tackle some of your most demanding reporting issues.

The book is organized to build on topics in a logical sequence. However, if you are trying to solve a specific issue, such as writing formulas in VBA, you can skip to the appropriate section. In addition, the code examples in the book illustrate each of the topics where VBA is used. All of the screenshots are produced from MS Office 2003, so your screen may look different, depending on which operating system you use, but most of the topics can be used in Office 97, 2000, and XP as well.

If you are interested in stretching your skills in the individual applications, I suggest reading *Access Hacks* and *Excel Hacks*, also from O'Reilly. Both books give great examples of how to use the applications to tackle problems.

What's in This Book

This book consists of 12 chapters. Chapters start with the basics and move to more complex topics. Here is a summary of the chapters:

Chapter 1, *Introduction to Access/Excel Integration*
  Introduces the general topics in the book and explains some of the thought process that goes into integrating the applications.

Chapter 2, *Using the Excel User Interface*
  Covers the tasks that you can complete using only the Excel GUI, as well as discussing some VBA topics.

Chapter 3, *Data Access from Excel VBA*
  Covers using ADO and DAO along with VBA to pull data into Excel.

Chapter 4, *Integration from the Access Interface*
  Covers both using Excel data in Access and exporting Access data into Excel from features in the Access GUI.

Chapter 5, *Using Access VBA to Automate Excel*
  Covers controlling Excel from Access and pushing data into Excel. Automation examples of many Excel formatting and formula topics are given.

Chapter 6, *Using Excel Charts and Pivot Tables with Access Data*
  Covers building charts and pivot tables in Excel using data that originates in Access.

Chapter 7, *Leveraging SQL Server Data with Microsoft Office*
  Covers using SQL Server Data, as well as using DTS and ActiveX scripts to automate Office applications from SQL Server.

Chapter 8, *Advanced Excel Reporting Techniques*
  Covers using VBA from Access to automate reporting in Excel.

Chapter 9, *Using Access and Excel Data in Other Applications*
  Covers data integration and automation from Access and/or Excel in Word, PowerPoint, and MapPoint.

Chapter 10, *Creating Form Functionality in Excel*
  Covers how to build forms in Excel similar to those in Access.

Chapter 11, *Building Graphical User Interfaces*
  Covers some basic topics to help you build a functional GUI in Access.

Chapter 12, *Tackling an Integration Project*
  Covers a project, complete with source code, that requires integration of Access and Excel.

This book covers hundreds of tasks you'll need to do at one point or another with Office. If you feel something important has been left out that should be included, let us know. We'll work to get it in a future edition. For contact information, see the We'd Like Your Feedback! section later in the Preface.

Conventions in This Book

The following typographical conventions are used in this book:

Italic

> Introduces new terms and indicates URLs, commands, file extensions, filenames, directory or folder names, and UNC pathnames.

`Constant width`

> Indicates command-line elements, computer output, code examples, methods, variables, functions, properties, objects, events, statements, procedures, values, loops, and formulas formatted as equations.

`Constant width italic`

> Indicates placeholders (for which you substitute an actual name) in examples and in registry keys.

`Constant width bold`

> Indicates user input.

 Indicates a tip, suggestion, or general note. For example, we'll tell you whether you need to use a particular software version or whether an operation requires certain privileges.

References in VBA

There are many places in the book where VBA uses specific objects that may not be loaded by default. These include ADO, ADOX, DAO, Excel, Word, PowerPoint, and MapPoint. When you see these objects in the VBA code, check in Tools → References while you are in the module to ensure that you have the objects referenced, keeping in mind that you may have more than one version available.

We'd Like Your Feedback!

The information in this book has been tested and verified to the best of our ability, but mistakes and oversights do occur. Please let us know about errors you may find, as well as your suggestions for future editions, by writing to:

> O'Reilly Media, Inc.
> 1005 Gravenstein Highway North
> Sebastopol, CA 95472
> 800-998-9938 (in the U.S. or Canada)
> 707-829-0515 (international or local)
> 707-829-0104 (fax)

You also can send us messages using email. To be put on our mailing list or to request a catalog, send email to:

info@oreilly.com

To ask technical questions or comment on the book, send email to:

bookquestions@oreilly.com

For corrections and amplifications to this book, check out O'Reilly's online catalog at:

http://www.oreilly.com/catalog/integratingea/

Safari Enabled

 When you see a Safari® Enabled icon on the cover of your favorite technology book, it means the book is available online through the O'Reilly Network Safari Bookshelf.

Safari offers a solution that's better than e-books. It's a virtual library that lets you easily search thousands of top technology books, cut and paste code samples, download chapters, and find quick answers when you need the most accurate, current information. Try it for free at *http://safari.oreilly.com*.

Acknowledgments

I would like to thank O'Reilly for publishing this book. And, I'd also like to give a special thanks to Simon St.Laurent for all of his help, from the book concept to signing and then through the editing process. In addition, Ken Bluttman and Geoff Andrikanich were both very helpful in their technical review of the book.

This book would not have happened without the understanding of my wife and daughter throughout the writing process.

Finally, I'd like to thank all of my prior clients and employers who gave me the projects that forced me to stretch and develop my programming skills.

CHAPTER 1

Introduction to Access/Excel Integration

Most business users understand Excel; its power and practically universal acceptance make it a key application to learn. While Excel is a powerful tool on its own, you can do a lot more with it when you add the power of a relational database. Whether you store your data in a simple Access database or link an Access database to your corporate data warehouse, you'll be able to do a lot of things more easily. A simple query combined with an Excel workbook can supply many of the benefits of expensive reporting packages using the tools you already have on your desktop.

Consider the following scenario. Your company stores sales information in a database, and each sales record carries an identifier that tells who sold the item. You also have a table of salespeople that tells what region they are in and who supervises them. Senior management wants to find out how each salesperson, sales manager, and region performs on a daily basis. Since they want to see the reports so frequently, it will be necessary to automate these reports as much as possible. This book will show you how to gather the information and build the reports, charts, and supporting details that are necessary to meet these business objectives.

If you consider the other uses of corporate data, you will begin to understand how useful these skills can be. Here is a short list of fairly common uses of data:

- Producing a monthly commission schedule
- Reporting sales by product, region, sales manager, or salesperson
- Doing financial reporting
- Producing invoices
- Performing analysis of data (average profit per sale, sales by month, etc.)
- Producing trend information to aid corporate planning
- Populating financial models and storing results
- Graphing financial and sales information

Building systems that can simplify and automate these tasks can make complex projects much simpler. Fortunately, you likely already have the tools you need to do this on your computer and just need to assemble the parts correctly.

Communications Between Excel and Access

There are several ways to exchange data between Access and Excel. Automation (formerly called OLE Automation) is a method of communication that gives you access to another application's objects. Using Automation, you can actually take control of the other application and send and retrieve data, set properties, run methods, and perform many other tasks. This book will explore in depth how automation can be used to allow integration between Access and Excel.

 One of the original ways to communicate between Windows programs was dynamic data exchange (DDE). While this can be useful, I do not recommend it between Office applications. It is sometimes necessary when you are communicating with a program that does not have a very useful object model. However, the object models for all of the programs in the Office suite allow you so much flexibility that I cannot imagine a situation when DDE would be preferable to Automation with VBA.

The other methods of communication treat Access or Excel simply as a data source and allow query access. This is accomplished through ActiveX Data Objects (ADO) or Data Access Objects (DAO). In addition to these programming methods, both Access and Excel offer data access methods from the standard user interface that work well for simple tasks.

Automation Objects

If you are new to programming, the mention of objects might not make sense. Objects are programming items that make your life much easier. As an example, one of the main Excel objects is the Worksheet. The Worksheet object is a container for many other objects, such as cells, pivot tables, and charts. By using the Excel object model, you can perform many tasks with one line of code that would have taken hours if there were not another method available. Let's assume that you want to press a button on an Excel worksheet to print it. The following code prints the worksheet when you press the CommandButton1 button:

```
Private Sub CommandButton1_Click( )
Dim xlws as Worksheet
Set xlws = ActiveSheet
xlws.PrintOut
Set xlws = nothing
End Sub
```

In this very short procedure, you declare a variable that is an Excel Worksheet (if you were automating Excel from another application, you would declare this as Excel. Worksheet and declare another variable as Excel.Application, but while in Excel this step is not needed). Next, you set this variable equal to the active worksheet—ActiveSheet represents the current worksheet in the active workbook. Once there is a reference to the active worksheet, you can call any of the methods that are part of the object. In this example, you call the PrintOut method of the worksheet. There are several objects in Excel that have a PrintOut method; in each case, it simply prints the object. The final step sets the xlws variable to nothing, which tells Excel to no longer store a reference to the object. The xlws variable in this procedure still exists, even though you are no longer using it—if you were in a procedure that used several worksheets, you could set xlws to nothing and reuse that variable with any other worksheet.

 This code may still look complicated, but if you did any programming in MS-DOS where you had to understand how each printer worked and how to send commands to it, you would see how simple this is by comparison.

In future chapters, you will see how to set a reference to each application and how the object model of each can be used to accomplish even the most demanding tasks. You can also get context-sensitive help while working with the VBA project, and when you are not sure how to tackle an Excel task with VBA but know how to do it with the user interface, you can always record a macro and then review the code. Please see Appendix A for a review of the most commonly used objects and their usage in Excel and Access.

ADO and DAO

As stated earlier, ADO and DAO are the two primary methods of data access. For the purposes of connecting to a data source and simply extracting data, the two may be used interchangeably. According to Microsoft, DAO was designed specifically for the Microsoft Jet database at the heart of Access, but it is still able to access other databases while taking a performance hit. There are also some differences in features when it comes to making changes to a data source (adding tables, fields, etc.) and performing more complex query functions, such as data shaping, turning the query result into XML, and using cursors. I generally use DAO when dealing with Access (Jet) databases and ADO when dealing with SQL Server or other databases.

If you have done any work in Microsoft Access, you are probably familiar with queries. When you build a query in the design mode in Access, you are really making a graphical representation of the SQL. To see how this works, you can change the query view in Access to SQL View and see what this looks like.

When you use ADO and DAO, you can reference queries and tables and simply open them. Eventually you will need to modify queries or write them from scratch. In those cases, you can get a head start by designing the query graphically in Access, changing the view to SQL view, and copying the text to your VBA project. You can then make any changes that you need to.

While you can simply copy the text of a query and use it in your code, you can also write SQL on the fly within VBA. This is useful when you want to give users the option to bring in certain fields from the database, change the field used to sort, modify the sort order, etc. Also, there are times when you want to place criteria for a query directly in the query instead of using parameters.

In both ADO and DAO, the primary objects that you will work with are queries, recordsets, fields, and parameters. When using DAO, you also have an object called a QueryDef that performs specific tasks in the book. The QueryDef object references a query. When you assign a variable declared as a QueryDef object and refer to a query, you can perform certain tasks, such as changing the SQL of the query, setting the parameter values, and opening the recordset.

There are some specific differences between ADO and DAO regarding how you set up the connection to the data source. You will see examples of each method throughout this book. When making a decision about which one to use, I suggest deciding based on ease of use. For example, if I am working in an Access database and writing VBA code to modify data structure, I find it much easier to use the DAO object model to accomplish those tasks rather than using ActiveX Data Objects Extensions for DDL and Security (ADOX). With ActiveX data objects, there are different object models for data manipulation, data definition and security, and Remote Data Services (RDS) and multidimensional data (ADOMD). In addition, you can download software development kits (SDKs) from Microsoft that explain both object models. Visit *http://www.microsoft.com* and search for MDAC (the short name of Microsoft's data access software).

Tackling Projects

This is probably an appropriate time to discuss how to tackle a project that would benefit from integrating Access and Excel. If this discussion doesn't make sense at first, go through the first couple of chapters and come back to it.

The very first step that you need to take, prior to starting a project that integrates Access and Excel, is to determine whether you need the power of both applications. I wouldn't suggest using both applications if you can accomplish the same task with one application and few compromises. If you decide that you do need both applications, the following model should help you perform the initial planning.

The first step in the actual project is to determine which application will serve as the primary application for the user interface. Generally, this decision should be driven by end user needs and preferences. Although there are some exceptions to this, during your initial planning, assume that the program the users see should be the one that they are most comfortable with.

The second step is to determine what information you will need from your end user. It is important to note that in some cases a project will support multiple end users with different needs. A good example is an application that has one end user who wants to input sales data and another end user who wants to create reports based on that sales data. In this example, the two users will share the same data source but will need completely different user interfaces.

Once you have determined those items, your next step is to determine how you will communicate with the other application. Several factors influence this decision. First, the layout of the data makes some types of communication impossible or, at a minimum, silly to try. For example, an Excel spreadsheet with five data points on two worksheets in multiple rows and columns that are not contiguous would not be a candidate for using ADO or DAO, since they expect tabular structures. Likewise, if you need to pull 500 records from an Access database into an Excel sheet that mimics a database table, you probably want to let DAO or ADO do most of the work. This choice is also driven by how much control you need over the other application and the amount of processing that you need to perform on the data.

The next step is to determine whether there will be an end product and what it will look like. In a project about sales data, the end product for a salesperson might be an Access report used as an invoice for the customer. The end product for a sales analyst might be a report in Excel with a pivot table and pivot chart. In cases when there is no end "product," you would want to define what actions you want to accomplish. Examples include accumulating data, updating data, and transmitting data.

Once you reach conclusions about which application will be automating the other, what information you need, and how it will be communicated, you are ready to take the first steps in designing the user interface. This might seem premature, but it is a good idea to prepare a prototype to ensure that you capture the necessary information. This prototype will be a work in progress and may change during the writing of the code (if you are using VBA).

This user interface is probably going to be an Access form, an Excel user form, or an Excel worksheet with protection enabled to only allow data entry into specific cells. If you don't do this, you will end up writing your VBA project twice—the first time to make sure your code works, and the second time to change the references to your user interface. You can do this if it makes you more comfortable, but it will cost you some programming time. Another option is to write your procedures to accept parameters, allowing you to test the procedures and then call them with your user interface. This also makes it easier to reuse code where it makes sense to do so.

When you have thought through your user interface, your next step is to write the code. It is very helpful if you know what the results should be for a few simple data points so that you can effectively test the application. As you write the code for your first couple applications, keep an eye out for recurring items. For example, if you find yourself writing multiple lines of code to set up an Excel reference from Access, you can save that code somewhere and copy and paste it into applications as you need it. Another thing to keep in mind as you write code is to watch out for what might change in the future. For example, if you have some code that builds a 35-line report in Excel with formulas and subtotals, you might note that it is likely that this report could expand or contract in the future. You can prepare for that now by creating a table that holds the necessary data and allows you to change the report without rewriting any code.

The example steps above are simplified, but regardless of the complexity of your project, these steps will need to take place at some point if you want your integration project to be successful.

Designing Applications

If you are writing code simply to make your own projects easier, thinking of them as applications might not be especially relevant. However, if you are building Microsoft Office applications that will be used by others, it is important to think about how the applications might change and how those changes can be dealt with. If you build an application that creates a set of reports and emails them to users, you could hardcode all kinds of information into the code. If you do that, though, any time the reports or recipients change, you will need to change the code.

I try to put elements that might change into tables that can be easily changed. To manage outgoing email, you could have a table that lists the reports and email addresses of the recipients. The code would open that table and send the reports based on the information in the table. This would allow the end user to make the changes necessary to email new or existing reports to new recipients.

While this might not seem very important, if you do not consider factors like this, you will spend more time modifying and maintaining applications than developing them. The same thoughts apply to connection strings to data sources, report formats, and other items where information can change over time. I once helped change an application that was written to produce a report of general ledger accounts with transactions over $1,000. Over time, the company grew and wanted to look at accounts over $50,000. As it turned out, the $1,000 parameter was hardcoded in the application code. Instead of just changing that code, I added a table that held parameters for the general ledger accounts to be queried, the dollar amount to review, and the tables holding the information (each type of transaction had a different table). Once I did this, changes to these criteria could be made without programming.

Some developers seem to build applications that always require developer assistance to make changes. This isn't a strategy I recommend, as it is dangerous for the end user. There are countless requests on the project boards online to modify applications that say that they cannot locate the original developer, or the original developer does not have time to work on it, or other similar reasons. It is also a good idea to document what each procedure does so that if you look at something you made two years ago, you can still follow what you were thinking.

Designing a graphical user interface (GUI) is not covered until much later in the book. As you try to solve a business problem, consider what the information flow will be and the best way to get that data from the user. In addition, it is also useful to consider the best way to display information when that is the purpose of the GUI. For example, is it better to have a large input screen with scrollbars, or is it better to use a tabbed dialog (like many Windows applications)? The other question that comes up when you integrate Access and Excel is which application is best suited for each task. Sometimes the answer is very clear, and at other times there is no clear-cut best product. As you work, the GUI should be in the back of your mind.

Next Steps

In the next chapter, I will introduce you to accessing data from the Excel user interface. This will be very useful for simple tasks for which you need a table of data from a database or another spreadsheet. You can also write database queries with Microsoft Query if you need more specific information than a table or prewritten query. These tasks are all managed from Excel's External Data toolbar. At the end of the next chapter, I will introduce PivotTables as a method for summarizing the data.

To give you a feel for what is to come, you will first learn data access from the Excel user interface, followed by using Excel VBA. Once this is accomplished, you will learn the Access user interface and Access VBA. Next comes an introduction to using these concepts with SQL Server and other Office applications. The final chapters in the book will cover more advanced topics on building applications that integrate Excel and Access. Where applicable, code samples will be available for download online at O'Reilly's web site.

As you go through the book, I suggest having sample Excel and Access files that you can use to apply the concepts discussed. If you don't have your own data, use the sample files that accompany the book. You will most likely get more out of the book if you type the code yourself and get a feel for how to use the VBA interface in Excel and Access. But you can certainly also use (or reuse) the code in the sample files without retyping it. However you decide to use the book, the concepts illustrated are focused around solving common problems that come up in a business environment.

CHAPTER 2

Using the Excel User Interface

I first realized how powerful integrating Access and Excel could be while I worked for a company that calculated incentives. A database housed all of the data required to calculate the incentives. Before I took over the process, a report was printed from the database and rekeyed into an Excel workbook that performed all of the calculations. Eventually we moved from rekeying, to using Microsoft Query to pull data from the database, to finally having the database fill in the Excel workbook. Using an automated process not only saved time, but it also dramatically reduced errors. In the years since, I have found many more opportunities to integrate Access and Excel.

While it is tempting to jump right into using VBA to perform data functions, understanding when and how to use the Excel interface is still very useful and can provide a springboard to using VBA. When you want to use External Data from the Excel user interface, use the Import External Data function under the Data menu. From here, you can open and edit saved queries or create a new query.

Using External Data

External Data refers to any data that does not reside in Excel. Using the Import Data function on the Data menu, you can import entire tables or queries from Access and other databases. You can access this function by going to Data → Import External Data → Import Data. In addition to importing data from a database, you can also use this feature to import text files, XML files, web pages, etc. This is a very simple way to bring in all of the data from a table or query. The nice part about this feature is that you can refresh the data at any time by pressing the refresh button on the External Data toolbar (Figure 2-1). Also, as with any external data range, you can set it up so that any formulas done at a row level will be copied as the data range expands (described later in the chapter).

There are several other features available when working with an External Data range. These are available on the External Data Range Properties, which can be accessed either by right-clicking in the data range and selecting Data Range Properties, or from the External Data Toolbar. Refer to Figure 2-2 to see these properties.

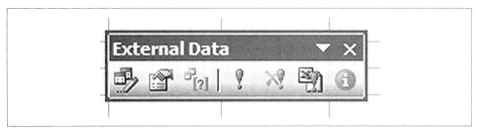

Figure 2-1. The External Data toolbar

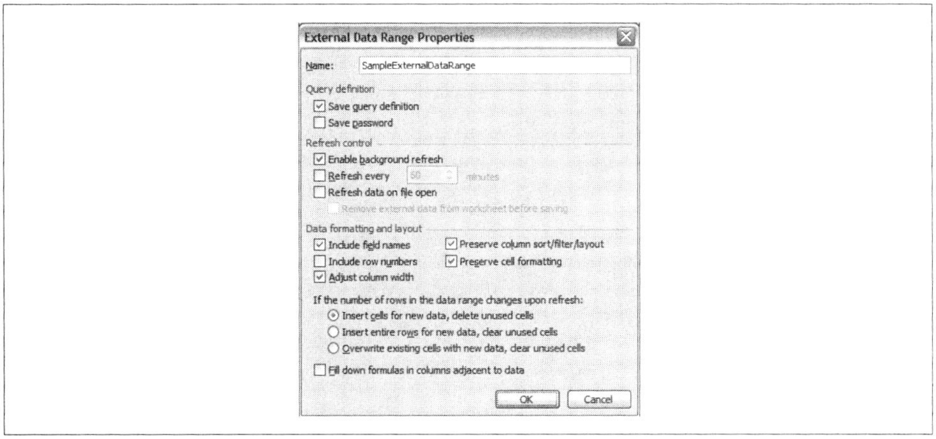

![External Data Range Properties dialog box]

Figure 2-2. The External Data Range Properties dialog box

While there are many options in the properties dialog, two key ones are "Refresh control" and "Fill down formulas in columns adjacent to data." Under the "Refresh control" section, there is a checkbox for "Refresh Data on File Open." This ensures that anytime the Excel workbook is opened, it will use the most recent data. If you are using a data source that is updated daily, this is probably enough; however, if you are using a data source that is constantly being updated, you can also select "Refresh every" for the amount of time that you want to elapse between each data refresh.

Under the "Refresh data on file open" checkbox, there is another checkbox that allows you to not save the data with the spreadsheet. This is useful if you are accessing data that is password protected and you want to ensure that no one can simply access the data in a saved Excel spreadsheet. For example, if Human Resources uses an Excel workbook to track salary or performance appraisal scores, checking this box ensures that the data does not get into the wrong hands. When you check this box, the Excel workbook opens with the data range cleared, connects to the data source, and pulls the most recent data. This prevents people who do not have access to the database— or more precisely, people who do not have access to that table or query in the database—from refreshing the data. If you do not have this checked, the data from the last refresh is visible when the Excel workbook is opened before the refresh.

The second option on the External Data Range Properties dialog box that you will find very useful is the option to fill down formulas. You will often perform calculations on the data at a row level. For example, you might pull some data from a sales table and want a formula that tells you whether the margin on each sale is acceptable. If you check the box to copy the formulas down, as the table (or query) grows, it will copy the appropriate formulas. It is important to note that the formulas must be adjacent to the data; formulas on another sheet or in non-adjacent rows need to be copied down using another method. The other thing to keep in mind is that the formulas must be to the right of the data. This point is not clear in the Excel documentation, but upon testing, you will find that formulas to the left of the data will need to be copied down.

Another advantage to using the Import External Data function is that the resulting External Data Range is defined as a named range. This allows you to use the name of your External Data Range in place of the cell reference for formulas like VLOOKUP. In addition, Excel also gives you the option of using the Column Label in your functions. For example, if you name a column Amount, and you want to create a summary on the same worksheet that sums that column, you can write the formula as =Sum(Amount).

However, by default, Excel does not allow you to use the names of your columns this way. To fix this, go to the Options dialog under the Tools menu and turn on the Manual option on the Calculation tab (Figure 2-3). To apply this feature to data that will refresh, type in the field names manually and bring in the data without them. In the External Range Properties Dialog (Figure 2-2), uncheck the "Include field names" checkbox in the "Data formatting and layout" section. By not linking the field names in Excel to the data, you can continue to use the column names in your formulas.

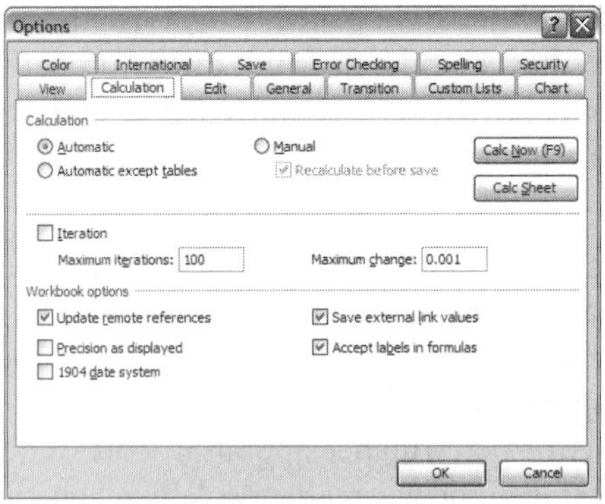

Figure 2-3. The "Accept labels in formulas" checkbox, which enables the use of column labels from Excel Lists and External Data Ranges in formulas

When you turn on this function, you also access another very powerful feature. If you are used to writing VLOOKUP statements, this will change the way that you write many of those in which the formulas reside on the same sheet as the data range. Let's assume that you have a list of Social Security numbers, employee names, and salaries, and assume that the salaries are in a column named Salary. If this was your External Data Range named EmployeeInfo, you could write a VLOOKUP function using the Social Security number (SSN) as the value, EmployeeInfo as the Table Array, column 3 (Salary) as the column index value, and False in the Range Lookup box to ensure that you only get a result for exact matches. Using this function would yield the salary of the person with the specified Social Security number. If Excel did not automatically create this named range for you, you would need to constantly update your VLOOKUP formula as the range expanded or contracted.

This works great when the first column in your data range is the range that you are looking up. When this is not the case, you either need to change your query so that the column you want to use is first, or you need to use the following function. Turn on the "Accept labels in formulas" option on the Calculation tab. Using the same example, if you wanted to look up an employee's salary but only knew his name (or did not want to use his Social Security number), you can write this formula: =Joe Smith Salary. This goes to the row where Excel finds Joe Smith and pulls his salary. You can also put Joe Smith in single quotes to be certain that Excel knows which row you want to pull. In this case, Excel is using the intersection of the row and column that you chose. I want to caution you again that you can only use labels in formulas on the same sheet. To do this on another sheet, use the named range with VLOOKUP and put the Employee Name in the first column.

The primary reason to use named ranges and column labels in your functions and lists is that it enables you to refer to the data without having to change the cell references when the data set gets larger or smaller. Some people get around this by making their formula ranges large enough to not have to update them. While this is possible, it can create performance issues, and it also means that you cannot write formulas directly below your data. Also note that when you create a named range, you cannot put spaces in the name. If you try to, Excel gives you an error message that the name is not valid. The default named range for an external data query places underscores for the spaces. To break up the names to make them more readable, use underscores or capital letters at the beginning of each word, as shown previously in the EmployeeInfo named range.

In addition to Excel creating a Named Range for your External Data Range, the result set is also a QueryTable object that can be referred to by VBA, whether it is a simple import of external data or a database query. Within VBA, you can perform many tasks on the QueryTable object, including changing the table or query, setting a refresh timer, and refreshing the data. In addition, you also gain access to the properties exposed by the QueryTable object, including connection string, source file name, command text, etc. Another way to use the QueryTable object in VBA will be discussed later in this chapter, and you will use QueryTables at other times throughout the book.

When you right-click anywhere in a data range, a menu of options appears. You can use the Edit Query option to change the table that you are accessing. You can also change the SQL there if you are not using a table.

While the Import Data function is relatively simple to execute, it is very useful when you need to use entire data sets that are already defined in the database or file.

Using Database Queries

Database Queries are valuable when you need more control over the data that is returned. Here is a quick example scenario where you can use a Database Query; this example uses the Northwind Database that comes with Access. Let's assume that your job is to review orders where the freight cost is over $100. There is a Query already designed in the Northwind Database called Orders Qry where the freight column is defined. You could bring in the entire table and search for records where the freight is over $100, but that would be time-consuming and error prone. It's simpler to make the computer do the work.

Choose New Database Query from the Import External Data submenu of the Data menu to get the screen shown in Figure 2-4. Since we want to use the Northwind Database, select MS Access Database from this dialog box and press OK, making sure that the box at the bottom of Figure 2-4 is checked to have the Query Wizard write the queries. The Northwind Database is in the Microsoft Office Samples Folder, as shown in Figure 2-5. After you select the Northwind Database, you get a list of all the tables and queries available in the database. For this example, you want to select the query called Orders Qry. You can expand a table or query to see all of the available fields, enabling you to select only the fields that you want. For this example, we want all of the fields, so click once on the name of the query and press the > button to place all of the fields in the query (Figure 2-6). To remove any of the fields, click on the field to remove and press the < button. In this case, since we want all of the fields, simply press the Next button.

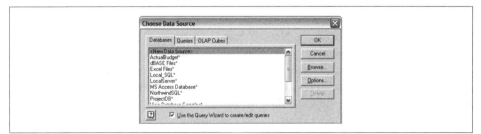

Figure 2-4. The Data Source selection box used to create a new database query

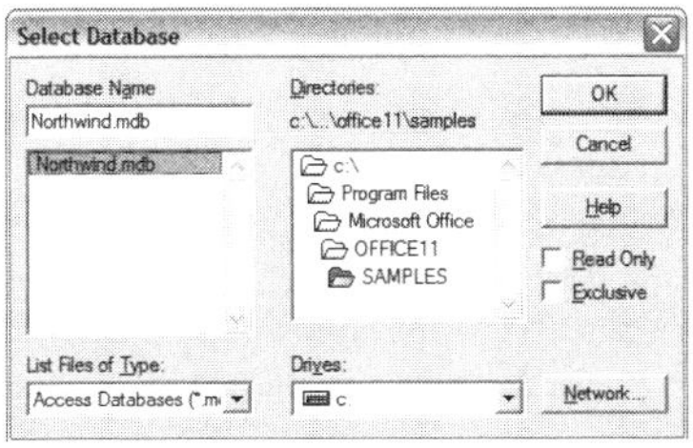

Figure 2-5. The Select Database dialog box

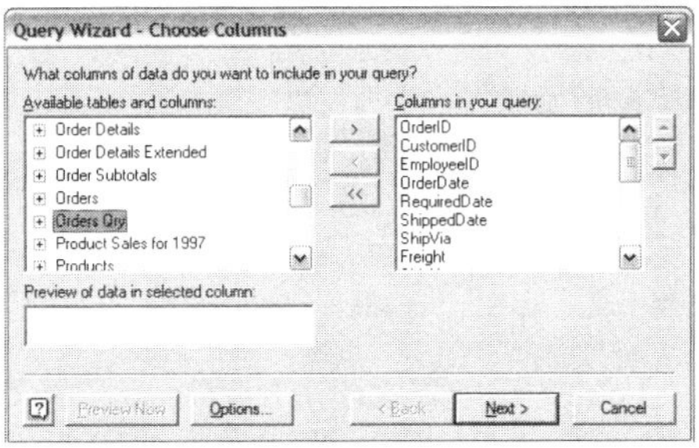

Figure 2-6. The first screen of the Query Wizard

The next screen in the Query Wizard is the Filter Data screen (Figure 2-7). On this screen, pick a column to filter and select the criteria. For this example, select Freight as the column, "is greater than" as the comparison operator, and enter **100** as the amount. The drop-down box to the right of the comparison operation shows the values in the database; you can override these by just typing in the box. Once you have done this, press the Next button.

The next screen (Figure 2-8) sorts the records. Select Freight as the "Sort by" field, and select Descending to sort the records from the most to the least freight cost. When you have done this, press the Next button. On the final screen, select whether to return the records to Excel, edit the query, or create an OLAP Cube. In addition to these choices, you may also choose to save the query so that you can easily access it from other Excel workbooks. For this example, select "Return Data to Microsoft Excel" and press Finish (Figure 2-9).

You are now out of Microsoft Query and back in Excel. Excel brings up a dialog box asking where to put the data (Figure 2-10). You can chose either an existing worksheet or a new worksheet. If you select an existing worksheet, you can select the cell where the import begins. The resulting records can also produce a PivotTable, which will be covered later.

This, again, is a relatively simple example; you can perform much more complex queries. However, this gives you a good example to try with the data that is already

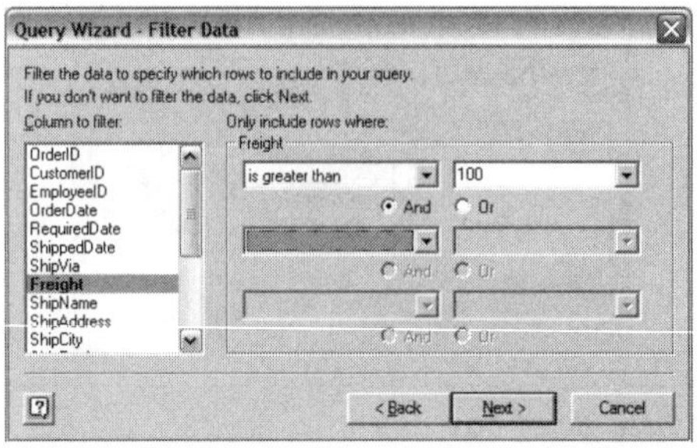

Figure 2-7. The Filter Data screen of the Query Wizard

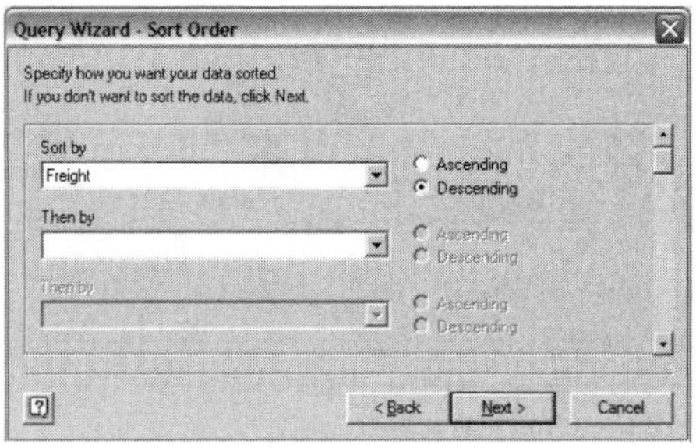

Figure 2-8. The Sort Order screen of the Query Wizard

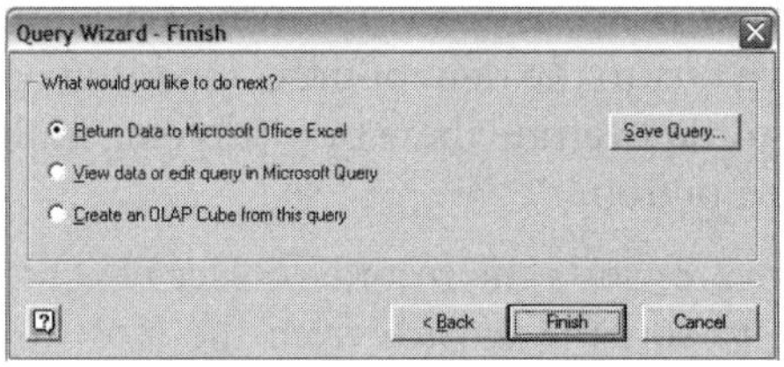

Figure 2-9. The Finish screen of the Query Wizard

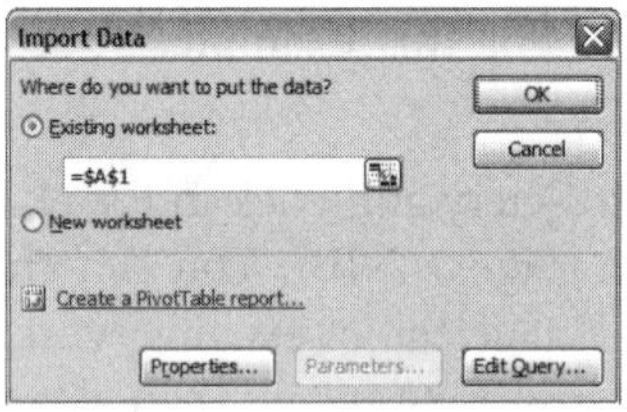

Figure 2-10. Directing Excel as to where to place the data pulled from Microsoft Query

on your computer. This method also makes it very easy to change criteria. Right-click anywhere in the result set and select the Edit Query option to bring the wizard back up and make changes to the query, such as selecting different columns, changing the criteria, adding new criteria, etc. If you change the criteria, you'll notice that any field that has criteria selected is in boldface. In addition to using the wizard, you can also change the query through VBA. The object created by a New Database Query is also both a QueryTable object and a named range. If you do not like the default name, you can change it in the Data Range Properties dialog box, which is accessed by right-clicking in the data range and selecting Data Range Properties.

Returning a PivotTable to Excel

Although collecting the data through the query is great, you may want to import data in a more analyzed form. Even if you are unfamiliar with PivotTables, you may find them preferable to Subtotals or any other summarizing capabilities that you currently use. When you use PivotTables, Excel makes it very easy to use their data to create a chart called a PivotChart. While you could always create a PivotTable on your own and select the name of your Data Range as the source, there may be situations when you want to see the PivotTable.

When you have gone through the previous example and are at the Import Data dialog box, click on the hyperlink for "Create a PivotTable report." You are now in Step 3 of 3 in the PivotTable Wizard (Figure 2-11). Before the PivotTable can be created, you need to click the Layout button, which brings up the screen in Figure 2-12. If you are unfamiliar with PivotTables, you can select fields to be used for Pages, Rows, Columns, and Data. For this example, let's assume that you want to see the number of shipments with freight over $100 that were shipped to each country and the total amount of the freight. To do this, click and drag Country to the Row section, and click and drag Freight to the Data section. Notice that Freight defaults to Sum; double-click on the Freight box and change it to the summarize by count option. Then click and drag the Freight field into the Data section, which defaults to Sum again. This gives you the selections for the PivotTable (Figure 2-12). Press OK, and it brings you back to the screen in Figure 2-11. Take the default of putting it into an existing worksheet beginning in cell A3 and press Finish. Your default location may vary, depending on which cell you started in. Just keep in mind that you can change the location of where the data will be placed before pressing Finish.

To add additional functionality, in the screen shown in Figure 2-12, put Country as a Page field and City as a Row field. This allows you to limit the PivotTable to one country in which you could see the cities. You could also make a PivotChart out of these results by right-clicking on the PivotTable and selecting PivotChart from the menu. However, you will notice that the chart does not present very meaningful results because you have both the count and the sum on the same axis. You can fix this by clicking on the drop-down box for data and unselecting either the Count or Sum field.

Figure 2-11. The PivotTable and PivotChart Wizard final screen

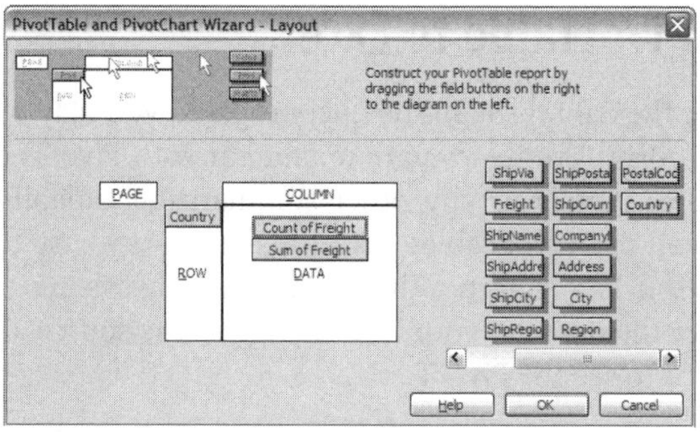

Figure 2-12. The Layout screen of the PivotTable and PivotChart Wizard

PivotTables also provide the ability to see the underlying data simply by double-clicking on any result. To support this feature, select all of the fields that you want included in your query, even if they will not be shown in the PivotTable. The data shown by double-clicking on the result field is every column and row from the query that is represented by that result. This can be a very powerful feature for analyzing data. Imagine a situation when you have general ledger transactions on one Excel worksheet and a PivotTable that summarizes the information by expense category on another worksheet. If you were using any other summary report, you would need to individually identify the rows from the general ledger to research an expense category. This would be very time-consuming and might introduce errors, but using a PivotTable allows you to simply double-click on any number to get the related rows. It also makes producing summary reports and charts a snap.

Using Microsoft Query to Gather Data

Now that you have tried the Excel user interface, I want to introduce you to the Microsoft Query interface. Use the Microsoft Query interface instead of the Query Wizard when you need more control over the query. For example, you might want to add a calculated field or perform a complex join in your query. Also, while you can create a parameter query with the query wizard, you must edit a parameter query with the Microsoft Query interface. So, let's try a simple example to demonstrate how to change the query to a parameter query. Go back to your Query results from the first example, or go through the steps again (see Figure 2-10). Once you see the results, right-click in the result data and select Edit Query. Get to the final screen and select "View data or edit query in Microsoft Query." You will see the screen in Figure 2-13. In the "Criteria Field and Value" section, select Freight for the field and >100 for the value. To change this to a parameter, replace >100 with >[Amt] (you can use any name that does not represent a column in the Query in brackets). After you click off of that field, it will ask you for the parameter amount. This time, type in **500** for the amount, and press Enter. When you are finished, go to the File menu and select "Return Data to Microsoft Office Excel."

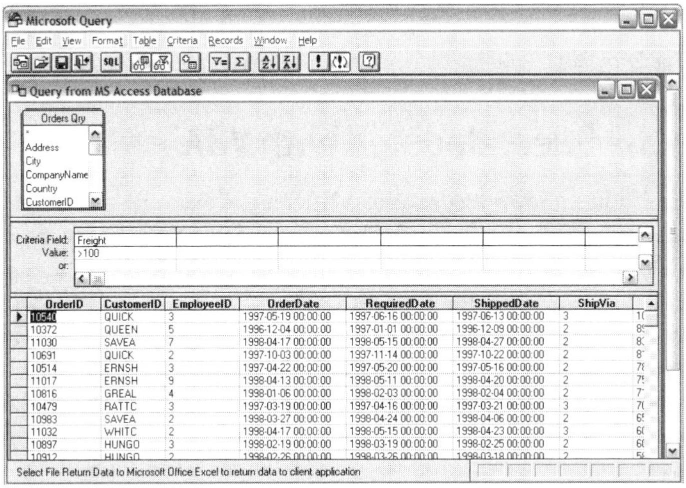

Figure 2-13. Microsoft Query screen

Creating a query as a parameter query is useful for changing the data that you look at regularly; using a parameter query is much easier than continuously editing the query in Microsoft Query. You can bring up the Parameters menu at any time by right-clicking in your data range and selecting Parameters. Excel allows you to choose whether you want to be prompted for the parameter, to use a particular number, or to refer to a cell to obtain the value. If you are going to change the value on a regular basis, I suggest using the option that looks in a cell for a value. This avoids prompting and also allows you to use VBA to refresh the query whenever you change the value of that cell.

Now that you are back in Excel with a parameter query, to set your parameter to come from a cell within Excel, select rows 1 through 3 and select Insert → Rows from the top menu to move your data down three rows. In cell A1, type **Amount** and in cell B1, type **300**. Then right-click in your data range and select Parameters from the menu. Click on the "Get the value from the following cell:" box, and click on cell B2 (Figure 2-14). Right-click on your data and select Refresh Data, and Excel will pull in the additional records (additional as compared to the original parameter of 500). Once you have done this, you will be able to change the criteria on the fly and refresh the result set.

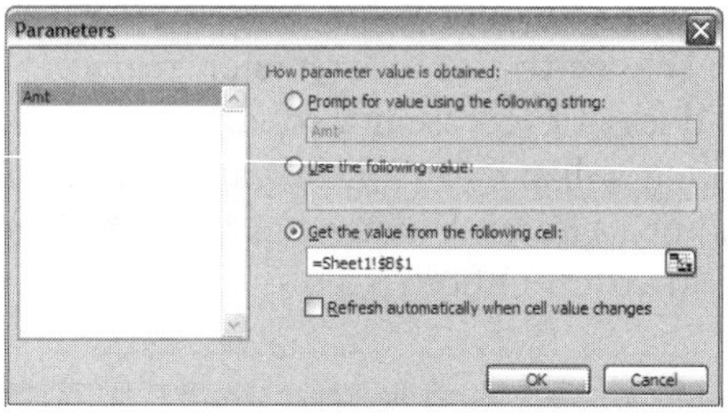

Figure 2-14. The ExternalDataRange Parameters dialog box

Keeping the Query Updated with VBA

This is an ideal time to introduce you to VBA. In the example above, you might not want to have to continue pressing refresh for your data. You may want the Query to automatically refresh itself with the new parameter each time you change cell B1. If you use VBA for programming Excel, you probably know that worksheets in Microsoft Excel have events that can have code associated with them. Events, as the name indicates, are triggered when certain events happen within Excel. Generally, these events are triggered from some type of user action. The event that you want here is the Worksheet_Change event. To set up Excel to automatically refresh your query each time you change the criteria, from your worksheet, press Alt-F11 to open the Visual Basic Programming Environment. You will see several sections; focus on the Project Explorer (Figure 2-15). If you do not see it, press Ctrl-R. Next, double-click on your current worksheet in the Microsoft Excel Objects list. There should be no code in the code window on the right side of the screen. Going from left to right on the top of the code window, go to the first drop-down box and select Worksheet, and on the second drop-down box, select Change. Excel fills in the opening and closing lines of the procedure; although the opening and closing lines are shown in the following code excerpt, they should not be typed in. Refer to the code below and type it into your procedure (Figure 2-16).

```
Private Sub Worksheet_Change(ByVal Target As Range)
Dim wks As Worksheet
Set wks = ActiveSheet
If Target.Row = 1 And Target.Column = 2 Then
  wks.QueryTables(1).Refresh
End If
Set wks = Nothing
End Sub
```

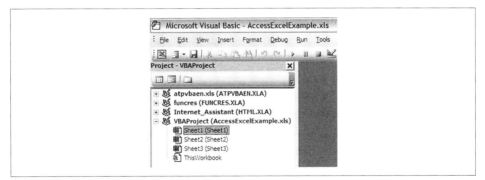

Figure 2-15. The Project Explorer treeview

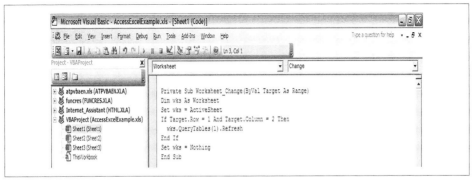

Figure 2-16. Typing in the code, with Project Explorer on the left and the code window on the right

Excel sends a reference to the range being updated (the *Target*) to this procedure. Normally, this is a single cell, but it can be multiple cells since it is a range object. In the past, I have run into problems in code when I didn't anticipate people updating a range of numbers simultaneously. In the part of the procedure that you control, you declare a variable (WKS) and make it a Worksheet object. Then you set this variable to be equal to the ActiveSheet, the currently active sheet. Remembering that the parameter is in B1, note that B1 is in row 1 column 2. Since you don't want to refresh the query every time the sheet changes, the If statement tests to ensure that the Target (the cell that is changing) is cell B1. If it is, in fact, cell B1, it will refresh the QueryTable. You may replace the 1 in wks.QueryTables(1) with the name of your DataRange in double quotes. This is important if you have more than one QueryTable on the same worksheet and you are not sure which number refers to a particular QueryTable. You can also use a For Each...Next loop to iterate through all of the QueryTables. By doing this, you can refresh every QueryTable on the Worksheet. (If you are unfamiliar with VBA, Appendix B covers the use of loops, or you could use a book on VBA as a reference to become more familiar with it). In the current example, you are using only one QueryTable, so you can refer to it with the number 1. After you have completed this code, go back to your worksheet, change the value in cell B1, and press Enter. The query updates automatically.

A more traditional VB method would be to place a command button on the worksheet and use the `Button_Click` event to fire the code. While that method would certainly work, having the query automatically update makes this method a lot more user friendly. If you had multiple criteria and the query took more time to run, you might want to wait for a `Button Click` to run the query. You could still use the `Worksheet_Change` event to change the caption on your button to let the user know that after she changes an amount in a criteria cell, the criteria on the screen are not what the query represents.

When you are dealing with changing query criteria, I suggest taking advantage of the functionality of Excel to take query parameters from Excel cells. The possibilities for this are endless. You can have a field for a date to review data for a certain date. You can have multiple parameters represent a range of dates, values, etc. The important thing to take away from this last example is that using the Excel user interface to pull your data in no way prevents you from using VBA to extend the capabilities.

Another important concept to take away from this chapter is the difference between the Import Data menu item and the New Database Query menu item. Use the Import Data menu item when you need to bring in an entire table or use a query that is already defined (either in the database or saved in a file); you do not have the ability to filter this data. You use the New Database Query menu item when you want to apply criteria to filter the data prior to bringing it into Excel. The procedure described in this section is a good example of how you can use VBA to extend the features that you are using from the Excel user interface. In many cases, it is easier to use VBA to extend the User Interface than it is to code the functionality from scratch.

Next Steps

Now that you have seen the External Data features available from the Excel user interface and have been introduced to VBA, the next chapter will build on these features and also introduce some functionality that can only be accomplished through VBA. The next chapter will also show you how you can automate the formatting of data once it is extracted. As you go through the next chapter, start to think about the ways that you manipulate the data you bring into Excel today and how the functionality being introduced can be applied to that data to automate or add functionality to a task.

CHAPTER 3

Data Access from Excel VBA

Up to this point, all interaction with the data source has been through the Excel user interface. I hope that you have seen how effective it can be in certain situations. You have also used VBA to enhance data access from the user interface. VBA gives you the opportunity to take more control of the data; it performs queries that are not possible from the user interface, and you can now automate many operations.

There are numerous situations when VBA is not only the preferred way to obtain data, but the only way. For example, you may run into situations in which you want to control access to the data by the time of day or another variable. Giving the user the ability to pull the data straight from the user interface limits your ability to restrict access to that data. You do not want people running queries that join a table with several hundred thousand customer records and a couple million financial transactions during the middle of the day. At the same time, though, you also cannot shut down the database to block the users' queries when the database needs to be available to perform official transactions. When a developer runs into a situation like this, an easy solution is to write code to pull data from the database while ensuring that the moment the query runs doesn't interfere with performance. The developer can then protect the code so that this restriction cannot be bypassed.

Another situation when it is preferable to use VBA to pull the data is when you need to perform actions based on information at the row level. While you could certainly pull the data in through the user interface and then write code to perform the actions within Excel on another worksheet, that method would result in duplication of data. When I am writing reports where I need to perform calculations at several subtotals, calculate ratios, and/or weighted averages, I control all of that through VBA. The other issue that will become more relevant as you move through this book is the choice between using Excel to pull the data from the data source and using the data source (Access) to automate Excel. This choice makes a large impact on application design.

Another consideration when using Excel to pull the data is macro security. At some organizations where Excel is not used heavily, or at least VBA is not used heavily, Excel's security will not enable macros that are not signed (high) or that are not installed in trusted locations (very high). This is a great precaution to avoid getting infested with macro viruses, but it makes it difficult to create a home-grown application for use in Excel. You can find out how your security is configured by going to Tools → Macros → Security from the Excel user interface (Figure 3-1). If your security is set at low, I suggest moving it to medium. If it is set to high or very high, I would change it to medium or speak with your system administrator about moving it to medium. At medium, you can choose whether or not to run macros each time you open up an Excel workbook. If you are unable to persuade your system administrator to allow you to change the setting, you will have to perform the automation from Access.

Figure 3-1. The Excel macro security dialog box, which tells Excel how to handle workbooks with macros

While this book focuses on integrating Excel and Access, most of the content in this chapter can be applied to other enterprise data sources such as SQL Server, DB2, and Oracle. For the purposes of this book, I will stick with Access and occasionally SQL Server.

Writing a Reusable Module for Data Access

While some people argue that writing a reusable module creates some additional overhead, this is a good way to get introduced to pulling data using VBA. I suggest building a module that returns a database connection when you pass it certain parameters. A module holds procedures and functions and can be saved as a text file, which makes it very easy to use in other applications. While it is certainly easy enough to write the code to access a data source each time you need it, having a module written that you know works can reduce the variables when building an application. Even if you do not use it in production, you can always copy the code from the module to use in future applications. I use this same concept of writing a generic procedure to perform actions like dropping tables, running action queries, and other database tasks that will be done the same way on multiple objects. This way, I only have to write the code once.

The key to using this method is passing the parameters by reference (with ByRef). When you pass parameters to a procedure, you can either pass the value of the parameter or pass a reference to the variable. When you pass the value, the procedure gets the value and cannot change the original value for the calling procedure (provided that it is not a global variable). When you pass the variable ByRef, any action done on that variable in the called procedure is done on that variable in the calling procedure.

For example, let's assume that you have an integer variable x, and you want to pass it to a procedure to perform some math function on it. Then you want to use the result, and you do not need to know the original value later. You could write a function called DoMath and pass it your variable. You would create a variable in your original procedure to hold the value of the function that is returned. The other method is to create a procedure called DoMath but pass the variable x as ByRef. Then when you change the value of x in that procedure, the value of x is also updated in the original procedure. While that is a simplistic example, I hope it explains how this can be useful. In the project in the final chapter, you will see an example of how both of these concepts work in a sample application.

 Example 3-1 uses ActiveX Data Objects (ADO), but you could also write it using Data Access Objects (DAO). When you decide which one you want to use, you must set a reference to either ADO, ADOX, or DAO by going into the Visual Basic Editor and pressing Alt + F11 from the Excel User Interface. Then you go to Tools → References and select the appropriate reference.

The procedure in Example 3-1, called GetCn, creates a new data connection with ADO and opens a recordset with the specified SQL. Once this procedure finishes running, the calling procedure can reuse the Connection and Recordset objects because the connection and recordset variables are passed ByRef.

Example 3-1. ADO connection

```
Public Sub GetCn(ByRef dbcon As ADODB.Connection, ByRef dbrs As ADODB.Recordset, _
    sqlstr As String, dbfile As String, usernm As String, pword As String)

  Set dbcon = New ADODB.Connection
  dbcon.Open "PROVIDER=Microsoft.Jet.OLEDB.4.0;Data Source=" & dbfile & ";", _
            usernm, pword
  Set dbrs = New ADODB.Recordset
  dbrs.Open sqlstr, dbcon

End Sub
```

In any procedure where you need to create a connection to an Access database and return a recordset, you can call this procedure. In order to use it, declare variables for the ADO connection and recordset to be passed to the GetCn procedure. You can either use variables for the SQL string and the filename or simply pass them as strings. The same thing applies to the username and password. If your Access Database is not password-protected, you can pass an empty string (" ") for the username and password.

Example 3-2 shows a procedure that returns all of the records from a table called Table1 in a database called *sampledb.mdb*. This example also introduces a method of the ExcelRange called CopyFromRecordset. This method places all of the records from the recordset in the Excel worksheet.

Example 3-2. Introducing CopyFromRecordset

```
Public Sub getrs()
Dim adoconn As ADODB.Connection
Dim adors As ADODB.Recordset
Dim sql As String
Dim filenm As String

sql = "Select * from Table1"
filenm = "C:\Data\sampledb.mdb"

Call GetCn(adoconn, adors, sql, filenm, "", "")

Dim xlsht As Excel.Worksheet
Set xlsht = Sheets("Sheet1")
xlsht.Range("A1").CopyFromRecordset adors

adors.Close
adoconn.Close
Set adors = Nothing
Set adoconn = Nothing
Set xlsht = nothing
End Sub
```

Keep in mind that anytime before you close the ADO connection, you can use it to open additional recordsets or perform any other functions. Again, this procedure is really only for demonstration purposes, but you could certainly use it if you had multiple features that needed to obtain recordsets.

Choosing Between ADO and DAO

In Chapter 1, I gave a brief description of ADO (including ADOX) and DAO. In this chapter, the biggest differences between the two methods of accessing data come with the use of queries. When you develop an Access Database, you will often have many different types of queries. For example, you might have one query that simply retrieves data (Select Query) or one that appends data from one table into another (Append Query).

When you are dealing with DAO, each type of query is a `QueryDef` object. Once you have a DAO database connection, you can simply cycle through the `QueryDefs` collection with a `For Each...Next` loop and get information about each query; you can then make changes to the queries, if necessary. The `QueryDefs` collection contains every query in the Access database. When using DAO, you do not need to know what type of query you are dealing with to take actions on it.

This is not as easy a task when using ADO and ADOX. ADOX categorizes queries similarly to the way SQL Server does. Specifically, ADOX considers *action* queries (Append Queries, Make Table Queries, etc.) to be procedures and *select* queries to be views. To loop through all of the queries in an Access Database using ADOX, you would cycle through the `Procedures` and `Views` collections. The other major difference between ADOX and DAO is that in ADOX, the Views are also part of the `Tables` collection, while in DAO they are not. The collection of tables in DAO is called the `TableDefs` collection. A single table is a `TableDef`.

The difference between accessing a select query as a view and as a table is that if you access a query in the `Views` collection, you have access to the Command and CommandText. This is what gives you the SQL of the View. When you access a View as a Table, you do not have access to the Command or CommandText.

I have included two samples below that show you how to loop through the queries and tables in an Access Database. Example 3-3 uses ADO, while Example 3-4 uses DAO. When I need to make changes to queries, I tend to use DAO when working with Access, and ADOX when working with SQL Server. The reason why I tend to use DAO when working with Access queries is that on many occasions when I am working with queries and I am writing SQL on the fly, the query may change from a select query to an action query. I find it is easier to just use the `QueryDefs` collection, as opposed to determining whether the query is now in the `Views` or `Procedures` collection. But, as you will see below, you are not limited to doing that. Also note that in the ADO example I am using the `GetCn` procedure from above. I am just ignoring the recordset that is returned.

Example 3-3. Using ADO and ADOX to loop through queries and tables

```
Public Sub getinfo()
Dim adoconn As ADODB.Connection
Dim adors As ADODB.Recordset
Dim sql As String
Dim filenm As String

Dim adocat As adox.Catalog
Dim adovw As adox.View
Dim adozz As adox.Procedure
Dim adotbl As adox.Table
```

Example 3-3. Using ADO and ADOX to loop through queries and tables (continued)

```
Dim x As Integer
Dim xlsht As Excel.Worksheet
Set xlsht = Sheets("Sheet1")

sql = "Select * from Table1"
filenm = "C:\Data\sampledb.mdb"

Call GetCn(adoconn, adors, sql, filenm, "", "")

Set adocat = New adox.Catalog
adocat.ActiveConnection = adoconn
x = 2
xlsht.Cells(1, 1).Value = "Views"
For Each adovw In adocat.Views
  xlsht.Cells(x, 1).Value = adovw.Name
  x = x + 1
Next
x = 2
xlsht.Cells(1, 2).Value = "Procedures"
For Each adozz In adocat.Procedures
  xlsht.Cells(x, 2).Value = adozz.Name
  x = x + 1
Next
x = 2
xlsht.Cells(1, 3).Value = "Tables"
For Each adotbl In adocat.Tables
  xlsht.Cells(x, 3).Value = adotbl.Name
  x = x + 1
Next

Set adocat = Nothing
Set adozz = Nothing
Set adovw = Nothing
Set adotbl = Nothing
adors.Close
adoconn.Close
Set adors = Nothing
Set adoconn = Nothing
Set xlsht = Nothing
End Sub
```

Example 3-4. Using DAO to loop through queries and tables

```
Public Sub getDAOinfo()
Dim wrk As DAO.Workspace
Dim db As DAO.Database
Dim qry As DAO.QueryDef
Dim tbl As DAO.TableDef
Dim x As Integer
Dim xlsht As Excel.Worksheet

Set wrk = DAO.CreateWorkspace("myworkspace", "admin", "")
```

Example 3-4. Using DAO to loop through queries and tables (continued)

```
Set db = wrk.OpenDatabase("C:\Data\sampledb.mdb")

Set xlsht = Sheets("Sheet2")

xlsht.Cells(1, 1).Value = "Queries"
xlsht.Cells(1, 2).Value = "Query Type"
x = 2
For Each qry In db.QueryDefs
  xlsht.Cells(x, 1).Value = qry.Name
  xlsht.Cells(x, 2).Value = qry.Type
  x = x + 1
Next
xlsht.Cells(1, 3).Value = "Tables"
x = 2
For Each tbl In db.TableDefs
  xlsht.Cells(x, 3).Value = tbl.Name
  x = x + 1
Next
Set tbl = Nothing
Set qry = Nothing
db.Close
Set db = Nothing
wrk.Close
Set wrk = Nothing
Set xlsht = Nothing

End Sub
```

In the DAO example, I place this information into Sheet2. This lets us compare the results of the DAO and ADO/ADOX methods. I also added the query type to the DAO method. This comes across as an integer. To find out what the values are, go to the Immediate Window on the Visual Basic Editor and type ? <constant to determine the values, or go to the object browser and look at the QueryDefTypeEnum collection; the object browser will show you the value if you click on a member of the collection. I have included a table of the values in Table 3-1.

Table 3-1. Query type values

Query type	Value
Action query	240
Append query	64
Compound query	160
Crosstab query	16
Data Definition query	96
Delete query	32
Make table query	80
Select query	0

Table 3-1. Query type values (continued)

Query type	Value
Union query	128
Pass-through query	112
Update query	48

The type of query is useful if you expect a query to return records or make a table. For records, check the query type to ensure that it returns records. Likewise, to make a table, make sure that the query type is 80.

While it is unlikely that you would use either of the examples above for anything other than potentially documenting a database that you are unfamiliar with, I think that these examples are a good introduction to ADO and DAO and how you can connect to databases using each one. In addition to connecting to Access databases, you can connect to enterprise databases, such as SQL Server or Oracle, using these methods. Since DAO was designed specifically for Jet databases, Chapter 7 will only cover connecting to SQL Server with ADO. However, if you feel more comfortable with DAO, you can connect to an SQL Server database using DAO. When dealing with remote data sources like SQL Server, DAO uses more resources than ADO and therefore runs slower. For this reason, it's frequently better to use ADO with SQL Server.

There are plenty of examples in the help file that comes with DAO to show you how to connect to data sources other than Access. One other thing to keep in mind is that you can use both ADO and DAO in the same application. You will notice when you read over the code above that when I referred to a recordset, I called it an `ADODB.RECORDSET`. If you only had a reference to ADO, you could simply refer to it as a `RECORDSET`. However, if you decided later that you needed the functionality in DAO for a specific item, you would have to go to all of your recordset references and change them to `ADODB.RECORDSET`. So, my recommendation is to always declare your variables with `ADODB.ObjectType` or `DAO.ObjectType`. I even do that with Excel items that I'm unlikely to use in any other applications (worksheets, workbooks, etc. as Excel.Worksheet, Excel.Workbook, etc.).

CopyFromRecordset Versus Looping

When pulling data from a data source into Excel, you need to decide how you want to process the recordset. For example, if you need all of the fields and records, you have already been introduced to a simple method that does this: the `CopyFromRecordset` method places the results of a recordset for Excel Range objects in the range in an Excel worksheet. Sometimes, however, you bring in the results of a query but want only a few of the fields. You can accomplish this by looping through the records.

When dealing with ADO and DAO recordsets, there are several methods of record navigation. In most examples, I go to the first record in the recordset and move through the recordset until there are no additional records. You accomplish this by using the MOVEFIRST method of a recordset to go to the first record, and then the MOVENEXT method to move through the recordset. There are several strategies to figure out when you have cycled through all of the records. When you move past the last record, the recordset's EOF flag is set to TRUE. I suggest using a While...Wend loop. Assuming your recordset is a variable named rs, you write the While...Wend loop like this:

```
rs.movefirst
While Not rs.eof
  <Code to work with your Recordset>
  rs.movenext
Wend
```

Since you have already been introduced to CopyFromRecordSet, let's take a look at an example of where you would want to loop through a recordset. Consider a table of employee information that has 15 fields. Assuming that you need only three of the fields (Last Name, First Name, and Salary), you have two choices for how to accomplish this.

The first method is to simply write your query to pull in only the fields that you want using the criteria that you want. This sounds easy, but in some cases it might be difficult if you are not familiar with how to write SQL and if you do not have the appropriate access rights to make changes to the database. In that case, you would need to find out the field names, loop through the records, and test for criteria, if necessary. You could also pull the records by position.

For this example, assume that the fields that you want are called LName, FName, and EmpSalary and that you already have a variable, rs, which is the recordset object; a variable, x, which is an integer; and a variable, xlws, which is an Excel worksheet. You want those fields for people who have a salary of more than $60,000. This example is the same for both ADO and DAO.

```
x = 1
rs.movefirst
While Not rs.eof
  If rs.fields("EmpSalary").value > 60000 then
  xlws.cells(x,1).value = rs.fields("LName").value
  xlws.cells(x,2).value = rs.fields("FName").value
  xlws.cells(x,3).value = rs.fields("EmpSalary").value
  x = x + 1
  End if
  rs.movenext
Wend
```

The most important part of this Example is that you have the x = x + 1 inside your If statement. If not, you bring in only the records that you want, but you have blank spaces between the records. If you place the x = x + 1 outside the If statement, each time a record is evaluated, x is incremented by one. In this procedure, the variable x determines the row to place the data. After looking at this example, you probably wonder how you get the titles of the fields on the Excel worksheet. When you pull the values by field name, this is very easy to do, either by simply writing the title that you want directly or by accessing the `.NAME` property of the field object. However, when you perform a `CopyFromRecordset`, you may not know all of the fields.

Fortunately, there is a very easy method to cycle through the fields. Again, assume that you have a recordset (`rs`), you also have a variable called `fld` that is defined as a Field (same for ADO and DAO—`ADODB.Field` or `DAO.Field`), and finally you have your Excel worksheet defined as `xlws`. Let's put the titles in the first row and paste the recordset starting in row 2. Here is the code:

```
x = 1
For each fld in rs.Fields
  xlws.cells(1,x).value = fld.name
  x = x + 1
Next
xlws.range("A2").CopyFromRecordset rs
```

In general, `CopyFromRecordset` is quicker than cycling through the records; however, you do give up some control. If you do not see any benefits to moving through the records one at a time, I suggest writing your query to pull the records and fields that you need and then using `CopyFromRecordset`. You may also have a situation when you want to use the same recordset for multiple purposes, and moving through the records is your best bet. In the previous example, for instance, we wanted to pull only the records where the salary was greater than $60,000. If you wanted to, you could use that same recordset to look at salaries less than $60,000 and place them in another location.

Formatting Techniques

There are essentially two formatting methods, which are on a worksheet using VBA. The first method is to learn where all of the formatting options are and write the code from scratch. This method is most effective when doing the same thing many times (formatting numbers as currency, for example); however, trying to remember how to perform every type of formatting becomes a daunting task. So, this brings us to the second method: using the Macro Recorder.

To access the Macro Recorder from the Excel user interface, go to Tools → Macro → Record New Macro. If all you need is the formatting, pick one cell for each type of formatting that you need to perform. When you are done doing the formatting, press the Stop button to stop recording, or go to Tools → Macro → Stop Recording. Go to the Visual Basic Editor to view the code that the Excel Macro Recorder wrote to perform the formatting. This gives you the syntax needed for your code. If you always have the same number of rows, etc., you can just do all the formatting and then save the macro to run in the future. If you need to customize it, the next couple of examples show you how.

Determining how to refer to your range becomes tricky. For example, let's assume that you want to format a column as currency ($0.00). If you are certain that you want every cell in that column to be currency, you can set your range to be that column. In Excel, there is a property called Columns that is available on a Range object and a Worksheet object. If your range is already defined in a variable called xlrng, and you want to perform formatting on the third column, refer to this column as xlrng.columns(3). If you do this, I suggest having an additional range object that you can refer to. If you have a range object called xlrng2, you can write a line that says set xlrng2 = xlrng.columns(3). I like to do this so that the range properties and methods will be available as I write the code.

To explain that a little, if you have a worksheet that is currently active that you refer to as ActiveSheet, you can write ActiveSheet.Range("A1").Value = 100, and it will put 100 in cell A1. However, as you type, VBA will not help you. If you say set xlws = ActiveSheet and type xlws., as soon as you type the . you will see all of the properties and methods available. Using this technique for your objects will make coding much easier. If you have ever tried to script an Excel worksheet in VB script, you can appreciate how useful the help is while typing.

In addition to using the RANGE object, you can also use the Worksheet object to refer to a column. So, if you have a variable xlws that is defined as the ActiveSheet, you can refer to column B by writing xlws.columns(2) or xlws.columns("B:B"). You can also refer to columns B through D by writing xlws.columns("B:D"). If you do not want to refer to entire columns and the range with your data has not been defined yet, you need a method to refer to this set of data. The following example will show you how to select from cell A1 to the end of the worksheet that has data in it.

```
Public Sub SelActiveRange()
Dim rng As Excel.Range
Dim xlws As Excel.Worksheet

Set xlws = ActiveSheet

Set rng = xlws.Range(xlws.Range("A1"), xlws.Cells.SpecialCells(xlCellTypeLastCell))
rng.Select

Set rng = Nothing
Set xlws = Nothing
End Sub
```

The first thing you will notice is that you can refer to a range by using the A1 notation. So, to refer to cell A1, you can write xlws.Range("A1"). You could also do this by writing xlws.cells(1,1)—the cells collection also returns a range object that refers to a single cell.

The second method is called `SpecialCells`. The `SpecialCells` method returns a range object based on constants built into Excel. I use `xlCellTypeLastCell`, a special cell that refers to the last cell being used. Of the others you can use, two that I find particularly useful are `xlCellTypeFormulas` and `xlCellTypeComments`. These return a range that includes all of the cells that have either formulas or comments, respectively.

Often, I want to send an Excel Worksheet to someone, but I don't want the recipient to change something on one sheet that will affect formula results on another. For example, if you show a scenario of net income based on sales assumptions, and you do not want that net income scenario to be changed if the sales assumptions change, you can change all of the formulas to values using the following procedure. This allows you to maintain a history of the results at various stages. For example, if you make a copy of the scenario with one sales assumption and then remove the formulas, you can maintain the results while still having a second worksheet that will change when the sales assumptions change. Note that the following example assumes that your report is in cells A1 to D100. (You could also build that first range dynamically by using the `xlCellTypeLastCell` method used above instead of building it directly into the code if you needed more flexibility or if the size of your spreadsheet will grow larger.)

```
Public Sub FormulatoConstant()
Dim rng As Excel.Range
Dim xlws As Excel.Worksheet
Dim rng2 As Excel.Range

Set xlws = ActiveSheet
Set rng = xlws.Range("A1:D100").SpecialCells(xlCellTypeFormulas)
For Each rng2 In rng.Cells
  rng2.Copy
  rng2.PasteSpecial xlPasteValues
Next rng2
xlws.Range("A1").Select
Application.CutCopyMode = False
Set rng = Nothing
Set rng2 = Nothing
Set xlws = Nothing
End Sub
```

This procedure uses a `For Each...Next` loop to loop through every cell in the Range variable rng. Each individual cell is copied and then pasted back onto itself with only the values. When it is done, cell A1 is selected and the `CutCopyMode` is set to `False` (if you do not set the `CutCopyMode` to `False`, cell A1 will be selected, but the last cell copied will still have the marquee box around it as if it is being copied). You could select the entire sheet and use Copy and Paste Special Values, or a `For Each...Next` loop can be placed into code and set to a particular range by changing it like this:

```
Public Sub FormulatoConstant(targetrange As Excel.Range)
Dim rng As Excel.Range
Dim xlws As Excel.Worksheet
Dim rng2 As Excel.Range
```

```
Set xlws = ActiveSheet
Set rng = targetrange.SpecialCells(xlCellTypeFormulas)
For Each rng2 In rng.Cells
  rng2.Copy
  rng2.PasteSpecial xlPasteValues
Next rng2
xlws.Range("A1").Select
Application.CutCopyMode = False
Set rng = Nothing
Set rng2 = Nothing
Set xlws = Nothing
End Sub
```

Using For Each...Next allows you to target just the range of cells that you want to find formulas in and change them to values. You could take this code, put it into any of your Excel workbooks, and with a simple call to the procedure, perform this action.

Since this section is about formatting, let's take a look at how you can apply the currency style to the results of any formula that returns a number. (Remember that formulas can return numbers, Boolean values, text, or errors.) We will modify the procedure in the previous example to use currency.

```
Public Sub FormulatoCurrency(targetrange As Excel.Range)
Dim rng As Excel.Range
Dim xlws As Excel.Worksheet
Dim rng2 As Excel.Range

Set xlws = ActiveSheet
Set rng = targetrange.SpecialCells(xlCellTypeFormulas, xlNumbers)
For Each rng2 In rng.Cells
  rng2.Style = "Currency"
Next rng2
xlws.Range("A1").Select
Set rng = Nothing
Set rng2 = Nothing
Set xlws = Nothing
End Sub
```

You can see that we've changed the setting of the style. Excel has some predefined styles, which you can refer to more easily than you can write a number format. In addition, you can create a new style and refer to it, as you would one of Excel's predefined formats, to format cells the way you want. Let's assume that column D includes numbers, and you want to create a style that is:

- A number with commas
- A whole number (has no decimal places)
- Blue when positive
- Red when negative
- A bold Arial size 14 font

Formatting that several times in your code or by hand would get repetitive and annoying. Instead, you can create code for a style and apply it from the Format → Style menu or refer to it in code.

The beauty of creating a style is that you can also modify styles that you've already applied using the Format → Style screen. So, if you wanted to change every cell that has a particular style, rather than having to find each cell on your worksheet, you could simply modify the style you've applied. The style dialog box is in Figure 3-2. The next example shows you how to create the style. The following example shows you how to apply that style to column D.

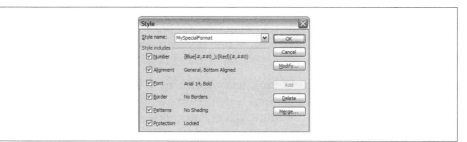

Figure 3-2. The Excel Style dialog box

```
Public Sub CreateStyle( )
ActiveWorkbook.Styles.Add "MySpecialFormat"
With ActiveWorkbook.Styles("MySpecialFormat")
    .Font.Bold = True
    .NumberFormat = "[Blue]#,##0_);[Red](#,##0)"
    .Font.Name = "Arial"
    .Font.Size = 14
End With
End Sub


Public Sub ApplyStyle( )
ActiveSheet.Columns("D:D").Style = "MySpecialFormat"
End Sub
```

Note that all of the boxes are checked in the style dialog box in Figure 3-2. If, for example, you don't want to apply a style to Protection, uncheck that box. In addition, you could modify the code in the With clause to say .IncludeProtection = False. You can also do that with the other options in the figure.

Formatting Techniques Example

So far you've seen how to pull in a recordset and how to do some formatting in Excel. The first couple of chapters show many examples of how to pull in recordsets because pulling is the primary method for bringing in data.

This example brings formatting and recordset pulling together. There is a query in the Northwind database that is called [Sales by Category], which is in brackets because there are spaces in the name. That data is not updated daily, but assume that you have a query named that on your system that *is* updated daily (or monthly, weekly, etc.). You also have a user who wants to see an Excel report that shows that data and produces subtotals by category. I will show you several methods to give the user the desired report, and you can pick the one that suits you best.

Getting to the Data

The first choice you have to make is whether to use ADO or DAO. Since Access will be my only source of data, I will use DAO. The next option is to decide where you want to put the data. I am going to default to the active worksheet starting in cell A4. This will give you room to put a title on the report. Once that is done, determine what you want to do with the data. The program offers two options: using the Subtotal feature in Excel or using a PivotTable. You could also use an input box and have the user type in a number, etc. I will use a message box to ask the user whether she wants a PivotTable. If she clicks Yes, it pulls the data and puts in a pivot table. If she clicks No, it pulls the data and uses Subtotals. If she presses cancel, it stops execution. This example also uses a button placed on the worksheet to allow you to run the code.

Your first step is to go into Excel and turn on the Visual Basic toolbar by going to View → Toolbars and checking Visual Basic. On the Visual Basic toolbar, click on the button that says Control Toolbox when you hover over it to bring up a box with the standard controls that you can place on your Excel Worksheets. We want to use the Command button. When you click the Command button box, your mouse cursor changes to a plus sign. Go to the top of your worksheet and click and drag a box to a size that you want.

Next, right-click on the Command button and select Properties. There are several properties to change so that this worksheet will look and print the way you want it to. First, change the PrintObject property to False so that the button will not show when you print the report. Next, change the Caption property to Pull Data or something similar. You can also change the system name that VBA uses to refer to the Command button to something more meaningful, so let's call it DataButton. Change the name on the box called Name (the first box on the alphabetical list or under Miscellaneous in the categorized list). You can also change the font, color, etc., but it is not necessary for this example. Once you have finished modifying the button, close the Properties box, right-click on the button again, and select View Code. When you are in the VBA screen, go to Tools → References and select a reference to Microsoft Data Access Objects. I am using Version 3.6. Put the code in Example 3-5 in for the `DataButton_Click` Event.

Example 3-5. Summarize data with a PivotTable or SubTotal

```
Private Sub DataButton_Click( )
Dim wrk As DAO.Workspace
Dim dbconn As DAO.Database
Dim rs As DAO.Recordset
Dim fld As DAO.Field
Dim msgoption As Long
Dim x As Integer
Dim xlws As Excel.Worksheet
Dim xlws2 As Excel.Worksheet
Dim xlrng As Excel.Range

Set xlws = ActiveSheet

Set wrk = DAO.CreateWorkspace("myworkspace", "admin", "")
Set dbconn = wrk.OpenDatabase("C:\Program Files\Microsoft Office\OFFICE11\" & _
            "SAMPLES\Northwind.mdb")
Set rs = dbconn.OpenRecordset("Select * from [Sales by Category]")

msgoption = MsgBox("Do you want a PivotTable?", vbYesNoCancel, _
            "Report Type")

Select Case msgoption
  Case vbYes
    Set xlrng = xlws.Cells(4, 1)
    On Error Resume Next
    xlrng.RemoveSubtotal
    x = 1
    For Each fld In rs.Fields
      xlws.Cells(4, x).Value = fld.Name
      x = x + 1
    Next
    Set xlrng = xlws.Cells(5, 1)
    xlrng.CopyFromRecordset rs
    xlws.Columns.AutoFit
    Set xlrng = xlws.Columns("D:D")
    xlrng.NumberFormat = "$#,##0.00"
    Set xlrng = xlws.Range(xlws.Cells(4, 1), _
                xlws.Cells(rs.RecordCount + 4, rs.Fields.Count))
    Set xlws2 = ActiveWorkbook.Sheets.Add
    xlws2.Name = "PivotTable"

    xlws2.PivotTableWizard xlDatabase, xlrng, xlws2.Cells(3,1),"SalesbyCategory", _
        False, True, True, True, False, , True, True, , , True
    xlws2.Cells(3, 1).Select
    xlws2.PivotTables("SalesbyCategory").AddFields RowFields:="ProductName", _
        ColumnFields:="CategoryName"
    With xlws2.PivotTables("SalesbyCategory").PivotFields("ProductSales")
        .Orientation = xlDataField
        .NumberFormat = "$#,##0.00"
    End With
    ActiveWorkbook.ShowPivotTableFieldList = False
    Set xlws2 = Nothing
```

Example 3-5. Summarize data with a PivotTable or SubTotal (continued)

```
  Case vbNo
    Set xlrng = xlws.Cells(4, 1)
    On Error Resume Next
    xlrng.RemoveSubtotal
    x = 1
    For Each fld In rs.Fields
      xlws.Cells(4, x).Value = fld.Name
      x = x + 1
    Next
    Set xlrng = xlws.Cells(5, 1)
    xlrng.CopyFromRecordset rs
    xlws.Columns.AutoFit
    Set xlrng = xlws.Columns("D:D")
    xlrng.NumberFormat = "$#,##0.00"
    Set xlrng = xlws.Range(xlws.Cells(4, 1), _
                xlws.Cells(rs.RecordCount + 4, rs.Fields.Count))
    xlrng.Subtotal 2, xlSum, 4, True, False, xlSummaryAbove
    xlws.Outline.ShowLevels 2


  Case vbCancel
    GoTo ExitStuff
End Select

ExitStuff:
    Set xlws = Nothing
    Set xlws2 = Nothing
    Set xlrng = Nothing
    rs.Close
    Set fld = Nothing
    Set rs = Nothing
    dbconn.Close
    Set dbconn = Nothing
    Set wrk = Nothing
End Sub
```

There is a lot going on in this procedure. First, the code sets up the DAO connection. This example uses the Northwind database and, provided you installed it in the default location, this path should work if you are using Office 2003. If you are using another version of Office, the path will be different. If the given path does not work, search your hard drive to find the correct path. As an aside, I will mention that I find the Select Case...End Select statement much easier to read than multiple If... Then statements. The Select Case statement allows you to write code that will be executed based on the value of your variable.

In the example above, you store the result of the message box in a variable called msgoption. The message box returns a value that is most easily deciphered by using the constants provided by Excel. The only options we gave were Yes, No, and Cancel. Excel VBA recognizes these as vbYes, vbNo, and vbCancel.

If the user clicks Yes, saying that she wants a pivot table, the code between Case vbYes and Case vbNo runs. The first few lines of both are the same. Remove subtotals if they exist. I put a line that says On Error Resume Next above this line; it will be in effect for each line after that. I suggest putting this in as the very last thing when you are writing code. This way, you know where your errors are occurring. As a general rule, I like to see all errors while I am writing and testing code. Then, when I put the code into production, I like to use On Error statements to try to avoid having the end user see error messages.

In addition to this command to add error-checking to the Remove Subtotals command, it is useful to have the On Error Resume Next line in for the occasion when someone runs the report twice and asks for a PivotTable both times. When this happens, Excel generates an error message that the sheet named "PivotTable" already exists. By having the code bypass that request, Excel simply skips the step of renaming the sheet, and it stays the default sheet. Returning our focus to the data, after the subtotals are removed (or the step is skipped, in the case where there are no subtotals to remove), you need to add the titles of the columns to the sheet by cycling through the Fields collection of the recordset. Use the CopyFromRecordset method of the range object to pull in the data from the recordset. With the data in place, the procedure formats the data in column D using a dollar sign, commas, and two decimal places. Those steps are the same for both vbYes and vbNo. In vbYes, the next step is to make the PivotTable.

There are two general methods for creating a PivotTable. The first method uses the PivotCaches method of the Workbook object. While I find the PivotCaches method to be less intuitive, it is the method that you see if you record a macro of making a PivotTable. The second method, used in the code above, is the PivotTableWizard method of the Worksheet object. Prior to this method being called, the xlrng Range Object is set up to reference the data worksheet, and the Cells object is used so that the data can be referred to by rows and columns. You could also use R1C1 notation, but this method is a little cleaner to read since we are pulling the values from rs. Fields.Count, etc. It is important to set up this Range first because you will build the PivotTable on a new worksheet, and the data resides on another sheet; by setting the range reference first, it becomes a simple matter of using that variable for the data range. The other steps are putting on the row, column, and data fields, as well as formatting the data to be like the data on the original worksheet.

For the vbNo option, go through the same steps as vbYes up to the point where column D is formatted. The Subtotal method is very easy to use. First, the Range object needs to be set up to refer to the range. Next, the Subtotal method of the range object is called by using Range.Subtotal—VBA helps you write the rest as you type. The first argument asks which column you want to group on. In Example 3-5, column 2 is selected instead of column 1 because it has the actual names. The consolidation function being used is xlSum. You can select from 12 different functions, including Average (xlAverage), Count (xlCount), etc. If you are not sure which one you want to use, you can highlight Subtotal with your mouse and press F1. Microsoft Help describes each function.

The next argument asks what column(s) you want to apply the function to. In this case we are using only one, so we can simply write 4. If there were multiple columns, say you wanted 4, 5, and 6, you would write Array(4,5,6). The next two arguments want to know whether it should replace the subtotals and whether you want page breaks between groups. The final argument asks if you want the totals to be above or below the group. In Figure 3-3, I have selected above the group. If you select xlSummaryBelow, the grand total appears at the bottom, and all of the details above the subtotals. This is really a user preference. Thinking back to the original reason for this report, the user wanted a summary of the data. It is unlikely that she wants to see all the details by default, but she probably wants to have the option to see the details if she chooses to. Assuming that, the ShowLevel method of the Outline property of the Worksheet object is being used to set the opening level to 2. In this case, 1 is the grand total, 2 is the total by category, and 3 is the detail. If the user wants to expand any subtotal, Excel places plus signs to the left of the row. Click on the plus sign to expand the subtotal. Also, press 1, 2, or 3 at the top left of the worksheet to get to the subtotal level that you want.

The vbCancel line simply sends it to the ExitStuff marker. In this case, you could have placed nothing in that line. However, since in many cases you will have code running after the Select Case statement, I added it. At the end of the procedure all of the objects are closed and/or set to nothing.

Summary

This chapter introduced you to the power of integrating Excel and Access. There is still a lot of ground to cover. At this point, my hope is that you understand how to build a recordset by using ADO and DAO. The rest of the chapter discussion and examples were meant to illustrate additional features already built into Excel. Our code just automated it. A side goal is that you are becoming familiar with the objects used in Excel VBA. When you read Chapter 5 on automating Excel with Access VBA, your familiarity with these objects will greatly increase your understanding of that chapter.

The Northwind database will not be used again until we use SQL Server in Chapter 7. For the rest of the examples, you will need to obtain the sample files available at *www.oreilly.com*. In these sample files, you will find the Excel example above and the other necessary databases and Excel workbooks, although I encourage you to try to enter the code for yourself, as it will help you get a better feel for VBA.

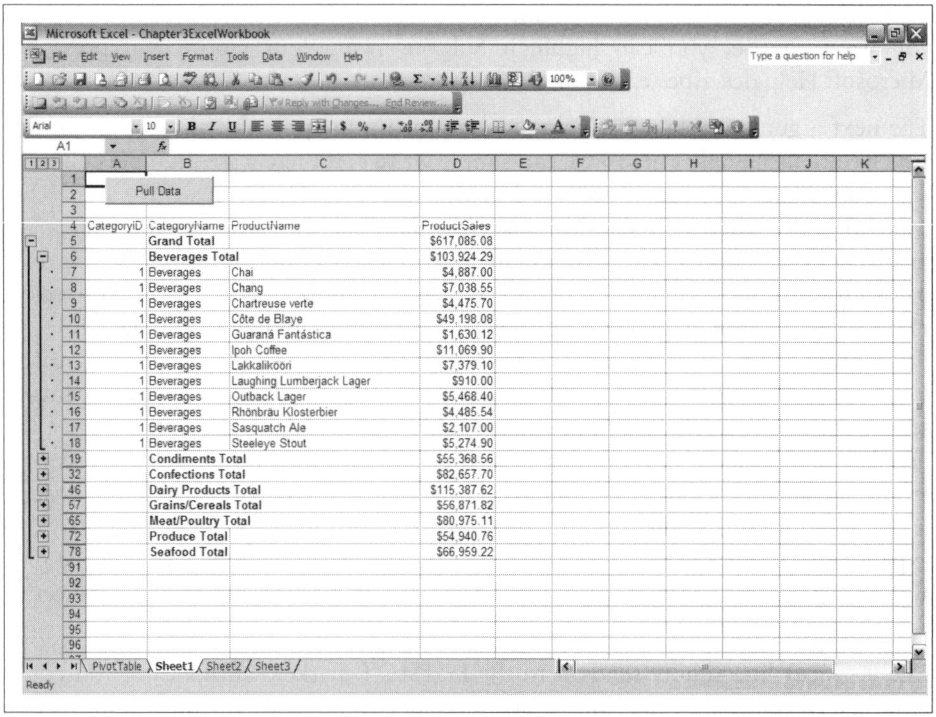

Figure 3-3. The resulting Excel file when the code in Example 3-5 is run showing subtotals instead of a pivot table, as well as details of the beverages category demonstrating how that works with subtotals

Note that there are appendixes at the end of the book that describe the commonly used Excel and Access objects that you use when doing this type of work. If you need help with VBA, there is a very complete language reference available from O'Reilly called *VB & VBA in a Nutshell: The Language*.

CHAPTER 4

Integration from the Access Interface

Using VBA from Access is very powerful and will be covered fully throughout the rest of the book. However, Access has some very powerful features available right from the user interface for importing, exporting, and linking data with Excel. The ability to do this from the Access user interface makes many tasks easier. For example, suppose you have two Excel spreadsheets of customer data, and you want to know which customers are on one sheet but missing from the other. You could try to use Excel's VLOOKUP functions and possibly even write some code in Excel to search the other worksheet. From Access, though, you can simply link the two worksheets and run the Find Unmatched Query Wizard; this technique will be discussed later in the chapter.

There are many other easy-to-use features covered in this chapter. By the end of this chapter, you will know how to do the following things:

- Import data from Excel into a new or existing table
- Link an Excel worksheet or named range and treat it like a table in Access
- Export an Access table to be analyzed with Excel
- Use the Save As feature to export a table or query
- Save a report in an Excel format

Performing these tasks requires only a few mouse clicks. After using these features, you'll begin to see other possibilities for integrating these applications. Also, you can use Access to perform these tasks on DBF files, fixed-width text files, delimited text files, and ODBC data source tables. Our examples, however, will be focused on Excel.

Importing Excel Data

Excel is commonly used to build a workbook that performs a series of calculations and returns a result set for analysis. Whether you think about it that way or not, that boils down to Excel's core functionality. The convenient thing about leaving data in Excel is that the result set changes as you make changes to the data. However, that is also the inconvenient thing about leaving data in Excel. There will be times when you will want to take a snapshot of result data and not want to have it changed by new data. Consider the input parameters in Figure 4-1 and the resulting data in Figure 4-2.

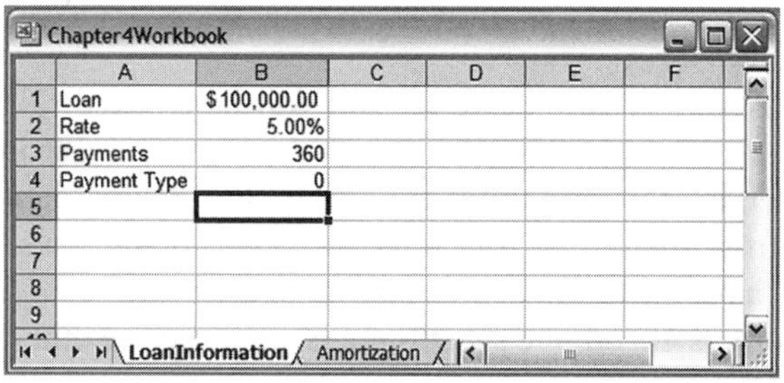

	A	B
1	Loan	$100,000.00
2	Rate	5.00%
3	Payments	360
4	Payment Type	0

Figure 4-1. An Excel worksheet providing inputs that drive calculations on the amortization page

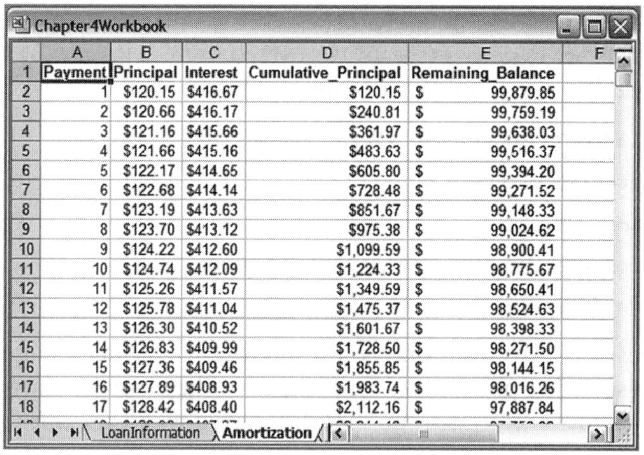

	A	B	C	D	E
1	Payment	Principal	Interest	Cumulative_Principal	Remaining_Balance
2	1	$120.15	$416.67	$120.15	$ 99,879.85
3	2	$120.66	$416.17	$240.81	$ 99,759.19
4	3	$121.16	$415.66	$361.97	$ 99,638.03
5	4	$121.66	$415.16	$483.63	$ 99,516.37
6	5	$122.17	$414.65	$605.80	$ 99,394.20
7	6	$122.68	$414.14	$728.48	$ 99,271.52
8	7	$123.19	$413.63	$851.67	$ 99,148.33
9	8	$123.70	$413.12	$975.38	$ 99,024.62
10	9	$124.22	$412.60	$1,099.59	$ 98,900.41
11	10	$124.74	$412.09	$1,224.33	$ 98,775.67
12	11	$125.26	$411.57	$1,349.59	$ 98,650.41
13	12	$125.78	$411.04	$1,475.37	$ 98,524.63
14	13	$126.30	$410.52	$1,601.67	$ 98,398.33
15	14	$126.83	$409.99	$1,728.50	$ 98,271.50
16	15	$127.36	$409.46	$1,855.85	$ 98,144.15
17	16	$127.89	$408.93	$1,983.74	$ 98,016.26
18	17	$128.42	$408.40	$2,112.16	$ 97,887.84

Figure 4-2. Result data that changes when you make changes to the inputs on the LoanInformation worksheet

Assume that you want to load that data into a new table in Access, and you don't want it to change. In Access, create a blank database application by going into Access and selecting File → New. Depending on the version of Access, you will either get a brand new empty database or a menu like you see in Figure 4-3. If you see the menu in Figure 4-3, click on Blank Database and it will bring up the dialog box that you see in Figure 4-4. Next, give the database a name.

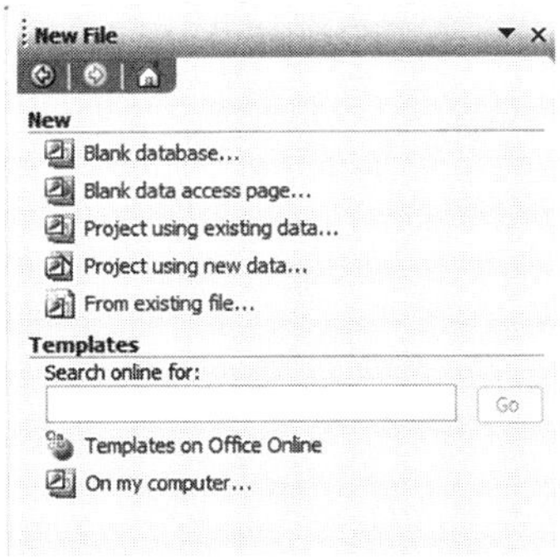

Figure 4-3. The new database menu that comes up in Microsoft Access 2003 when you select File →
New

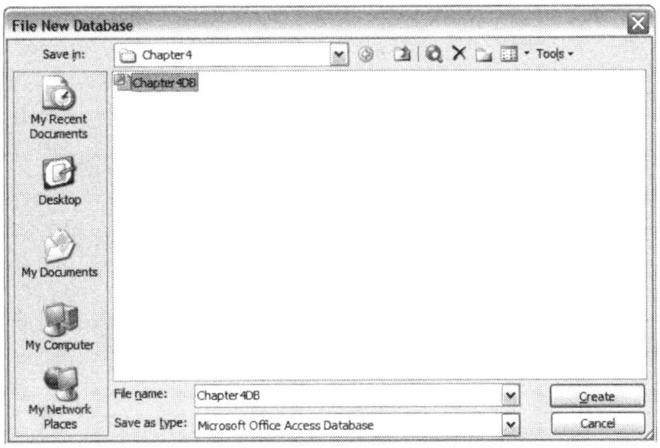

Figure 4-4. The dialog box that comes up when you want to create a new database, similar to the
Save As dialog box that you would see in other Office applications

Unlike Excel, Access continually saves your progress as you update the data. This is helpful in the sense that you don't work all morning and lose your work due to a power outage or a network drive going down. But it also means that you can't do work and later go back to the point of your last save. The result is that in Excel, you can work in a workbook called Book1 which you don't need to save, while in Access a file must be created and saved.

Once you have done this, you will have a blank database as shown in Figure 4-5.

Figure 4-5. A brand new blank database in Microsoft Access 2003, showing the Tables tab of the database

Now you are ready to import data into this new database application. To accomplish this, right-click on whitespace when you have the Tables tab selected, and you will see the menu in Figure 4-6. On that menu select Import. Access brings up a File Dialog box like the one in Figure 4-7. In the Files of Type box, select Microsoft Excel and then the file that you want. Access brings up the Import Spreadsheet Wizard shown in Figure 4-8. You will notice that you can choose to bring in entire worksheets or named ranges. Using named ranges is very useful if you have data resembling tables throughout one worksheet. However, generally I try to keep data from tables on its own worksheet. In this example, the data needed is in the worksheet called Amortization, so to import it, click it and then Next.

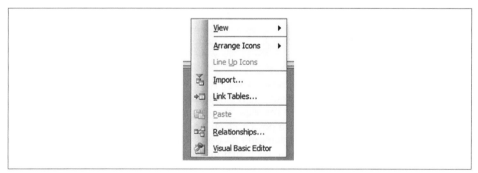

Figure 4-6. A context dialog with Import

Access brings up the screen shown in Figure 4-9. In this case, check the box that says the first row contains column headings and click Next. (If you have headings and do

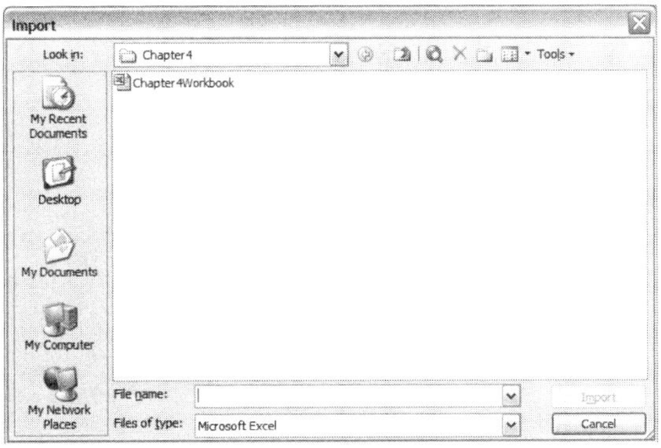

Figure 4-7. The import file dialog

not check this box, you run the risk of your data types being incorrect.) This brings up the next step in the wizard, shown in Figure 4-10, where you select whether you want to import the data into a new table or an existing table. Since this is a blank database, select In a New Table and click Next. The next step in the wizard, shown in Figure 4-11, allows you to select columns and either change the name or choose not to import it.

> In some cases, you can change the data type, but in many cases you can't. For this example, accept the defaults and click Next. You might have noticed that the Excel worksheet did not have spaces in the column headings; underscore characters were used instead. While this is not necessary, it makes writing queries much easier. If you have spaces in your field names in an Access table, you will need to place brackets —[Table Name]—in your query when you refer to the field in calculations, etc. So if you were forced to import an Excel spreadsheet that did not have good field names as a table, you could edit them in this step.

The next step of the wizard allows you to either pick the field that is the primary key or select the option that there is no primary key. Normally, I let Access add the primary key. However, since you won't have two payments with the same number in this example, you can select Payment as the primary key, as shown in Figure 4-12. The final step in the wizard, shown in Figure 4-13, is to give the table a name. The table will default to the name of the worksheet or named range. I prefer to place the identifier "tbl_" in front of table names, "qry_" in front of query names, "frm_" in front of form names, etc. So my suggestion is to name this table tbl_Amortization.

While this may seem like a lot of steps, the wizard makes it very quick, particularly if you accept the defaults. Also, you will find this to be a welcome change if you ever had to enter the information already in a spreadsheet into a database.

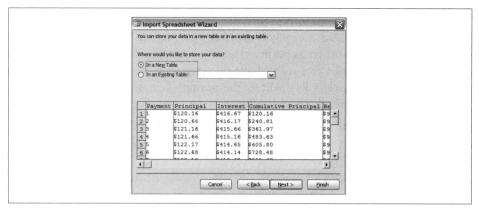

Figure 4-8. *The first step of the Import Spreadsheet Wizard, when you can select importing worksheets or named ranges*

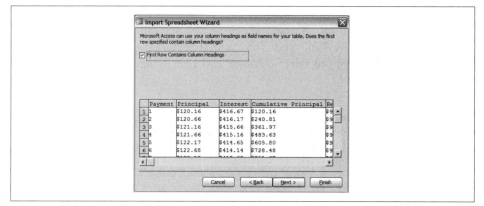

Figure 4-9. *The second step of the importing process, when you can select whether the first row contains the column headings*

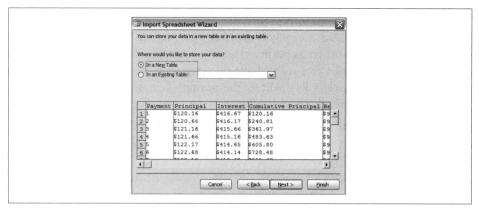

Figure 4-10. *The third step, when you select whether you want the spreadsheet imported into a new table or an existing table*

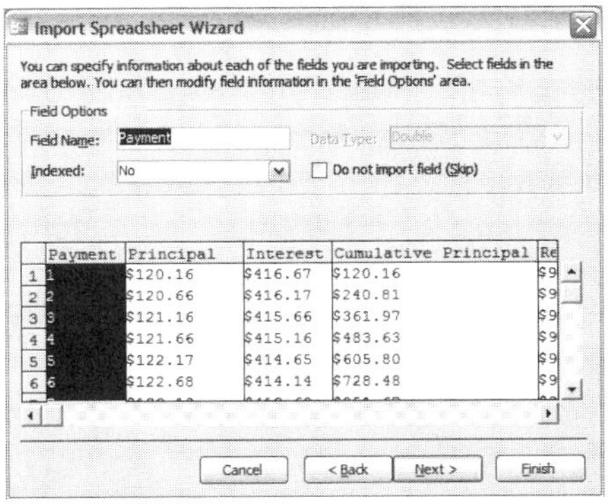

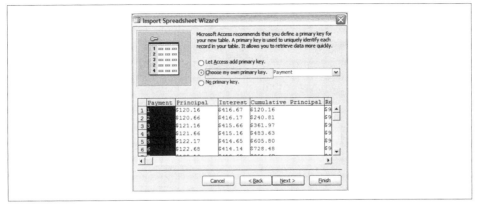

Figure 4-11. The step when you can change field names and choose whether you want to skip importing a particular field

Figure 4-12. The step when you choose which field, if any, to use as the primary key of the table

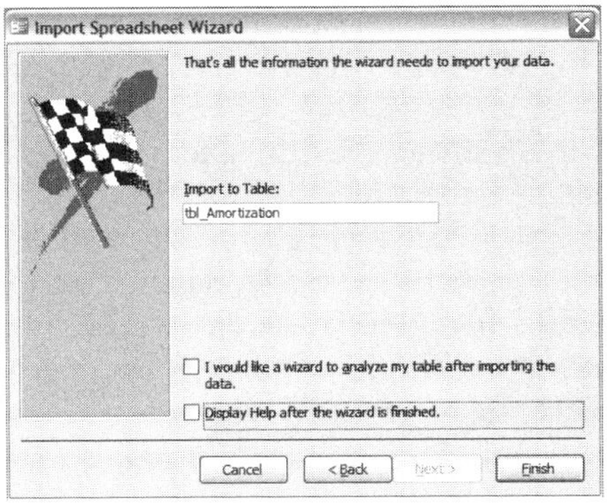

Figure 4-13. The final step in the wizard, when you choose the name of the table and have the choice of two options for Access to help you and/or analyze your new table

The other benefit to importing data into a new database is that you don't have to go through the grueling process of creating a table using Design View. Access uses the information that you load to determine whether the field should be text, integer, double, currency, etc. This feature can be a real time saver if you have many fields. Sometimes when I am creating a new database, I mock up a few records in Excel and import the spreadsheet just to save time creating and naming tables. Also, if you are working with database novices, they are often more comfortable in Excel. If you need to obtain data from someone who is not familiar with Access, you can give them an Excel worksheet and have them type in the data using the Excel user interface where they feel comfortable. Then you can take the spreadsheet and import the data into your Access database.

Using Excel to Ease Importing

As you saw in Figure 4-10, you can import data into an existing table. Unless the spreadsheet was designed to work with the existing database, however, you will often work with database tables that may not have the same field names (columns) and data types. For example, a cost center in Excel might be a number without leading zeros, while the same column in Access might be text and expect leading zeros.

You can deal with this in Excel. Create a new worksheet and references to the cells that you need on the original worksheet. Once you have done that, create formulas to modify the data so that the field names and data types match those in Access, and save the workbook. Now it is as simple as importing the new worksheet from Access.

An Easy Way to Add Leading Zeros

One of the most common data conversion items is to put leading zeros on a number and treat it like text. Some people simply edit each record by using an apostrophe to signify that they are entering text and then adding zeros where they are needed. Other people attempt to accomplish this by using a format in Excel that appears to add leading zeros. This does not change the underlying data, however. I have also seen people write a series of If...Then statements checking to see how many zeros are needed. While that works, there is a much easier way. Using the RIGHT function, available in Excel and in VBA, you can easily add leading zeros. If you wanted leading zeros for five digits, the formula is =RIGHT(number + 100000,5)—all you need to do is put a 1, the number of zeros needed, and the number after the comma is the number of digits that you want. This works because if you have the number 123 and you need it to be 00123, by adding 100,000 you get the number 100,123. When you take the right 5 digits, you end up with 00123. This accomplishes a task that many people do as several steps in one.

Another easy way to put data from Excel into Access is to use the Copy command in Excel and then, with the table open in Access, use the Edit → Paste Append command from Access. (If you attempt to use the paste command, Access gives you an error message.) You might find that Paste Append still gives you errors. However, Access does create a table of the paste errors for you to review.

You should carefully review the errors to make sure that your tables are not too restrictive. For example, you might find a field in the database listed as required when there are times it is OK for it to be blank. In addition, you also want to determine what is more important, having some of the data for all of the rows or having all of the data for some of the rows. I have been asked to work on many projects where data integrity was an issue, and things like missing customer records, missing billing records, and so forth were problems. Often, there were data issues causing records to not load. While these issues could have also been found by reviewing a log, it is sometimes easier to loosen restrictions so that you can load the data you have and then use exception reports to find out where you need to fill in the data gaps.

You can also end up with unexpected logic errors when importing or pasting data from Excel into Access. In some cases, Access performs the import without noticing the error. This is a particularly large problem when you inadvertently load a number with decimals (double) into an Integer field. When importing data, some common errors to look for are:

Importation of numbers of type double into a field with a field size of integer
  Say you are loading a number with decimals, such as prices of raw materials, into a field that was mistakenly created as an integer field. Aside from all of the prices being wrong, it is a difficult item to catch, particularly if you are working with queries that use that data and not at the base table.

Text in an Excel sheet with more characters than the field size allows
  This issue is important because you might end up losing data. I have dealt with issues like this on many occasions, particularly with mailing address fields.

Spaces at the end of text
  This problem is common when the Excel file was created as an extract from a mainframe or another database. Some database applications will write spaces at the end of each field until it reaches the field size. This will cause problems if you are attempting to join this field with another. Using the TRIM function `Trim([FieldName])` in an update query makes quick work of this.

Duplicate primary keys
  Sometimes this error lets you know that there are problems with the data, but other times you will find that what you thought was the primary key really wasn't. For example, on many general ledger systems, it might make sense for

the Account Number field to be a primary key on a chart of accounts, but you might find that the primary key is really Company Number and Account Number. You can accomplish this in Access, but you would most likely skip the primary key step in the import and set the primary key in Design View.

If you have successfully addressed the issues, this type of integration with Access and Excel can lead to significant savings of data entry time. Keep in mind that if your Excel workbook's primary function is to provide data to a database, it should be designed with ease of importing in mind. If, on the other hand, the database is secondary to the form and functionality of the workbook, I suggest creating an extra worksheet linked to the primary worksheet in the workbook that will be used specifically for importing/exporting data.

Linking Excel Data

There are many occasions when you want to work with Excel data as if it were in a table in Access, but you need to keep the source of the data in Excel. (This happens frequently at companies where Access is not on every desktop but everyone has Excel.) I worked with one company who maintained their product list in Excel, although many of the people who needed that information used Access. While you could simply import the data each time you needed it, this could cause problems if you forgot the importing step, causing someone to use old data. Linking to the Excel worksheet instead of importing it allows you to take advantage of the ability to query the data using Access while ensuring that you always have up-to-date information.

The steps for linking versus importing are virtually the same, except that when you right-click on the tables area, you select Link Tables instead of Import. What you have to be careful with and always keep in the back of your mind when linking to a worksheet is that *any changes you make will also be made and saved within Excel*. Normally, this would be a very good thing, but if you forgot about this feature, you could be very surprised when changes occur. For importing versus linking, I suggest determining how the information will be updated and how important the updates are. Consider the risks of linking and making inadvertent updates. It is easy to forget that you are dealing with data that, in reality, exists outside your application, so you might want to abbreviate a product name in your database and upset the person in charge of maintaining the product list in the Excel workbook.

As mentioned at the beginning of the chapter, it is also helpful to link Excel worksheets when you want to find items that are exclusively in one worksheet. Access provides a Find Unmatched Query Wizard that allows you to easily find items in one list that are not in another. Let's say you have an Excel worksheet with product information and a primary key of a Product Number, and another worksheet with sales information by product number, sale date, and amount sold. If you want to know which products had no sales, link to the two worksheets and run the Find

Unmatched Query Wizard on the linked tables. The resulting query result set would give you the answer, and you could build a report using this data.

Sometimes I use Access as a place to hold data on which to perform analysis, and all of the data entry and validation are done in different places. Access makes easy work of linking, importing, and combining information from various sources, so it is ideal for these types of tasks. A good example is corporate budgeting. Many companies use Excel as a data entry tool for budget information. Assume you are dealing with 100 individual budget files; if you had to look in every workbook to determine whether a particular account was budgeted, or some other nugget of information like that, you would search for a better solution. By using Access and importing all of the information, you can quickly run queries, produce reports, and update data. You can even take the updated data from Access and update the Excel workbooks using VBA.

Combining Linking and Importing

If you want to import data so you do not need to worry about accidentally making changes while you are working with it, but you also want to ensure that you have the most up-to-date information, you can have both. Taking the product list example, if you want to make changes without affecting the original Excel workbook, import the table first and create a link to it. You can then use the imported data in your application while still being able to view and retrieve the data in the original Excel workbook. You must give these tables different names; I sometimes use tbl_TABLENAME and lnktbl_TABLENAME. If you don't, you will be given tbl_TABLENAME and tbl_TABLENAME1. These might be OK, but I have had to go back to the database window enough times while writing queries to figure out which name is which that I find making more descriptive names to be a time saver.

Once you have the two tables in the database, create a Find Unmatched Query to determine what records are missing. This gives you the information in the linked table but not in the local database table. If you need the data locally, create an Append Query using the Unmatched Query as the source and the local table as the destination where you'll put the missing information. If you have to worry about values in the individual fields changing, you could also create an Update Query and update all of the fields of the unconnected table with the values in the linked table. You could have a few lines of code in the Open event of your startup form that would run these queries to automate this process.

While this is useful in Excel, it is also useful when dealing with data from databases. Sometimes you have a large table on a database server, and you want to run a lot of queries locally to reduce impact on server performance. Link to the data and run Import and Update Queries described previously to make sure you have the most up-to-date information.

Using Export and Analyzing It
with Microsoft Office Excel

Now that you have tried to import data, assume you need to go the other way and send data to Excel. This method has far fewer steps than the import method, but before attempting to export data, you need to answer a few questions. First, find out how many rows are being exported. If there are more than 65,536 rows, you need to break the table up into pieces before exporting it. Next, consider the importance of the data format. If the data must be in a particular format, you can export the data, have an Excel report read it, and present it in another sheet. Another option is to use VBA to automate Excel. In this case, neither of these is a problem.

What if you need to put date information into the amortization table and email it to someone as an Excel worksheet? Sure, you could copy and paste from Access into Excel, format it, put in the formulas, etc.—or you could take advantage of the power of a query in the database. Where possible, I attempt to draw comparisons between how you would handle something in Excel versus Access.

In Excel, to add a payment date field that refers to the payment number, write a formula and copy it down to the end of your data. As new rows are added, continue to copy down the formulas. There is nothing stopping you from putting different formulas into every cell or not putting formulas in some cells. This can lead to problems with consistency.

If you contrast that with the Access solution, you see how the database makes this easier. In an Access database, you can write queries that can have calculated fields. If you want to have a field for the date of a payment based on the payment number, you could do so very easily with a calculated field. Since you know that the payment number is in a field named Payment, add a parameter for the begin date to make the calculated field work by placing the name of the parameter you want in brackets ([BeginDate], for example). You can go one step further by going to Query → Parameters when in Design View of the query, where you can declare the parameter and data type. You will be prompted for the parameter either way. The benefit to declaring the parameter is that Access validates that the data type is correct before running the query.

To implement a calculated field with a parameter, click on the Queries tab on the database and double-click on the Create Query in Design View on the query list. This brings up the Show Table dialog box shown in Figure 4-14. Click on tbl_Amortization, Add, and Close. In the query's first column, enter the following code in the text box:

```
PaymentDate: DateAdd("m",[Payment]-1,[BeginDate])
```

Then go to Query → Parameters and type BeginDate for the parameter and Date/Time for the Data Type (Figure 4-15). (Note that you will be prompted for all

---

declared perameters even if they are no longer in use in the query.) Select all of the fields and drag them down to the query, or double-click on each field in the field list. In either case, you should end up with the query shown in Figure 4-16.

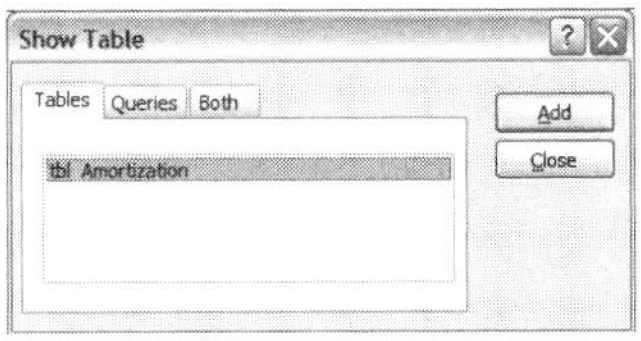

Figure 4-14. Dialog box allowing you to add one or more tables to a query

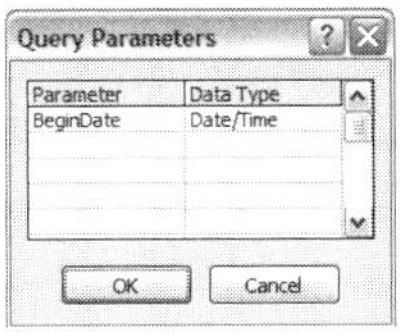

Figure 4-15. Dialog box allowing you to define parameters

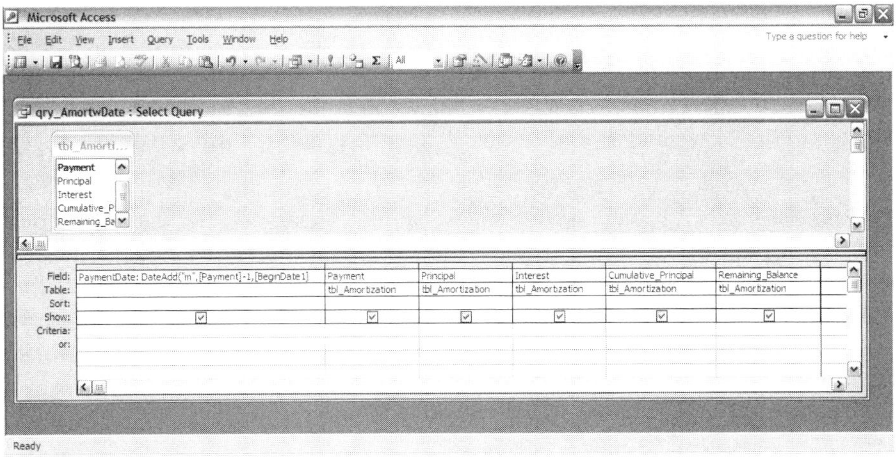

Figure 4-16. What the query should look like in design view with the calculated field

Take a moment and look at the DateAdd function that is being used in the query. This function adds a particular number of intervals to a date or time. You can add seconds, minutes, hours, days, months, years, etc. Here, the interval selected is "m" for month and the number is Payment—1, since we want the first payment to be the BeginDate, not a month later.

When you open this query, you are prompted for a date. The query gives you the date that each payment number refers to based on the begin date that you entered. If you attempt to enter a number instead of a date, Access stops you. However, if you don't declare the parameter, Access converts a number to a date. So, if you enter **1**, it starts at December 31, 1899; **2** would be 1/1/1900, etc. However, I suggest declaring the parameter and making sure it is the right type, since it is unlikely that anyone would count the days from 1899 to determine what today is.

Now that your query is done, go to File → Save As and call it qry_AmortwDate, make sure As Query is selected (default), press OK, and close the query. If you double-click on the query, it will ask you for the begin date and show you the results on the screen. Assuming that you want that data in Excel, you have three options: go to Edit → Select All Records and copy and paste into Excel, export the data from the File menu, or use Analyze with Microsoft Office Excel from the Tools → Office Links → Analyze from the Microsoft Office Excel menu. While all three work, I suggest choosing your approach based on the situation.

Let's say that you have Excel open already, and you just want the data—you don't care about formatting, etc. You can select all records in Access (Ctrl+A is the shortcut) and copy and paste into Excel. That is most likely the easiest method. If you want to export the data for someone else to use and don't care to see the data, you can select File → Export and when the File Name Dialog comes up, select Microsoft Excel from the Files of Type box. Select the highest version that is going to be available on all of the machines you have. Give it a file name and press Export All. This will create an Excel file with virtually no data formatting, except that it will be exported with the correct data type; currency would have dollar signs and commas, for example. (If the query is not open, you can right-click on the query and hit Export. It will ask you for the filename and parameter value and then export it.)

Consider next that you want to open it in Excel and do some things with the file, like run some formulas or review individual records. While you could do either of the other steps noted above and make it work, there is a very easy way to open up Excel, provide some basic formatting, and then save the new Excel workbook with the data. By using Tools → Office Links → Analyze it with Microsoft Office Excel, Access will open up Excel and create a new file as described above. You can select this method with the query open or closed. If the query is closed, you will be prompted for a parameter (if the query is a parameterized query) and if it is open, it will go right to Excel. If the file name already exists (the filename defaults to the query name), Access will ask you if you want to overwrite it. If you click No, it will prompt you for a new name. If you click Yes, it will simply clear the old file and replace it with the new one.

Using the Analyze it feature from Microsoft Office Excel makes quick work of many common requests. For example, if you have a table of products and someone from the marketing department calls you and wants an up to date product list, you can click on the products table and go to Analyze it with Microsoft Office Excel, and it will create a report for you.

Using Raw Exported Access Data in Excel

If you need to use information in Excel that comes from Access, you need to first determine if you want to pull the data from the database (covered in Chapters 2 and 3) or if you want to push the data into Excel from the database. Assuming that you want to push the data from Access into Excel, you have to then figure out how you will use the data.

There are no simple right answers (but there are certainly some wrong ones) as to what the best method is. I decide on the option where I have the most control. If I built the database, and I am charged with maintaining it, I would most likely choose to push the data into Excel and would probably opt to automate Excel from Access (covered in Chapter 5). Whatever you choose, keep in mind what you are doing with the data and make sure that the method you choose is easy to maintain. For instance, if you use Excel to pull the data from Access, the feature will often automatically create a named range (see Chapter 2). This can make using the data much more manageable. However, if you need a new Excel workbook each month and a macro can do your work for you within Excel, you can create a blank Excel sheet with your macro, paste in your data, run the macro, and do the processing from Access. In many cases, this will be easier than opening the correct workbook and pulling in the most current data.

I find that when I am trying to share data with other users in the basic database format with no formulas, using the user interface functions from Access is easiest. If, however, I need to manipulate the data in Excel for my own purposes, I generally use Excel to pull the data or Access VBA to automate the process.

Exporting an Access Report to Excel

Use this feature at your own risk. When you open up an Access report, you can use the Export function from the File menu to save the report in a variety of formats. When you select Export, Access will bring up the Export To dialog box that looks like the typical Save As Windows dialog. You can change the file type by changing the Save As Type drop down box. If you need to keep the formatting and want it to look exactly like it does on the screen, your best bet is to use the Snapshot format. At the time of writing this, users can get the Snapshot viewer free from Microsoft. The other option, outside of Office, is to use a PDF printer to print the document to a PDF file that can be opened with Adobe Acrobat. If you don't have that option, the Snapshot viewer is your only choice if you want it to look exactly the same. These two options are the only ones that preserve controls. This is very important if you have charts that you want to share.

If you just want the basic data to be presented, I suggest using the Export function from the File menu to save it in Rich Text Format. This allows the report to be opened in Microsoft Word. The next choice on my list would be to save it as an HTML file. Exporting a report into an Excel format works, but I have found that the formatting and the layout with the subtotals, etc. are very clunky. So, this is the one area that I suggest that you either automate Excel using the query results directly or use something other than Excel when dealing with reports.

Next Steps

This chapter covered some very basic functionality that exists in Access to deal with outside data sources, including Excel. Most of the functionality can be applied to other data sources as well. While these features can be very useful, I would guess that after you finish this book you'll use the more advanced functionality of Access VBA for most of your reporting tasks. The features covered in this chapter, therefore, will be used on a more ad hoc basis. Having said that, it is critical to understand how these features work because over time you will probably use each of them.

The other important item to note is that Access and Excel have very similar functionality with respect to data access. Because of that, people often use the feature that they know instead of the feature that will best solve the problem. It is because of those times that I think you should understand all of the features so you can make the best decision.

Finally, most of the features covered in this chapter can be automated by using Access VBA. This will be more relevant in future chapters, but if you have 20 or 30 Excel files to process, you would do yourself a big favor by learning a small amount of VBA to automate the process instead of doing each file individually.

CHAPTER 5

Using Access VBA to Automate Excel

While the earlier pieces of the book lay a good foundation, and the rest of the book certainly builds on it, if you were only going to focus on one chapter, this should be it. Access is a great application for building a front end. While Access provides some nice wizards for many of the functions that you can perform, this chapter focuses on VBA code that you write from scratch. If you have done any work in Visual Basic and have built forms, the form building tools in Access will be very familiar to you. The nice thing about using VBA is that the syntax is the same from application to application; the main difference is the objects that you are using.

This chapter is broken up into several distinct sections. The first part focuses on creating an Excel Workbook that can be used with Access VBA. The next part looks at some Access features with queries to create the data used for reporting, including using VBA to write SQL. The rest of the chapter focuses on how to use other Excel capabilities from Access.

High-Level Excel Objects

There are three primary objects that your Access VBA needs creating in order to automate Excel: the Excel Application object, the Excel Workbook object, and the Excel Worksheet object. These objects are created in that order.

In order to use the Excel objects, you need to create a reference to Excel from Access VBA. When you are in an Access database, click on the Modules table and then press the New button. This will bring up a new module. You can also do this from the Insert menu by going to Insert → Module. In the Module View, go to Tools → References, and Access brings up the References Dialog as shown in Figure 5-1. Scroll down to the Microsoft Excel Object Library and check its box. The library is Version 11.0 for Office 2003, but if you have different versions, choose the highest version available.

Figure 5-1. The References dialog box, which lets you set a reference to any applications that you want to automate, including Excel, Word, PowerPoint, or MapPoint

After creating that reference, go to Insert → Procedure. This brings up the dialog box shown in Figure 5-2. For this example, call the procedure GetExcel, and click the radio buttons for Sub and Public.

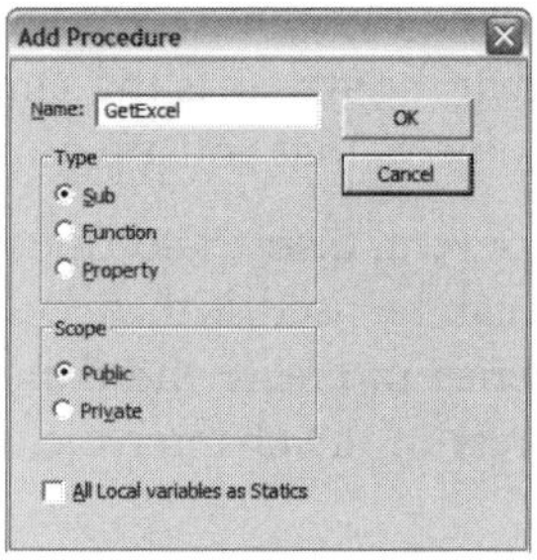

Figure 5-2. The Add Procedure dialog, which adds new subs, functions, or properties to a module

The Application Object

In order to use the Application object, you must first use the Dim statement to create a variable to access the object. Once you have created the object, you will use the Set statement to set the variable to a new Excel Application object. This opens Excel, although you won't be able to see it until you set the Visible property of the Application object to True, as shown in Example 5-1.

Example 5-1. Creating an Excel application object

```
Public Sub GetExcel()
Dim xlApp As Excel.Application
Set xlApp = New Excel.Application
xlApp.Visible = True
End Sub
```

This code is the starting point of any Excel automation task because you need the Excel Application object to use the other objects in Excel. The only risk of using this method of automation is that if you use a different version of Excel than the people using the application, your users would need to change the reference to their own version. While this is not that difficult, it makes distribution a challenge for some of your novice users since they would need to know how to change references in order to use the application.

You can eliminate this problem by using something called *late binding*. In late binding, you create a variable As object instead of specifying an exact object type, and then use Createobject to produce the required object. (Setting a reference to Excel and using the New keyword to set a reference is called *early binding*.) To use late binding, use the code in Example 5-2.

Example 5-2. Using late binding to create an Excel application object

```
Public Sub GetExcelLate( )
Dim xlApp As object
Set xlApp = Createobject("Excel.Application")
xlApp.Visible = True
End Sub
```

While it would seem like you could just use late binding all the time, it does make it more difficult to write the code, as some of the Visual Basic Editor's automation isn't available when you use late binding. For example, in the early binding example, when you type xlApp.Visible, by the time you got to vi, you would see the entire word, visible. At that point, press the tab key, and "visible" will be filled in. This is especially helpful when you search for a method or property to use.

When I am doing work for a client and I don't know their version of Excel or whether they have several versions of Microsoft Office running at their company, I use object and late binding to automate Excel. While this makes it more difficult to program, it is certainly easier for the user.

The Workbook Object

The Application object does very little on its own, but it is a necessary foundation for using the other objects in Excel. As you may know, when you use Excel and want a new workbook, go to either File → Open or File → New. When you automate Excel from Access, you need to use the Workbooks object, which is actually a collection of objects. When you do that, you will see several methods available.

The two main methods that will be covered here are the Add method and the Open method. The Add method simulates the File → New functionality that you access from Excel. The Open method is used less frequently, but can be helpful if you are using prebuilt templates, or just want to import data. However, just about anything that you could put into a template can be done from VBA in Access. And, while it adds to the programming, when creating the material in VBA, you do not need to be concerned about whether the user has the correct template available on his computer. Example 5-3 and Example 5-4 show how to create a new workbook and open an existing workbook. The code to create the application is also included.

Example 5-3. Workbooks collection add method example

```
Public Sub GetExcel()
Dim xlApp As Excel.Application
Dim xlWb As Excel.Workbook
Set xlApp = New Excel.Application
xlApp.Visible = True
Set xlWb = xlApp.Workbooks.Add
xlWb.SaveAs "Test.xls"
End Sub
```

Example 5-4. Workbooks collection open method example

```
Public Sub GetExcel()
Dim xlApp As Excel.Application
Dim xlWb As Excel.Workbook
Set xlApp = New Excel.Application
xlApp.Visible = True
Set xlWb = xlApp.Workbooks.Open("C:\Devwork\Chapter5.xls")
End Sub
```

The Add method example uses the SaveAs method of the Workbook object to save the workbook. In most cases, when you create a new workbook you will want to save it. When you want to save the workbook, you have several choices: Save, SaveAs, SaveAsXMLData or SaveCopyAs. The SaveAsXMLData method is new to Office 2003 and is only available in the Professional edition. After you have used the SaveAs method, you can use the Save method to continue saving the workbook. The SaveCopyAs method is useful if you want to save the workbook in its current state but continue working with the original. This can be useful if you are working with an Excel workbook that will be sent to various users and you want each to get progressively more information.

For example, if you are building a report that has divisional and corporate information, and you have one group of users that gets the divisional data and another group that gets divisional and corporate data, you can create a new workbook, use the SaveAs method, and call it *Corporate.xls*. Add the divisional data and save the workbook using the SaveCopyAs method, calling it *Divisional.xls*. When you add the corporate data, use the Save method to save it. If you had used the SaveAs method for the divisional data, you would have had to use the SaveAs method again. There are many other times when you want to save a workbook as a different name but want to continue working in the current workbook, and the SaveCopyAs method is the easiest way to do that.

As you can see in the Open method example, it is very simple to open an existing workbook. However, there are also many other options available, such as whether there is a password, whether you want to update links, etc. The Open method is useful when you are opening a workbook that will be used as a template. You also use the Open method when you have data in Excel that you want to bring into Access in an automated fashion.

An example of this is an Excel workbook that holds various types of information within each row. Let's say that you have an Excel workbook that holds the amount of time worked by each participant on a project, and column A specifies whether the person is an employee or a contractor. In an Access database, if you keep the time of employees in a separate table than that of contractors, you need to sort or filter in Excel to be able to import or cut and paste the data. This might be manageable, but if you get several of these each week, it quickly takes up more time than it is worth.

From Access, you could open up every workbook in a directory using VBA, and in an automated fashion, process them line by line, using the Select...Case statement to process each row. If the row held contractor data, you would have code to put it into the contractor table, and if the row were an employee record, you could put that data into the employee table.

If you are working with data that needs to go into multiple tables in exactly the same format, you can easily handle this with one line of code for each table, instead of recreating all of the code. Have one table for items ordered and another for items on backorder, with the same fields for each.

Another example is if you have separate tables for home addresses and business address. Using the example from the text, if you have an employee table and a contractor table, and the data being entered is the same for each, write a Select...Case statement and have all of the code in each Case. This results in duplication of code.

As an alternative, have the Select...Case statement set the reference to the correct table, and have the code run after the Select...Case statement. This reduces the amount of code that you have and also make it easier to maintain, since changes need to be made in only one place, instead of for each Case. This won't work if the data is different in each table, but when the data is the same, it makes coding much easier.

The Worksheet Object

The place where most of the code happens is with the Worksheet object. As with the application object, the Worksheet object has many objects, methods, and properties available. There is a Worksheets collection that holds all of the worksheets in a workbook and provides methods to add, copy, delete, move, etc. the worksheets in the workbook. When you add a new workbook to the Excel application object, it adds the number of worksheets specified on the General tab of the Excel options dialog. You can get to that dialog from within Excel by going to Tools → Options, as shown in Figure 5-3.

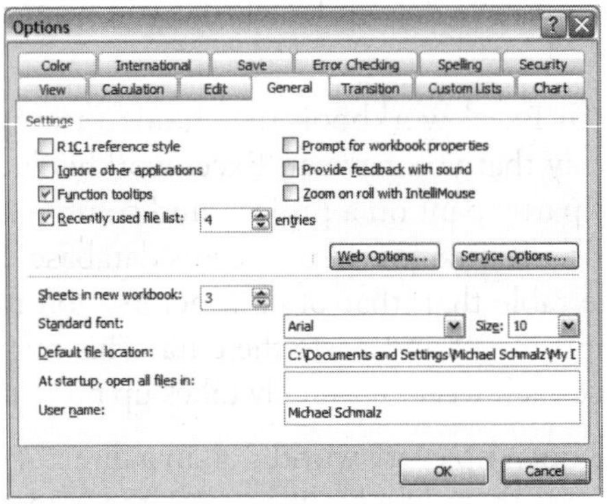

Figure 5-3. Excel dialog box allowing you to set various options, including the "Sheets in new workbook" option referred to in the text

This is important to know because you cannot assume that your user has the same number of worksheets as you do on your machine. I ran into a problem once in which I prepared three worksheets of data, and my machine had a default of three worksheets for a new workbook. I referred to each as Sheet1, Sheet2, and Sheet3. As it ran, it renamed each. This worked for a while until one day I was called about an error. I could not easily diagnose it over the phone so I went to the person's PC and found the problem was that their default was set to one worksheet for a new workbook. While I could have changed this setting for them, instead I changed the code to add worksheets instead of referring to the default blank worksheets, allowing the code to work on all machines.

The code below shows how to set a reference to a worksheet added to a new workbook. To use an existing sheet, you would use xlWb.Sheets("*SheetName*") instead of xlWb.Worksheets.Add. In addition to the Sheets collection, you can also use the Worksheets collection. As with other objects, the Worksheet object belongs to multiple collections. The Sheets collection holds all of the worksheets and chart sheets. The Worksheets collection holds only the worksheets. Each worksheet is a member of both collections. In Example 5-5, a new worksheet is added and renamed to MyNewWorksheet.

Example 5-5. Code to add a worksheet

```
Public Sub GetExcel()
Dim xlApp As Excel.Application
Dim xlWb As Excel.Workbook
Dim xlWs As Excel.Worksheet
Set xlApp = New Excel.Application
```

Example 5-5. Code to add a worksheet (continued)

```
xlApp.Visible = True
Set xlWb = xlApp.Workbooks.Add
Set xlWs = xlWb.Worksheets.Add
xlWs.Name = "MyNewWorksheet"
End Sub
```

Now that you have been exposed to the primary objects necessary to begin an automation project, the other objects will be discussed. By the time you finish with this chapter, you will be able to dump data from Access into Excel, format and perform calculations on the data, and print the result.

Other Excel Objects

Programming with the Excel object model is generally intuitive if you are familiar with Excel. For example, cell, range, columns, rows, etc. are all referred to by their common names. While the syntax might not be intuitive, the Visual Basic Editor helps you write it (provided that you use early binding). For these examples, assume that you used the earlier code to create an Excel application, workbook, and worksheet. Let's say that you want to put the text "Employee Data" in cell B4 and you want it to be bold with a border around it. You also want that column width to fit the text. You could do this in a number of ways.

The Range Property and Object

Using a `Range` object and the `Range` property of a worksheet is probably the most straightforward way of doing this task. Use the `Dim` statement to create a variable for an Excel range, or simply use `xlWs.Range("B4").value = "Employee Data"`. Your choice depends on what you need to do with the range. Since we have a stated goal of formatting this range, I suggest using the `Range` object as a variable. The code to do this in Access is in Example 5-6.

Example 5-6. Using the range object

```
Public Sub GetExcel()
Dim xlApp As Excel.Application
Dim xlWb As Excel.Workbook
Dim xlWs As Excel.Worksheet
Dim xlRng As Excel.Range
Set xlApp = New Excel.Application
xlApp.Visible = True
Set xlWb = xlApp.Workbooks.Add
Set xlWs = xlWb.Worksheets.Add
xlWs.Name = "MyNewWorksheet"
Set xlRng = xlWs.Range("B4")
With xlRng
   .Value = "Employee Data"
   .Font.Bold = True
```

Example 5-6. Using the range object (continued)

```
   .BorderAround xlContinuous, xlThick, 5
End With
xlWs.Columns("B").AutoFit
End Sub
```

As previously mentioned, there are several ways to accomplish this. Instead of the Range object, you could also use either the Cells property or Offset to refer to a range.

The Cells Property

When you know the range ahead of time, it is probably easier to refer to it as it is above. However, if you are writing to multiple cells or if you have variables that hold both row and column numbers, it is very difficult to use the Range property. To do so, you need to create some type of lookup to show that the third column is column C, and you need to create a string and concatenate the C with the row number. This difficulty is solved very easily by using the Cells property, which returns a Range object that you can handle as in the previous example. The syntax of the Cells property is Worksheetobject.Cells(Row Number, Column Number). You can also continue using the same properties and methods as you would a Range object, but you will not get help while typing it. For this reason, I generally use the Cells property with a Range object unless I am writing to the Value property.

Looking at the Example 5-6, you can change two lines to use the Cells property. In Example 5-7, changes have been made: first, the cells property is used to refer to cell B4—row 4 and column 2; and second, for the column's autofit, I refer to the column by number.

Example 5-7. Using the cells property to select a range

```
Public Sub GetExcel()
Dim xlApp As Excel.Application
Dim xlWb As Excel.Workbook
Dim xlWs As Excel.Worksheet
Dim xlRng As Excel.Range
Set xlApp = New Excel.Application
xlApp.Visible = True
Set xlWb = xlApp.Workbooks.Add
Set xlWs = xlWb.Worksheets.Add
xlWs.Name = "MyNewWorksheet"
Set xlRng = xlWs.Cells(4, 2)
With xlRng
   .Value = "Employee Data"
   .Font.Bold = True
   .BorderAround xlContinuous, xlThick, 5
End With
xlWs.Columns(2).AutoFit
End Sub
```

Using Offset

When you have already referred to a range, and you want to move a certain number of rows and columns, you can use the Offset method of the Range object to return a new Range object. The syntax of the Offset method is *Rangeobject*.Offset(Row Offset, Column Offset), which returns a range. In the next example, the range object is set to A1. To move to B4, offset the row by 3 and the column by 1. This is useful when you do not have a variable for the column or row and you want to continue moving by a certain number of rows and/or columns. I am less likely to use this than the Cells property, but I am more likely to use this than a reference directly to a range. Understanding this property is important for later possible uses of R1C1 notation when writing formulas with VBA. The other change in Example 5-8 is that I refer to the column to auto fit by using the Column property of the Range object. The Row property can also be referenced if you need to know which row a range refers to.

Example 5-8. Using Offset to select a range

```
Public Sub GetExcel2()
Dim xlApp As Excel.Application
Dim xlWb As Excel.Workbook
Dim xlWs As Excel.Worksheet
Dim xlRng As Excel.Range
Set xlApp = New Excel.Application
xlApp.Visible = True
Set xlWb = xlApp.Workbooks.Add
Set xlWs = xlWb.Worksheets.Add
xlWs.Name = "MyNewWorksheet"
Set xlRng = xlWs.Range("A1")
Set xlRng = xlRng.Offset(3, 1)
With xlRng
  .Value = "Employee Data"
  .Font.Bold = True
  .BorderAround xlContinuous, xlThick, 5
End With
xlWs.Columns(xlRng.Column).AutoFit
End Sub
```

Many other Excel objects will be used throughout the book. Understanding the basic objects presented here and their common properties and methods is a good basis to begin automation. The difficulty with automation is that you can do the same thing a variety of ways. For the most part, there are no right answers as to which is the best way. Usually, the objects, methods, and properties used are determined by what the programmer is familiar with. I show multiple methods so that you do not get stuck using a more difficult property.

 If you want to auto fit all of the columns on a worksheet, use Worksheetobject.Columns.AutoFit instead of referring to each column individually.

Writing and Using Queries in VBA

One of the nice things about working in Access is that you can write queries in a graphical design mode and save them for use in VBA. While that is useful, you might also want to modify the queries from VBA. This can be as simple as changing the query to a parameterized query, or it can be a situation when you want the VBA to choose which columns of data the query should return. In other cases, you might want to change the query from a query that uses the Sum function on the rows to one that takes an Average or Standard Deviation.

Referring to Queries

You can refer to queries with DAO or ADO. I am going to focus on using DAO in the next examples. However, there is no reason why you can't use ADO and ADOX to do the same thing. I believe that DAO is a little more intuitive and easier to use, but use the one you are most comfortable with.

Earlier in the book, you saw how to pull data from Access when you are in Excel and use the CopyFromRecordset method of the Range object to put the data into the Excel worksheet. You do the exact same thing in Access when you automate Excel; refer to Chapter 3 to refresh your memory if necessary. While in Access, you need a few variables to use the DAO objects: one variable for the database, one variable for a recordset to hold the results of a query, and possibly a QueryDef object if you are going to create and/or modify queries, as we will do in the next examples. Example 5-9 shows how to create a new query that selects all of the records from a table called tbl_CostCenters and calls the query "Query1."

Example 5-9. Creating a new query

```
Public Sub MakeQuery1()
Dim db As DAO.Database
Dim qry As DAO.QueryDef
Dim sqltxt As String

Set db = Access.CurrentDb

sqltxt = "Select tbl_CostCenters.* from tbl_CostCenters"

Set qry = db.CreateQueryDef("Query1", sqltxt)
qry.Close

Set qry = Nothing
Set db = Nothing
End Sub
```

The biggest difference between getting a DAO database connection from Excel and from within Access is that in Access, the CurrentDB method is a pointer to the current open database that you are working in. This makes creating the connection much easier. If you are using ADO, use the `Access.CurrentProject.Connection` property to return a reference to the open database as an ADO connection.

Another topic that often comes up is what to do in situations when you need data that is in multiple databases. I suggest keeping it simple. Unless there are serious performance issues, link the data from the other data sources into the Access database you are working in and query them as though they were tables in your database. You will not be able to create queries in the other database, but you will be able to perform most other tasks. If you absolutely need to have a second connection, you can create the connection using the method shown in Chapter 3.

You may have noticed that in Example 5-9, the DAO database object has a `CreateQueryDef` method. This does exactly what it sounds like it does: creates a new query definition. The syntax is simply a name and the SQL text separated by commas. The `CreateQueryDef` method is useful, but I find that in most cases you will modify queries that already exist. Example 5-10 shows how to modify Query1 to select only centers that are storefront locations, as identified in the field LineofBusiness2.

Example 5-10. Modifying an existing query

```
Public Sub ModifyQuery1( )
Dim db As DAO.Database
Dim qry As DAO.QueryDef
Dim sqltxt As String

Set db = Access.CurrentDb

sqltxt = "Select tbl_CostCenters.* from tbl_CostCenters " & _
    "Where tbl_CostCenters.LineofBusiness2 = ""Storefront Locations"""

Set qry = db.QueryDefs("Query1")
qry.SQL = sqltxt
qry.Close

Set qry = Nothing
Set db = Nothing

End Sub
```

This example illustrates the use of the `QueryDefs` collection of the DAO Database object. When you set a variable of type `DAO.QueryDef` to an existing query in the database, you can modify the query, open it using the `OpenRecordset` method, or, if it is an action query, run it with the `Execute` method. The `SQL` property of the `QueryDef` object allows you to change the query by writing SQL, assigning it to a string variable, and assigning the `SQL` property the value of the string. You also might notice the quotation marks in the `sqltxt` variable code; I want to ensure that double quotes are used in the query so that using an apostrophe will not affect the code. I find more errors for SQL code breaking down because an entry using an apostrophe—when the code was written using single quotes—than any other single error with SQL.

While this example seems to work well, you might not want to continue modifying the query each time that you change the criteria for LineofBusiness2. You can accomplish same things by changing the query to a parameterized query and then setarameter with the code. See the new SQL in Example 5-11; it is saved as rameter.

11. Parameter SQL example

```
CostCenters.*
stCenters
l_CostCenters.LineOfBusiness2)=[LOB]));
```

as the SQL, every time the query opens, it asks the user for the parameter. ot want your user prompted when he runs your code, but the entry of the can be handled through code. Example 5-12 shows the value of the parameter being passed to the procedure when it is called.

Example 5-12. Parameter code example

```
Public Sub UseQuery1Parameter(Ptext As String)
Dim db As DAO.Database
Dim qry As DAO.QueryDef
Dim rs As DAO.Recordset

Set db = Access.CurrentDb

Set qry = db.QueryDefs("Query1Parameter")
qry.Parameters("LOB").Value = Ptext
Set rs = qry.OpenRecordset
qry.Close

If Not rs.BOF And Not rs.EOF Then
  rs.MoveFirst
  While Not rs.EOF
    Debug.Print rs.Fields(0).Value & " " & rs.Fields(1).Value
    rs.MoveNext
  Wend
End If

Set qry = Nothing
Set db = Nothing
End Sub
```

This example opens the recordset and writes two of the fields to the Debug window, provided that there is data; check for this by determining that you are not at both the beginning and end of the recordset. A very easy way to cycle through a recordset is to use the While Not rs.EOF...Wend statement. Be sure to have the rs.Movenext line inside the While statement, or it will continue to run the code until you force a break, because it will never get to the end of the recordset until you move to the next record. Also note that since there is only one parameter, you could refer to the parameter as `qry.Parameters(0).value` instead of using the name of the parameter, but I think it is best to use the name of the parameter anytime you know it.

Querying Data with Form Input

What if you want to create a generic form that allows you to select a table, select a field from the table, and enter in criteria for the selected field? The input would return all records from the table that met that criteria. This is actually a fairly straightforward task when using an Access form. We will add an extra step by dumping the result to a new Excel workbook. Use this if you have a database of addresses and want to send a mailing to every person on the list in a particular zip code on some occasions, every person added after a particular date on other occasions, etc. Having to build static queries to do that would be very time consuming. Also, having the data in multiple tables would add to the complexity. The generic form example is a simple solution to a complex problem.

In Access, go to the Forms tab and create a new form in Design View. When the blank form comes up, click on View → Form Header/Footer to add a header and footer to the form. Next, go to the Properties dialog by pressing Alt+Enter. On the Format tab of the Properties dialog, set Record Selectors, Navigation Buttons, and Dividing Lines to No. (This step is for appearance only, since this form will not be doing any record navigation, so record selectors and navigation buttons are unnecessary and actually make the form look cluttered.) If you don't see the control toolbox, click on View → Toolbox to bring it up.

You need a drop-down box that holds the names of the tables and queries in the database, a list box that holds the fields in the selected table or query, and a text box to hold the criteria. First, create a query that gives you the names of the tables and queries in the database by querying the Name field of the MSysobjects table where the Type is 1 or 5 (to give you Tables and Queries) and the Flags value is 0. Set the Flags value to 0 because you want only regular tables and select queries, not system tables or action queries. Save this query as qry_TablesQueries:

```
SELECT MSysobjects.Name
FROM MSysobjects
WHERE (((MSysobjects.Type)=1 Or (MSysobjects.Type)=5) AND ((MSysobjects.Flags)=0));
```

Now, go back to your form and place a combo box on the form. The wizard comes up, as shown in Figure 5-4. In order for the wizard to recognize the field in qry_TablesQueries as valid, you must have Access set to show system objects by going to Tools → Options and checking the "System objects" box in the Show section of the View tab. This only needs to be checked while you design the form. When you are finished, uncheck the box.

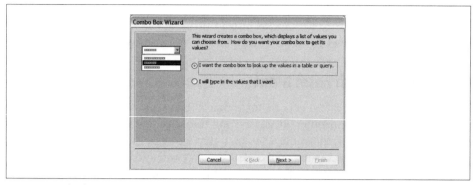

Figure 5-4. The first step in creating a combo box, when you can select whether you want to use a table or query to look up the values or enter in a list

 If you become familiar with the MSysobjects table, you can write queries that fill in combo boxes and list boxes with names of tables and queries. You can also do this with reports, forms, or other Access objects. It allows you to build code that does not need to be maintained as often. For example, assume that you build a form to run reports from an Access database. If every report had a separate button, you would need to maintain the buttons each time a report was created. However, if you used a query of the MSysobjects table and filled a combo box with the report names, you would not need to maintain the form every time a new report was created.

In the wizard, select "I want the combo box to look up the values in a table or query," and press Next. On the next screen, click the Radio button for queries, select the query called qry_TablesQueries, and click Next, as shown in Figure 5-5. On the next screen, click the right arrow to move the Name field to the Selected Fields list, as shown in Figure 5-6. There is only one field available in the figure, but if there were multiple fields, you would select the one holding the data you want to retain. On the sort screen, select a field to sort, or just press Next. The next screen shows the values in the query, which will be all of the regular tables and the select queries; just press Next again. On the final screen, pick a label for your combo box—in this example, I chose Data Selection—and press Finish. The final screen is shown in Figure 5-7.

Next, put a list box on the form. I suggest drawing the list box big enough to hold the names of your queries and to have enough room for at least four or five rows of data—you can always resize it later. When the wizard comes up, press the Cancel button. The Properties dialog should be open for the list box; if it isn't, press Alt+Enter to bring it up. On the Properties dialog box, click on the Data tab and set the Row Source Type to Field List. Next, click on the label for the list box and set the caption

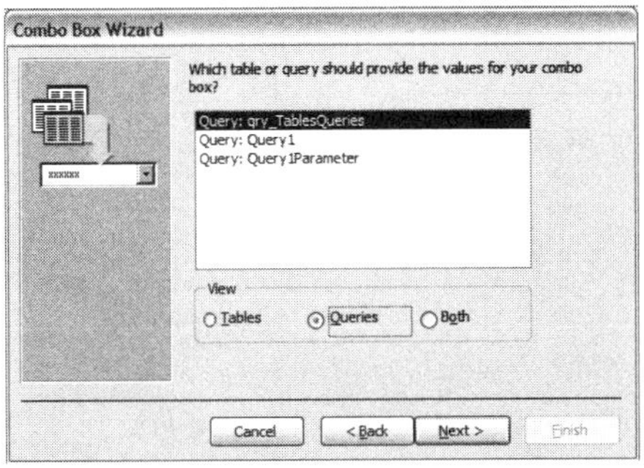

Figure 5-5. Selecting the table or query that holds the data you want to show in the combo box

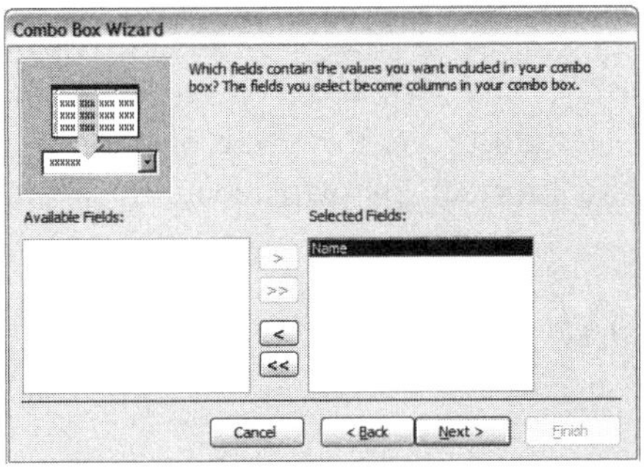

Figure 5-6. Selecting the field name

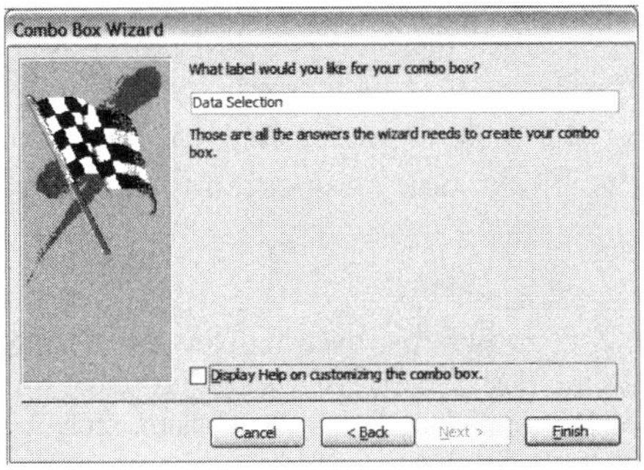

Figure 5-7. The final step, when you enter specific text that you would like to use to label your combo box

to Field Selection, either by setting the caption property on the Format tab of the Properties dialog for the label or by double-clicking on the label and editing the text.

Next, put on a text box to hold your specified criteria. Set the label for this text box as Criteria, click on the Other tab on the Properties dialog, and set the name to be PText.

Now you are ready to write code. Click on the Combo box, and go to the Event tab on the Properties dialog. On the drop-down menu for the On Change event, select Event Procedure, and click on the ellipsis to the right of the menu. This brings up the code window, where you enter Example 5-13.

Example 5-13. Combo box change example

```
Private Sub Combo0_Change()
Me.List2.Enabled = True
Me.List2.RowSource = Me.Combo0.Value
Me.List2.Requery
Me.PText.Value = ""
Me.PText.Enabled = False
End Sub
```

This enables the list box and sets the row source to be equal to the selected table or query. The Requery method of the list box updates the list box with the field list of the new selection. The PText box is set to an empty string and is not enabled until a field name is selected. Next, go to the Event tab of the list box, select Event Procedure on the After Update event drop-down menu, click on the ellipsis, and enter Example 5-14.

Example 5-14. List box After Update example

```
Private Sub List2_AfterUpdate()
Me.PText.Enabled = True
End Sub
```

Now, go to the toolbox, put a Command button on the form, and press Cancel when the wizard comes up. On the other tab of the Properties dialog for the Command button, change the name to RunButton. Then go the Event tab of the properties dialog for the PText text box, select Event Procedure for the After Update event, click on the ellipsis, and enter the code in Example 5-15. Note that the user will have to move the focus from the PText box after entering the text before the RunButton becomes enabled.

 You could get around this by using the On Change event instead. However, I don't like the idea of the code running each time a character is typed. This code is very short, so it is unlikely to have any impact on performance, but if you had more substantial code running, it could.

Example 5-15. Text box After Update example

```
Private Sub PText_AfterUpdate()
Me.RunButton.Enabled = True
End Sub
```

Next, click on some of the gray space outside the form to get to the form's properties, or select Form on the drop-down menu at the top of the Properties dialog. On the Event tab, go to On Open, select Event Procedure from the drop-down menu, and click on the ellipsis. Then enter the code in Example 5-16.

Example 5-16. Form on Open Event example

```
Private Sub Form_Open(Cancel As Integer)
DoCmd.Restore
Me.List2.Enabled = False
Me.PText.Enabled = False
Me.RunButton.Enabled = False
End Sub
```

This code ensures that a user does not run the code before entering the correct information. Now you are ready to put the code into the Command button's On Click event. Go to the Properties dialog of the Command button, and on the Event tab, go to the On Click event. Select Event Procedure from the drop-down menu, and click the ellipsis. In the code window, click on Tools → References and add a reference to the object library for your version of Excel. Then enter the code shown in Example 5-17.

Example 5-17. Button code example

```
Private Sub RunButton_Click()
Dim xlApp As Excel.Application
Dim xlWb As Excel.Workbook
Dim xlWs As Excel.Worksheet
Dim xlRng As Excel.Range
Dim db As DAO.Database
Dim qry As DAO.QueryDef
Dim rs As DAO.Recordset
Dim fld As DAO.Field
Dim x As Integer
Dim sqltxt As String

Set db = Access.CurrentDb
Set qry = db.CreateQueryDef("")
sqltxt = "Select " & Me.Combo0.Value & ".* " & _
  "From " & Me.Combo0.Value & " Where " & _
  Me.List2.Value & " = [PValue] "
qry.SQL = sqltxt
qry.Parameters("PValue").Value = Me.PText.Value
Set rs = qry.OpenRecordset

Set xlApp = New Excel.Application
xlApp.Visible = True
Set xlWb = xlApp.Workbooks.Add
Set xlWs = xlWb.ActiveSheet
x = 1
For Each fld In rs.Fields
xlWs.Cells(1, x).Value = fld.Name
```

Example 5-17. Button code example (continued)

```
x = x + 1
Next fld
Set xlRng = xlWs.Cells(2, 1)
xlRng.CopyFromRecordset rs
xlWs.Columns.AutoFit
rs.Close
qry.Close
Set fld = Nothing
Set rs = Nothing
Set qry = Nothing
Set db = Nothing
Set xlRng = Nothing
Set xlWs = Nothing
Set xlWb = Nothing
Set xlApp = Nothing
End Sub
```

As you review this code, notice that a parameter called PValue holds the value of the criteria the user specifies; I don't know whether the user will pick a field that needs a string, number, date, etc. If I attempt to put the criteria in the SQL text, I need to know what the data type is. However, if I use a parameter, Access does this for me, so I don't need to check the type to determine whether I need quotes.

There are some other items that I would like to point out in this code. When you create a query definition with an empty string as a name, it is only a temporary query definition and will be dropped when the code is finished. Also, to create a parameterized query when writing SQL text in code, put the name of the parameter in brackets. Finally, I am not saving or closing the Excel document; instead I am setting the variables to be equal to nothing. This removes the reference to the Excel objects in the code but leaves the application open.

When you have finished testing your work, put a meaningful caption on the Command button and add a title. I also suggest adding a Command button to close the form in the footer. When the wizard comes up, select Form Operations and Close Form. Click Next, leave the default exit picture, and click Next again. Keep the default name and choose Finish. When you open the form, you should see something similar to Figure 5-8. Your form may vary in size, font, color, etc.

Save your form with a meaningful name when you are done. I have called mine frm_ GenericQuery. This form could be used in any database as long as the database had a reference established to the Excel object library and you brought along the query for the tables and queries. Generally, I suggest writing code like this that can be moved from one application to another. You might be tempted to have a list of tables built into your combo box or to create a form specific to each table, but then you won't be able to use past work in new applications you create.

Now that you have been introduced to creating interactive queries and are familiar with the syntax, you can write more complex queries and perform additional automation within Excel.

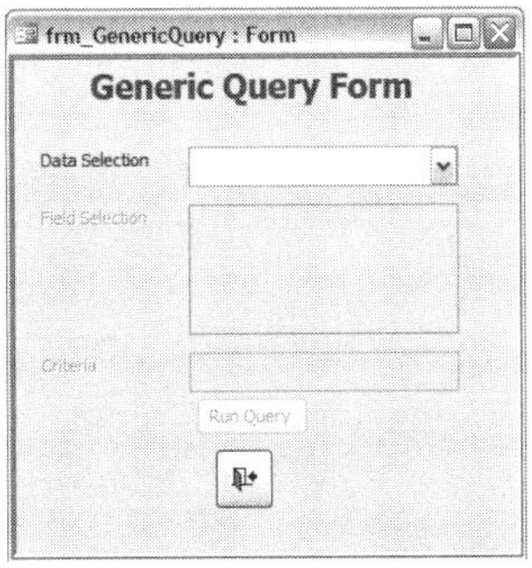

Figure 5-8. The completed form

Creating Crosstab Queries

In Access databases, it is very common to use crosstab queries for summarizing data. While this is their intended purpose, I generally recommend using a pivot table instead of a crosstab query for most purposes. You are limited to one field in a crosstab query. Despite this limitation, it is often necessary or just desirable to build a crosstab query to summarize data. For this example, assume you have three tables: one for centers, one for sales, and one for products, and assume you have a query called qry_BaseQuery that brings up the following fields:

- LineofBusiness1
- LineofBusiness2
- CostCenter
- CenterName
- SaleDate
- ProductCategory
- ProductName
- Quantity
- TotalCost

Let's assume that you want a crosstab report with Product Categories in columns across the top and Center Names as rows. In addition, you need two crosstab reports, one for Quantity and one for Total Cost. This report can be created easily through the wizard. Instead, go into Design View for a new query, and change the query type to crosstab by going to Query → Crosstab Query. Right-click in the gray space at the top of the query, select Show Table, and select the qry_BaseQuery table. On the field list, double-click (or drag down) the CenterName, ProductCategory, and Quantity fields so that they move into the query fields. Next, on the crosstab row, select Row Heading for CenterName, Column Heading for ProductCategory, and Value for Quantity, and change the Group By option in the Quantity column to

Sum. Finally, save the query as qry_QuantityCrosstab. Your query should look similar to Figure 5-9.

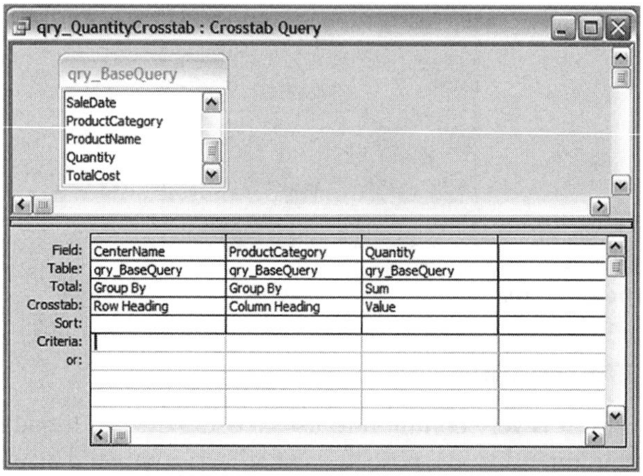

Figure 5-9. The design view of the crosstab query summarizing quantity by center and product category

Once you have saved the query, change the Quantity field to TotalCost, go to File → Save As, and name it qry_TotalCostCrosstab. You can now open either query and see either the quantity of each product category for each center or the total cost of each product category by center.

There are some limitations to this. For example, if you want the quantity and total cost by product category by center while also getting an average price per unit, you can use two crosstab queries that would join with a third query to bring in the fields that you need and perform any math. While this would work, you would need to maintain the query every time new product categories were added, and this type of query and join runs very slowly. This brings us to a query concept that I call the Created Crosstab Query.

Generating a Created Crosstab Query

This query is created by using VBA to write SQL for the query. The concept is rather simple, although the implementation can be tricky. To create this query, go to the Modules tab in Access and select New Module. Go to Insert → Procedure, call this procedure CreatedCrosstabPerUnit, and make it a Public Sub. When this query is finished, we will export it to Excel and perform a row and column sum.

Here are the basics of this query. First, perform a Group By query on the field that you want as the column headings to ensure that you get only column headings with values and that the query stays up to date. (If you want all possible column headings, query the source table for the field to get all possible values.) Next, write a series of immediate if (IIF) statements that bring in the value field if the value in the column heading field matches the column's value; otherwise it puts in a zero. Unlike a regular crosstab, it has zeros in unused cells instead of blanks. Once the immediate if statements are written for each column, add other fields that need to be selected, along with the appropriate Group By statement, and save the query.

To do this, you need DAO Database, Query, and Recordset objects, along with Excel Application, Workbook, Worksheet, and Range objects. In addition, you need several string and integer variables. The full code is listed in Example 5-18.

Example 5-18. Created Crosstab example

```vba
Public Sub CreatedCrosstabPerUnit(queryname As String, colfield As String, _
        rowstr As String, valfield1 As String, valfield2 As String)
Dim db As DAO.Database
Dim qry As DAO.QueryDef
Dim rs As DAO.Recordset
Dim fld As DAO.Field

Dim xlApp As Excel.Application
Dim xlWb As Excel.Workbook
Dim xlWs As Excel.Worksheet
Dim xlRng As Excel.Range

Dim w, x, y, z As Integer
Dim sqlstr As String
Dim numfmt As String
Dim sqlstrcol As Collection
Dim varitm As Variant

Set sqlstrcol = New Collection
Set db = Access.CurrentDb

Set rs = db.OpenRecordset("Select Name from MSysobjects Where " & _
   "Name = ""qry_CreatedCrosstab""")
If rs.EOF And rs.BOF Then
  Set qry = db.CreateQueryDef("qry_CreatedCrosstab")
End If
If Not rs.EOF And Not rs.BOF Then
  Set qry = db.QueryDefs("qry_CreatedCrosstab")
End If
rs.Close
Set rs = Nothing

Set rs = db.OpenRecordset("Select " & colfield & " From " & queryname & _
    " Group by " & colfield)
If Not rs.EOF And Not rs.BOF Then
  rs.MoveFirst
  While Not rs.EOF
    sqlstr = "Sum(IIF([" & colfield & "] = """ & rs.Fields(0).Value & _
     """,[" & valfield1 & "]),0)) As [" & rs.Fields(0).Value & "_" & valfield1 & "]"
```

Example 5-18. Created Crosstab example (continued)

```
    sqlstrcol.Add sqlstr
    sqlstr = ""
    sqlstr = "Sum(IIF([" & colfield & "] = """ & rs.Fields(0).Value & _
      """,[" & valfield2 & "],0)) As [" & rs.Fields(0).Value & "_" & valfield2 & "]"
    sqlstrcol.Add sqlstr
    sqlstr = ""
    sqlstr = "Sum(IIF([" & colfield & "] = """ & rs.Fields(0).Value & _
      """,[" & valfield2 & "],0))/(Sum(IIF([" & colfield & "] = """ & _
      rs.Fields(0).Value & """,[" & valfield1 & "],0))+.000001) AS [" & _
      rs.Fields(0).Value & "_PerUnit]"
    sqlstrcol.Add sqlstr
    sqlstr = ""
    rs.MoveNext
  Wend
End If

sqlstr = "Select " & rowstr
For Each varitm In sqlstrcol
  sqlstr = sqlstr & ", " & CStr(varitm)
Next varitm
sqlstr = sqlstr & " From " & queryname & " Group By " & rowstr

qry.SQL = sqlstr
qry.Close
rs.Close

Set rs = db.OpenRecordset("qry_CreatedCrosstab")

Set xlApp = New Excel.Application
xlApp.Visible = True
Set xlWb = xlApp.Workbooks.Add
Set xlWs = xlWb.ActiveSheet
x = 1
For Each fld In rs.Fields
  xlWs.Cells(1, x).Value = fld.Name
  x = x + 1
Next fld
Set xlRng = xlWs.Cells(2, 1)
xlRng.CopyFromRecordset rs
Set xlRng = xlWs.Cells.SpecialCells(xlCellTypeLastCell)
y = xlRng.Row + 1
w = xlRng.Column
x = 0
For z = 1 To rs.Fields.Count
  If xlWs.Cells(1, z).Value Like "*" & valfield1 Then
    x = z
  End If
  If x = z Then z = rs.Fields.Count
Next z
rs.Close
For z = x To w
  Set xlRng = xlWs.Cells(y, z)
```

Example 5-18. Created Crosstab example (continued)

```
  If Not xlWs.Cells(1, z).Value Like "*PerUnit" Then
    xlRng.FormulaR1C1 = "=Sum(R2C:R[-1]C)"
  End If
  If xlWs.Cells(1, z).Value Like "*PerUnit" Then
    xlRng.FormulaR1C1 = "=Sumproduct(R2C[-2]:R[-1]C[-2]," & _
      "R2C:R[-1]C)/Sum(R2C[-2]:R[-1]C[-2])"
  End If
  If xlWs.Cells(1, z).Value Like "*" & valfield1 Then
    numfmt = "#,##0"
  End If
  If Not xlWs.Cells(1, z).Value Like "*" & valfield1 Then
    numfmt = "$#,##0.00"
  End If
  Set xlRng = xlWs.Range(xlWs.Cells(2, z), xlWs.Cells(y, z))
  xlRng.NumberFormat = numfmt
Next z

Set xlRng = xlWs.Range(xlWs.Cells(y, x), xlWs.Cells(y, z - 1))
xlRng.Font.Bold = True
With xlRng.Borders.Item(Excel.xlEdgeTop)
  .LineStyle = Excel.xlContinuous
  .Weight = Excel.xlThin
  .ColorIndex = 3
End With

Set xlRng = xlWs.Range(xlWs.Cells(1, 1), xlWs.Cells(1, z - 1))
xlRng.Font.Bold = True
With xlRng.Borders.Item(Excel.xlEdgeBottom)
  .LineStyle = Excel.xlContinuous
  .Weight = Excel.xlThin
  .ColorIndex = 3
End With

xlWs.Columns.AutoFit

Set xlRng = Nothing
Set xlWs = Nothing
Set xlWb = Nothing
Set xlApp = Nothing

Set fld = Nothing
Set rs = Nothing
Set qry = Nothing
Set db = Nothing
End Sub
```

You can call this procedure from the Immediate Window in the design view of a
module. The syntax to call this procedure to get Quantity, Total Cost, and Per Unit
Cost by Center and by Product Category is:

```
Call CreatedCrosstabPerUnit ("qry_BaseQuery", "ProductCategory", "CenterName", _
  "Quantity", "TotalCost")
```

The syntax is the same whether you call it from within another procedure or from the immediate window. To show you how useful this can be, if you want to look at the actual products instead of only the product category, change the string that says ProductCategory to ProductName. Now you can imagine a reporting system that lets you pick the level of detail that you want to see and, at the press of a button, create a report. And, even though there are many different combinations of reports, the same module creates them all.

A lot happens in this example. After the declarations and the CurrentDB reference are set, it checks to see if there is a qry_CreatedCrosstab query in the database. If it exists, the code sets the qry variable equal to the existing query. If it does not exist, it creates the query definition. This step is useful because you never know what might be deleted on a given computer when you distribute an application. This step ensures that the code runs error-free.

The procedure could have created a temporary query and avoided saving, but I don't recommend it for reports where you are doing a lot of calculations in the query. If you use temporary queries and want to print out the query logic, you would have to put break points in the code and capture the query text. So, these few extra lines of code allow you to save the query without requiring that the actual query exist in the first place.

Next, query the `colfield` as a Group By query to get each unique instance of the values in that field. Once you have a recordset with all of the necessary columns, write the `immediate if` statements. In this example, each unique IIF statement is written to a collection.

While this step can be avoided by writing to the query string each time and concatenating, I like putting each one in the collection so that I can build the entire SQL string in one section, rather than writing to the string over several sections. I think this both makes debugging easier and ensures the commas are handled correctly.

Notice that on the IIF statement where division is being done, I have added .000001 to the denominator. By adding this small number, you can avoid a divide by zero error if for some reason the denominator were zero. While you could instead test for a zero, the code quickly gets very confusing with the additional test. Adding this very small number does not change the result except in very rare instances, and for business functions it has no impact.

Each column created by the IIF statement is named by the AS keyword. Use brackets on both sides of the name to ensure that no errors are caused by spaces in the name. After the statements are done, the SQL String is put together, the `.SQL` property of the query is set to the string, and the query is closed.

Next, set the recordset using the new query's `OpenRecordset` method, create the Excel objects, and drop the field names into the worksheet. Send the recordset to Excel using the `CopyFromRecordset` method of the ExcelRange object, and determine where the last row of data is so that totals can be done by column. Excel makes this very easy because each worksheet has a specially defined cell that tells you the last cell used, called `xlCellTypeLastCell`. If you set a range equal to this cell, you can use the `.Row` property of the range to determine the last row. Add one to this row to find out which rows your formulas belong in.

The formulas themselves may look strange to you if you have never used R1C1 notation, but once you figure it out, it is very easy to use and is much simpler than figuring out where you are to determine the column letter and row number. The R stands for row and the C for column. The syntax is ordered by R and then C. If you refer to the Row that you are in, you simply use R. The same idea works for column. If you put a number directly after R or C and don't put it in brackets, Excel treats it like an absolute reference. The formula has a $ in front of the row or column identifier. If you put a number in brackets directly after R or C, it moves the number of columns or rows specified. For rows, a negative number moves up the spreadsheet, so if you are in row 10 and you enter **R[-2]**, you refer to row 8; **R[2]** refers to row 12. For columns, a negative number moves left, so if you are in column D and you enter **C[-2]**, you refer to column B; **C[2]** refers to column F. Be careful not to refer to a column less than column A or a row less than row 1.

This makes it very easy to write `sum` formulas when you want to sum an entire recordset, because you want the second row of the column (R2C) and the row above the sum row (R[-1]C). Use this formula for all of the columns that are not per unit. If the column you are summing is per unit, you have two ways to do it. The first way would be to take the sums that you have just calculated and divide them. While this would certainly be easy, in some cases you have only the result and the weighting column, so I wanted to demonstrate how to take a weighted average. This is made easy by the `SumProduct` function in Excel. For this function, enter your two ranges set off by commas, and Excel will return the sum of the two ranges multiplied by each other. If you ever took a statistics class, you would have created a column that held the weightings, which were then added up and divided by the sum of the column that held the quantity. Excel lets you do this in one step by taking the `SumProduct` and dividing it by the sum of the quantity column.

Now that the formulas are taken care of, some formatting is needed. In this case, the top row is bold with a red border below. The formula row is bold with a red border above it. The quantity fields are given a number format without decimals but with commas if they go over 1,000. The total cost and per unit fields are formatted as Currency with a Dollar sign and two decimal places.

The columns are then auto-fit, and the object references are set to nothing. Again, this code does not close the Excel workbook. In production code, it is likely that I would have set the code to save and print the worksheet and then close Excel. Printing, page setup, and other formatting options are covered in detail in Chapter 8.

One note of caution: if you do not use the step where xlApp.Visible = True, the code will run, but you will see nothing. Excel will still be open in the background. You can see it happening if you go to the Processes tab on your task list (Ctrl+Shift+Esc in Windows XP).

When you run this code, you will see an Excel document that looks similar to Figure 5-10. You can change the colors, fonts, number formats, etc. Again, to code a formatting change, the easiest way is to use the Macro Recorder in Excel and then review the code.

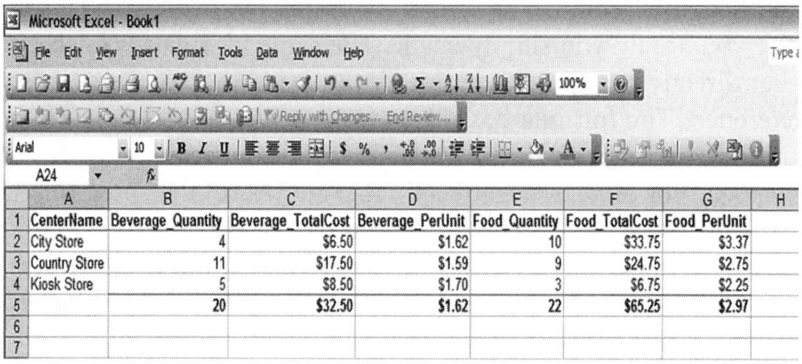

Figure 5-10. The Excel document that results from the created crosstab query code when summarizing by product category

After you have run the code and gained an understanding of how it works, play around with it to see how easy it is to change or add additional columns. Try to do the same thing with joined regular crosstab queries. You'll find that the extra coding now will be worth it to not have to maintain the application. The advantage is even more evident when changes happen infrequently. With staff turnover or just fading memories, you may end up with an application that does not tie to the real numbers, and people won't know how to fix it. Using this method ensures that each time there are new records, they will be put into the result set.

Referencing Sheets, Ranges, and Cells

When you use Access VBA to automate Excel, there are some simple ways to refer to Excel objects. In addition, there are easy ways to cycle through the objects. Let's begin with Sheets.

Working with Sheets

When you think about sheets in Excel, you generally talk about worksheets. However, there is another sheet object called a *chart sheet*. Each Excel worksheet is a member of two collections: the Sheets collection and the Worksheets collection. Both collections can be searched. Generally, I use the Sheets collection so that I use the same collection for all sheets in the application. However, if you cycle through the workbook and want to format regular worksheets a particular way, going through the Worksheets collection is your best bet. The chart sheets are in the Charts collection of the workbook object. Assuming that you have a variable called xlWs defined as an Excel.Worksheet, there are three basic ways to set the variable:

- Set xlWs = ActiveSheet
- Set xlWs = xlWb.Worksheets("Sheet1")
- Set xlWs = xlWb.Sheets("Sheet1")

Assuming that you just opened the workbook and Sheet1 is the active worksheet, any of these three methods will work. You can also cycle through the collection with the For Each...Next loop. For example, to print the name of each worksheet into the debug window, write:

```
For each xlWs in xlWb.Worksheets
   Debug.Print xlWs.Name
Next xlWs
```

This example assumes that you already have a reference to a workbook with a variable xlWb and that the variable xlWs refers to an Excel.Worksheet object. You can also refer to a worksheet by number, but I don't recommend it because the numbers are not constant if you move sheets around.

Working with Ranges

Ranges can refer to a single cell, a group of contiguous cells, a group of non-adjacent cells, or every cell on a worksheet(s). The interesting thing about working with ranges is that many other objects are based on the Range type. For example, a cell is a range. A range is also a collection of cells. If you wanted to look at every individual cell in a range, you could use a For Each...Next loop, as shown in Example 5-19.

Example 5-19. Working with ranges example

```
Public Sub CycleRange( )
Dim xlws As Worksheet
Set xlws = Sheets("Sheet1")
Dim xlrng As Excel.Range
Dim xlrng2 As Excel.Range
Set xlrng = xlws.Range("A1:B10")
For Each xlrng2 In xlrng.Cells
   Debug.Print "R" & xlrng2.Row & " - C" & xlrng2.Column
Next xlrng2
Set xlrng2 = Nothing
Set xlrng = Nothing
Set xlws = Nothing
End Sub
```

If you run this loop from Excel VBA, you can see that the distinct ranges in the `Cells` collection are individual cells, since two combinations print in the debug window. This is useful when automating Excel from Access because you can check all of the cells in a range without knowing where the range is. For example, if there were a named range called ProductData, you could set a range equal to `xlws.Range("ProductData")` and cycle through the ranges in that range's `.Cells` collection.

Working with Cells

Use the `.Cells` property of the worksheet object to return an individual cell based on the row and column number. In addition, when writing formulas, either refer to a cell as a string with A1 notation, using `.Range` with the worksheet object, or use R1C1 notation. Finally, as in Example 5-8, you can use the `Offset` function to return a cell reference that was offset a certain number of rows and columns from a particular cell.

Cells are the smallest data-holding object on an Excel worksheet available from the user interface. It is important to understand how to refer to each object type, particularly from Access, to make automation tasks easier.

Writing Excel Worksheet Functions from Access VBA

You have already been exposed to the `.FormulaR1C1` property of a cell in the created crosstab example earlier this chapter. When you use this property to write a function, the Excel worksheet stores it. When data changes in the Excel worksheet being referenced by the formula, the formula result also changes. Any functions that you can write from the Excel user interface can also be written from VBA.

You can use either A1 or R1C1 reference style based on the formula property. For example, `FormulaR1C1` and `FormulaArray` must be entered using R1C1 style, and the `Formula` property must use the A1 reference style. Set the workbook option to use labels in formulas from VBA and the `FormulaLabel` type for the range object.

In addition to actually writing formulas that end up in Excel, you can also use the functions available in the `WorksheetFunction` property of the Excel application object to return a value and place that value in the Excel cell. For example, if you write:

```
xlRng.FormulaR1C1 = "=Sum(R2C:R[-1]C)"
```

you end up with a formula in the cell, but if you write:

```
xlrng.Value = Excel.WorksheetFunction.Sum(xlws.Range(_
    xlws.Cells(2, xlrng.Column), _
    xlws.Cells(xlrng.Row - 1, xlrng.Column)))
```

you end up with only the formula result in the cell. Depending on the purpose of the application, you might not want your users to see your formulas. In addition, you might not want the results of your formulas to change if a user changes the base numbers.

Normally, I don't use the `WorksheetFunctions` unless I am calculating on the fly and won't want or need the formulas later. When I automate Excel from Access, though, I almost always use the actual formulas. If I am concerned about people changing the formulas, I can hide them, lock the rest of the worksheet, and protect the worksheet with a password. This way, I can go in later and make sure everything is calculating correctly without worrying about things changing that I didn't want to change.

Chapter Summary and Next Steps

There were a lot of items covered in this chapter that are critical to effectively using VBA automation with Access and Excel. Using Access to automate Excel is my preferred approach to integrating the two applications because you have much more control over the data and complete access to all of the built-in Excel functions. The only things you don't have access to from VBA within Access are any macros or user-defined Excel functions. When you open an Excel workbook from VBA, macros are not enabled. This feature is designed to protect you from macro viruses.

If you are confused about anything covered in this chapter, review it or go back to prior chapters. You must understand this chapter completely to be able to complete the project in Chapter 12. Also, the same concepts used to automate Excel from VBA are used to automate Word, PowerPoint, MapPoint, or any other VBA-enabled application.

You should understand:

- the difference between early and late binding
- how the objects needed to create a usable Excel worksheet can be manipulated from Access
- how to manipulate queries from within VBA

If you have those items down and have a general understanding of the other topics, the rest of the book will reinforce what you know. You will be exposed to other topics and will continue to build on your knowledge.

In the next chapter, you will learn how to use the data in Access to create Excel PivotTables, PivotCharts, and regular charts and graphs. In addition, you will learn how to manipulate existing charts and graphs by changing the data ranges, adding new ranges, or changing the underlying data.

CHAPTER 6

Using Excel Charts and Pivot Tables with Access Data

There is something about putting your information into a colorful chart or summarizing a tremendous amount of data in a pivot table that really adds to an analysis. Unfortunately, some Excel users struggle with putting together a simple chart, and many have never even heard of pivot tables. This chapter has two main goals: first, to explain why these built-in Excel features are important and how they can be used; and second, to show how to automate reporting of Access data through Excel charts and pivot tables with VBA.

Excel has many built-in standard chart types, as well as some custom chart types. There are several custom chart types that allow you to plot data on two axes, which is very useful for analytical functions. For example, you can graph sales on one axis and margin on another to see if periods of high sales correspond with lower margins. While you could see the same thing by looking at a numbers-only report, using a chart really illustrates the analysis. These are the standard types of charts that are built into Excel 2003:

Column	Line	XY (Scatter)
Donut	Surface	Stock
Cone	Bar	Pie
Area	Radar	Bubble
Cylinder	Pyramid	

Excel also offers a number of built-in custom charts:

Area Blocks	B&W Column	B&W Pie
Colored Lines	Columns with Depth	Floating Bars
Line-Column on 2 Axes	Logarithmic	Pie Explosion
Stack of Colors	B&W Area	B&W Line (Timescale)
Blue Pie	Column-Area	Cones
Line-Column	Lines on 2 Axes	Outdoor Bars
Smooth Lines	Tubes	

While there are many charts available, pick the chart type that shows your data most directly. Readers should be able to quickly see what the chart is trying to show. If you have something specific to highlight, try your data with a number of different types of charts and ask people what they think the graph is showing. After ensuring that the graph is easily understood by readers, consider whether the graph should be printed in color. I have been on the receiving end of a number of charts where you could not tell the difference between series because the graph was printed in black and white. Another good tip is to use different markers on line charts for each series to easily distinguish them, even if you are also using color.

 You can easily use graphs in conjunction with a pivot table. If you want to graph a pivot table in Excel 2003, right-click on the PivotTable and select PivotChart from the menu. While PivotCharts may seem many levels deep in the GUI interface, they can still be automated by VBA.

When creating charts, I generally recommend using named ranges instead of fixed ranges because they make it much easier to handle situations where the number of items being charted changes. Regardless of whether you use fixed ranges or named ranges, you can to open an existing Excel workbook from Access and update data used in an existing chart. You can then have code run to set your upper and lower bounds of each axis, etc. Many companies have monthly or quarterly analytics involving graphs that include things like cost per item, average hold time, customer satisfaction scores, etc. If you have a working Excel workbook that graphs information, simply open the workbook with VBA, push in the new data, and print the new graphs—all without leaving Microsoft Access. This is one of the easiest types of automation and will often save you hours of work each reporting period.

This chapter later covers automation of charts. However, because of the ability to easily create charts from pivot tables, automation of pivot tables will be covered first. Both creating charts from scratch with VBA and changing data and/or data ranges of existing charts will be covered. One other technique relating to charts covered in this chapter is using VBA to change a variable in a simple model and graphing the results. You will find this very useful for financial applications.

Automating Pivot Tables

In Chapter 5, you learned how to connect to an Access database from Excel and pull in data. Once the data is in Excel, spreadsheet users can produce a pivot table on that data. However, there will be times when users need to produce more pivot table reports than are practical to produce manually. One of the most efficient ways to do this is to push the data from Access into Excel and produce the pivot table using VBA from Access. For example, you want to summarize headcount by position for each department in a company with multiple departments. In many cases, Human

Resources won't want department managers to see the raw data about other departments. If you use Access to pull the data, you can populate an Excel workbook with each department's data and have Excel produce a pivot table. The database could then email the report to the department managers.

There are two ways to use VBA to build a pivot table. The first method is to simply use the PivotTableWizard of the worksheet object. By using this method in conjunction with a variable with the object type of PivotTable, you can produce a pivot table rather quickly. The second method, which you see if you use the macro recorder in Microsoft Excel 2003, is to use the PivotCaches object in the ActiveWorkbook. For this chapter, I focus on using the PivotTableWizard method of the worksheet object, as it is more direct.

You do not necessarily have to bring the data into Excel before creating your pivot table. Both methods of producing the pivot table allow you to connect to an external data source. I like to push the data into Excel, so that when users double-click on a number in the report, they can get the detail behind it. Using an external data source, however, can add to the complexity, particularly if the recipients do not have the same type of access to the source data, so it is a good idea in the beginning to reduce the variables.

 As long as you know how to do something through the Excel GUI, you can record the macro to get help writing the code; with a few changes, you can copy the Excel macro code into Access VBA to make it work. You will probably find that more often than not, you will look for some specific help, such as how to add a page field or multiple row fields to the pivot table, rather than trying to have all the code written for you. I think it is very effective to use the Macro Recorder to help learn how to use methods.

Example 6-1 shows a simple example of automating the production of a pivot table. For this example, you use the same table and query structure that you saw in Chapter 5. To refresh your memory, with that data we have tables for Cost Centers, products, and sales. Let's say that you are responsible for providing a weekly production report to management on how each type of store performed by product category, and you use a query called qry_BaseQuery, as shown in Figure 6-1.

Example 6-1. PivotTable example

```
Public Sub PivotTableExportData()
Dim xlApp As Excel.Application
Dim xlwb As Excel.Workbook
Dim xlws As Excel.Worksheet
Dim xlrng As Excel.Range
Dim xlPivot As Excel.PivotTable
Dim adors As ADODB.Recordset
Dim adofld As ADODB.Field
Dim x, y, z As Integer
```

Example 6-1. PivotTable example (continued)

```
Set xlApp = New Excel.Application
xlApp.Visible = True
Set xlwb = xlApp.Workbooks.Add
Set xlws = xlwb.ActiveSheet
xlws.Name = "BaseData"

Set adors = New ADODB.Recordset
adors.Open "qry_BaseQuery", CurrentProject.Connection, adOpenStatic, adLockReadOnly

x = 1
For Each adofld In adors.Fields
  xlws.Cells(1, x).Value = adofld.Name
  x = x + 1
Next adofld

Set xlrng = xlws.Cells(2, 1)
xlrng.CopyFromRecordset adors
y = adors.RecordCount + 1
adors.Close

Set xlws = xlwb.Worksheets.Add
xlws.Name = "SalesPivot"
Set xlrng = xlws.Range("A3")


xlws.PivotTableWizard Excel.xlDatabase, "BaseData!R1C1:R" & y & "C" & x - 1, _
  xlrng, "SalesPivotTable", True, True, True, True

Set xlPivot = xlws.PivotTables("SalesPivotTable")
xlPivot.AddFields "LineofBusiness2", "ProductCategory"
With xlPivot.PivotFields("TotalCost")
    .Orientation = Excel.xlDataField
    .NumberFormat = "$#,##0.00"
End With

Set xlPivot = Nothing
Set xlrng = Nothing
Set xlws = Nothing
Set xlwb = Nothing
Set xlApp = Nothing
Set adofld = Nothing
Set adors = Nothing
End Sub
```

You can see the resulting PivotTable in Figure 6-2. There are a few items of note. First, to define the range for the pivot table, I chose to use the R1C1 notation discussed in Chapter 5 because by cycling through the fields, I already have the number of columns and after pasting the data with the CopyFromRecordset method, I can store the number of rows of data in a variable. Since there is a header row, I need to add 1 to the row count and subtract 1 from the variable used to cycle through the fields

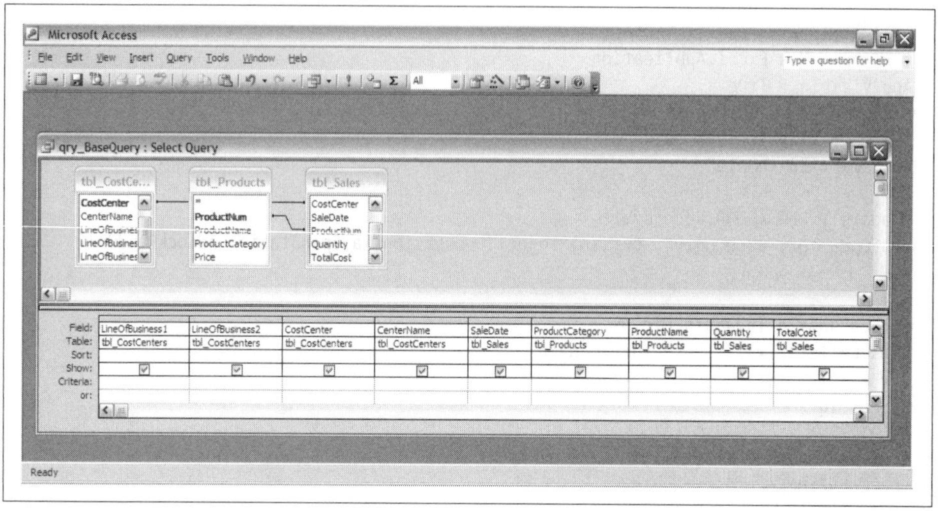

Figure 6-1. The query layout of qry_BaseQuery in Access, joining together three tables to provide the information needed for the pivot table

because the code will add 1 when it gets to the last field. The second item of note is that if you need to add multiple row or column fields, use the `Array` function in VBA. Beyond that, we are simply using the same techniques used earlier in the book to move data into Excel.

> When using Access to automate Excel, your users will not get the Macro warnings they would see if you built this in Excel to pull the data from Access.

Another way to tackle this would be to use an external data connection and just use the query. This has the effect of not having a table of data in Excel while still showing the results. Be careful using this method if your users do not have the same access to the data as you have. This is very important if they are used to double-clicking on a number to see the detail behind it. In any case, it is useful to learn this method if your data changes regularly. Once it is built this way, you would need only to refresh the pivot table to bring in the most current data. One could argue that using this method makes it unnecessary to automate with VBA because you would reuse the Excel workbook. However, I have often found that even though people use databases and can store data in a manner that allows them to see when records change; they make a copy for each month or do something else that results in the name of the database changing throughout the life of the database.

I use the `Add` method of the `PivotCaches` object of the Excel `Workbook` object, as shown in Example 6-2. Note that the values for the variables *dblocation* and *dbdir*, which hold the path and file names, will be different for you.

Example 6-2. External data PivotTable example

```
Public Sub PivotTableExternalData( )
Dim xlApp As Excel.Application
Dim xlwb As Excel.Workbook
Dim xlws As Excel.Worksheet
Dim xlrng As Excel.Range
Dim xlPivot As Excel.PivotTable
Dim dblocation As String
Dim dbdir As String

dblocation = "C:\BookInformation\Chapter6\Chapter6DB.mdb"
dbdir = "C:\BookInformation\Chapter6"

Set xlApp = New Excel.Application
xlApp.Visible = True
Set xlwb = xlApp.Workbooks.Add

With xlwb.PivotCaches.Add(SourceType:=Excel.xlExternal)
    .Connection = Array(Array( _
    "ODBC;DSN=MS Access Database;DBQ=" & dblocation & _
    ";DefaultDir=" & dbdir & ";DriverId=25;FIL=MS"), _
    Array(" Access;MaxBufferSize=2048;PageTimeout=5;"))
    .CommandType = Excel.xlCmdSql
    .CommandText = Array("SELECT qry_BaseQuery.* from qry_BaseQuery")
    .CreatePivotTable TableDestination:="", TableName:="SalesPivotTable"
End With

Set xlws = xlwb.ActiveSheet
xlws.Name = "SalesPivot"

Set xlPivot = xlws.PivotTables("SalesPivotTable")
xlPivot.AddFields "LineofBusiness2", "ProductCategory"
With xlPivot.PivotFields("TotalCost")
    .Orientation = Excel.xlDataField
    .NumberFormat = "$#,##0.00"
End With

Set xlPivot = Nothing
Set xlrng = Nothing
Set xlws = Nothing
Set xlwb = Nothing
Set xlApp = Nothing
End Sub
```

A couple of things need to be emphasized here. First, you cannot run this module from the same database where your data resides because when you run the module, the database will not allow database access from Excel. If you try it, Excel prompts you for login information, but you will not be able to connect. Second, the connection string looks difficult, but it is very easy to build by using the macro recorder from Excel. To make it easier to read, I create variables to hold the path of the database and the database directory. The other item that you may notice, if you use the macro recorder, is that when I reference Excel constants from Access, I always precede them with Excel.. While this step is not necessary, I do this to make it more clear. Also, if there are any other issues with references, you may receive an error if you are not explicit about which application the constant comes from.

To create a chart with either of these examples, right-click on the pivot table and select PivotChart from the menu. Doing the same thing with code requires only three extra lines. Example 6-3 modifies Example 6-2 and emphasized the code that changes.

Example 6-3. PivotTable and PivotChart example

```
Public Sub PivotTableChartExportData( )
Dim xlApp As Excel.Application
Dim xlwb As Excel.Workbook
Dim xlws As Excel.Worksheet
Dim xlrng As Excel.Range
Dim xlPivot As Excel.PivotTable
Dim adors As ADODB.Recordset
Dim adofld As ADODB.Field
Dim x, y, z As Integer

Set xlApp = New Excel.Application
xlApp.Visible = True
Set xlwb = xlApp.Workbooks.Add
Set xlws = xlwb.ActiveSheet
xlws.Name = "BaseData"

Set adors = New ADODB.Recordset
adors.Open "qry_BaseQuery", CurrentProject.Connection, adOpenStatic, adLockReadOnly


x = 1
For Each adofld In adors.Fields
  xlws.Cells(1, x).Value = adofld.Name
  x = x + 1
Next adofld

Set xlrng = xlws.Cells(2, 1)
xlrng.CopyFromRecordset adors
y = adors.RecordCount + 1
adors.Close

Set xlws = xlwb.Worksheets.Add
xlws.Name = "SalesPivot"
Set xlrng = xlws.Range("A3")


xlws.PivotTableWizard Excel.xlDatabase, "BaseData!R1C1:R" & y & "C" & x - 1, _
  xlrng, "SalesPivotTable", True, True, True, True
```

Example 6-3. PivotTable and PivotChart example (continued)

```
Set xlPivot = xlws.PivotTables("SalesPivotTable")
xlPivot.AddFields "LineofBusiness2", "ProductCategory"
With xlPivot.PivotFields("TotalCost")
    .Orientation = Excel.xlDataField
    .NumberFormat = "$#,##0.00"
End With

xlwb.Charts.Add
ActiveChart.SetSourceData xlrng
ActiveChart.Location Where:=Excel.xlLocationAsNewSheet


Set xlPivot = Nothing
Set xlrng = Nothing
Set xlws = Nothing
Set xlwb = Nothing
Set xlApp = Nothing
Set adofld = Nothing
Set adors = Nothing
End Sub
```

This example was easy because I already had a range object that referred to a cell in the pivot table. If I didn't have that, I would have either had to create one or write a range reference in the code after SetSourceData. Other than that, it is a very simple addition. Because most of the code to do pivot tables and pivot charts is the same regardless of data, I suggest keeping a text file of generic information and simply copying it into your module and changing the necessary parts. Figure 6-2 and Figure Figure 6-3 show the results of the pivot table and chart using this code. As with all Excel pivot charts, you can drag additional fields onto the charts or use the drop-down boxes to narrow the data.

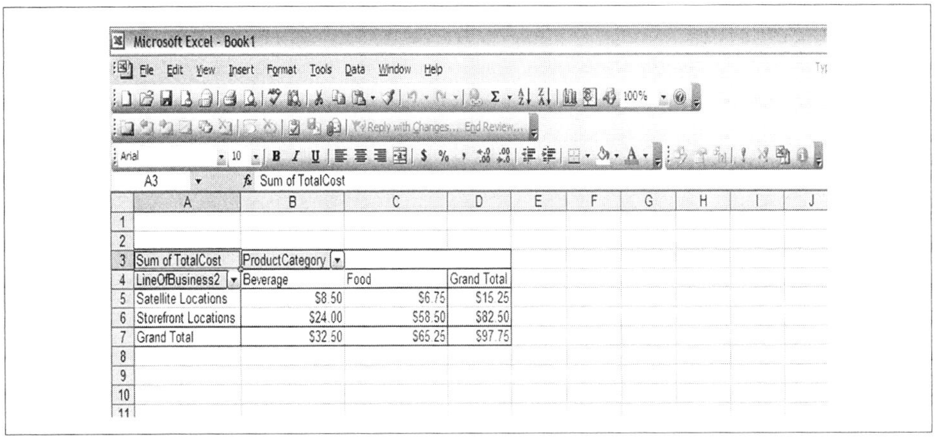

Figure 6-2. The resulting PivotTable produced by any of the three examples

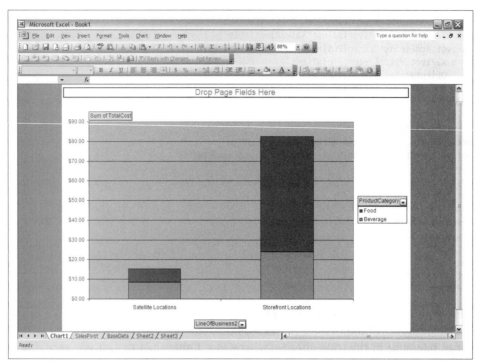

Figure 6-3. The resulting PivotChart

Building a Regular Chart

While pivot charts are very useful, sometimes you want to chart data using a regular chart, or you do not want your users pivoting the data. In these cases, you have a couple of choices. You can, of course, build the chart manually each time you need it. You can also build the chart manually and use automation from Access to push in updated data. If you're feeling ambitious, you can use VBA to build the chart from scratch.

If you already have a good chart, I recommend saving and opening it, using it as a template, and just changing the data. However, sometimes this is not practical, or you might not want to rely on having an Excel file available. Also, sometimes clients want a generic charting tool run from Access where they can choose the data they want and have it created in a chart. In cases like that, you have to build the chart each time with VBA.

To demonstrate building a chart with VBA, let's start with the data we exported earlier. Assume that you want to show the number of units and total sales of each product in one chart and total sales by location in another—on two axes on the first chart and one axis on the other. You can do this with two Group By queries; select the text fields as Group By and select Quantity and/or TotalCost using Sum as the function. For Example 6-4, the queries are saved as qry_SalesbyProduct and qry_SalesbyCenter.

Example 6-4. Chart from scratch example

```vb
Public Sub BuildCharts()
Dim xlApp As Excel.Application
Dim xlwb As Excel.Workbook
Dim xlws As Excel.Worksheet
Dim xlrng As Excel.Range
Dim adors As ADODB.Recordset
Dim x, y, z As Integer
Set adors = New ADODB.Recordset

Set xlApp = New Excel.Application
xlApp.Visible = True
Set xlwb = xlApp.Workbooks.Add
Set xlws = xlwb.ActiveSheet
xlws.Name = "MonthlyPerformance"
xlws.Range("A1").Value = "Center"
xlws.Range("B1").Value = "Quantity"
xlws.Range("C1").Value = "Cost"

Set xlrng = xlws.Range("A2")
adors.Open "Select * from qry_SalesbyCenter", _
           CurrentProject.Connection, adOpenStatic
xlrng.CopyFromRecordset adors
x = adors.RecordCount
adors.Close
xlws.Columns.AutoFit
Set xlrng = xlws.Range(xlws.Cells(1, 1), xlws.Cells(x + 1, 3))
xlrng.Select

xlwb.Charts.Add
With xlwb.ActiveChart
        .ApplyCustomType ChartType:=xlBuiltIn, TypeName:= _
            "Line - Column on 2 Axes"
        .SetSourceData xlrng, Excel.xlColumns
        .Location xlLocationAsObject, "MonthlyPerformance"
End With
With xlwb.ActiveChart
        .HasTitle = True
        .ChartTitle.Characters.Text = "Sales by Location"
        .Axes(Excel.xlCategory, Excel.xlPrimary).HasTitle = True
        .Axes(Excel.xlCategory, Excel.xlPrimary).AxisTitle.Characters.Text = "Location"
        .Axes(Excel.xlValue, Excel.xlPrimary).HasTitle = True
        .Axes(Excel.xlValue, Excel.xlPrimary).AxisTitle.Characters.Text = "Units"
        .Axes(Excel.xlCategory, Excel.xlSecondary).HasTitle = False
        .Axes(Excel.xlValue, Excel.xlSecondary).HasTitle = True
        .Axes(Excel.xlValue, Excel.xlSecondary).AxisTitle.Characters.Text = "Sales"
    End With
xlwb.ActiveChart.HasLegend = True
xlwb.ActiveChart.Legend.Position = Excel.xlTop
xlwb.ActiveChart.HasDataTable = False

xlws.Range("A1").Select
Set xlrng = Nothing
Set xlws = Nothing
```

Example 6-4. Chart from scratch example (continued)

```
Set xlwb = Nothing
Set xlApp = Nothing
Set adors = Nothing
End Sub
```

Running this code yields the chart shown in Figure 6-4, but it is not obvious how to move the chart around. From VBA, refer to the chart as a shape in the worksheet object and use the IncrementLeft and IncrementTop methods. While it is easy enough to use the methods, it is difficult to determine what values to use for those methods to move the chart where you want it because the values are entered as points. If you need to move the chart, you will most likely have to use the macro recorder and examine the results it produces. For IncrementLeft, positive numbers move it right and negative numbers move it left. For IncrementTop, positive numbers move it down the worksheet and negative numbers move it toward the top of the worksheet.

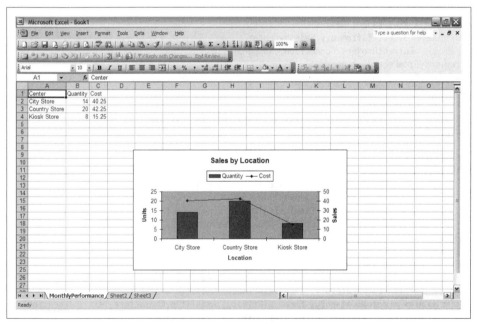

Figure 6-4. The chart from the BuildCharts procedure, formatted completely by code

Now that you have had a chance to try building a chart from scratch, let's take a look at a worksheet report published on a monthly basis by a fictional company. There are two charts on one worksheet with the data to the left of the charts, as shown in Figure 6-5. While building a worksheet like this is possible from VBA, it is easier to build it through the Excel GUI and modify the data from VBA.

To modify the data using VBA, first you need to determine whether the number of records will change during each refresh. For example, is it necessary to check how

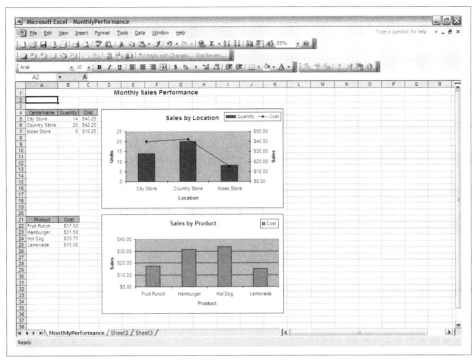

Figure 6-5. A worksheet that can be built from VBA, but would be more easily built through the Excel GUI

many products or centers are being output, or would a new product and/or center be a rare enough event that it makes sense to modify the template? Example 6-5 shows how to open this workbook and modify the data. Note that your values for the xlFile and xlSaveFile variables will be different.

Example 6-5. Modify Excel data example

```
Public Sub ModifyExcelData( )
Dim xlapp As Excel.Application
Dim xlwb As Excel.Workbook
Dim xlws As Excel.Worksheet
Dim xlrng As Excel.Range
Dim adors As ADODB.Recordset
Dim xlFile As String
Dim xlSaveFile As String
xlFile = "C:\BookInformation\Chapter6\MonthlyPerformance.xls"
xlSaveFile = "C:\BookInformation\Chapter6\MonthlyPerformance2.xls"


Set xlapp = New Excel.Application
xlapp.Visible = True
Set xlwb = xlapp.Workbooks.Open(xlFile)
Set xlws = xlwb.Sheets("MonthlyPerformance")
```

Example 6-5. Modify Excel data example (continued)

```
Set adors = New ADODB.Recordset
adors.Open "select * from qry_SalesbyCenter", CurrentProject.Connection
Set xlrng = xlws.Range("A5")
xlrng.CopyFromRecordset adors
adors.Close
adors.Open "select * from qry_SalesbyProduct", CurrentProject.Connection
Set xlrng = xlws.Range("A22")
xlrng.CopyFromRecordset adors
adors.Close
Set adors = Nothing

xlwb.SaveAs xlSaveFile
xlwb.Close
Set xlrng = Nothing
Set xlws = Nothing
Set xlwb = Nothing
xlapp.Quit
Set xlapp = Nothing
End Sub
```

Once you know where the data begins for each query, it is a simple matter of opening up the workbook (instead of using the Add method of the Workbooks collection) and using the CopyFromRecordset method to push the new data into the workbook. Then, to preserve the template, use the SaveAs method of the Workbook object to save the file under a new name. In this example, the axes are set to Automatic, so you do not need to make any changes with code to update either axis when new data is loaded. However, if you want to customize the axes, use the Axes method of the ActiveChart object. Because every type of change is different, it is easier to use the macro recorder and then move that code into your Access VBA code.

Using an Array Formula

Sometimes you have data that is already partially pivoted. For example, you might have data where you have some descriptive columns and then columns of sales data by year. If you were to use a pivot table to summarize some of the descriptive columns, you would end up having the data by year stacked—two data by year rows for each descriptive summary. When some data is stacked, it is often difficult to interpret the information in the pivot table. Even in the examples we used earlier in the chapter with units and quantity, if we summarize both fields with a pivot table, the data ends up stacked, which makes it difficult to interpret the data. If you do not want the data reported this way, you can either write a series of Union queries to unpivot the data, or you can use the following example.

First, let's start with an example in Excel. Go back to the Excel workbook where we exported the data from the qry_BaseQuery query into an Excel workbook. Assume you want to summarize the data by CenterName and ProductName. The `SumIf` function does not allow you to use multiple criteria, so you have to find another way to do this. I have worked with a lot of workbooks where someone has needed to do this. They usually sort their data and then perform a `SumIf` function on multiple subsets of data. While this works, using the same workbook the following month or other reporting period is a challenge.

To avoid this problem, you'll want to use an *array formula*. It's easiest to show this before explaining it. First, select the two columns of data that you want to summarize, copy them, and paste them starting in cell A23. Then, with that data selected, go to Data → Filter → Advanced Filter (see Figure 6-6).

Figure 6-6. The Advanced Filter dialog box, which pastes the unique records from a list into a new location

You will be copying the data to a new location using unique records only. Select cell C23 as the new location for your filtered list. You do not need to always place your filtered data beside the data being filtered, but the formulas we're using are dependent on this. Next, delete the list you filtered so you just have a list of unique center names and the products sold at each. To delete the list, use Edit → Delete and select "Shift cells left" when prompted. This puts the center names in column A and the product names in column B. Using the advanced filter to get unique records is very similar to a group by query from a database. Here is the function to type in cell C24:

    =Sum(IF($D$2:$D$21=A24,IF($G$2:$G$21=B24,$H$2:$H$21,0),0))

Here is the function to type in cell D24:

    =SUM(IF($D$2:$D$21=A24,IF($G$2:$G$21=B24,$I$2:$I$21,0),0))

After you type these formulas in, press Ctrl-Shift-Enter to enter them as an array formula. This uses an `IF` statement to determine whether the criteria are met. The array formula returns an array of values if you select a multiple cell range and do not use the `SUM` function. In our case, we just want to return the sum of the array. You may run into situations when you want to nest the `IF` function further than Excel will let you. In this case, multiply the Boolean results by the range that you want to sum:

    =SUM(($D$2:$D$21=A24) * ($G$2:$G$21=B24) * ($I$2:$I$21))

Note that in the Excel GUI, `FALSE` is 0 and `TRUE` is 1, which is why multiplying the results together works. If any come up false, the result is 0 and the sum doesn't change. Also notice that when you press Ctrl-Shift-Enter, Excel automatically puts braces around the formula, signifying that it is an array formula. Do not attempt to put the braces in yourself, or Excel will give you an error message. Figure 6-7 shows what the resulting worksheet looks like with the IF statement method.

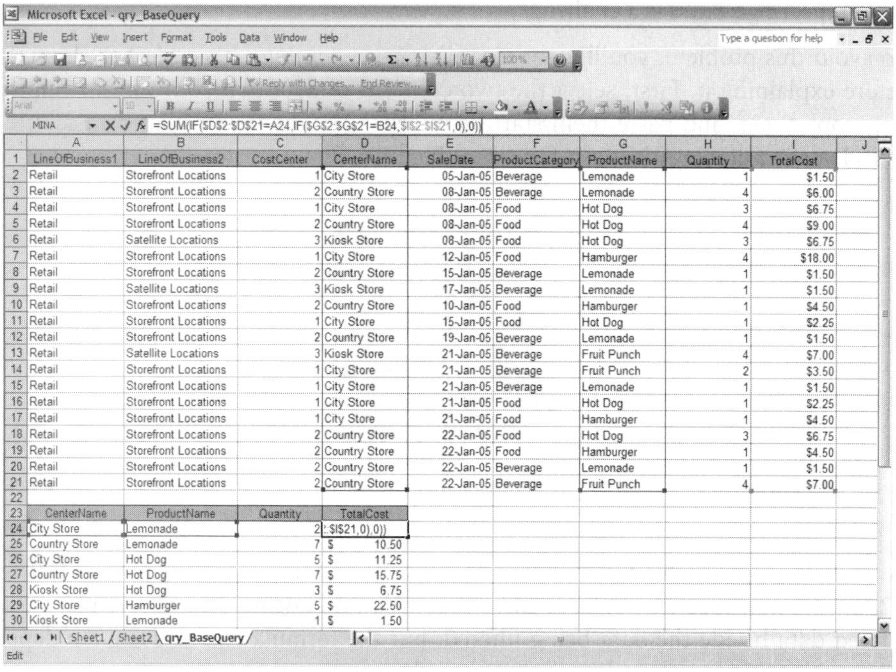

	A	B	C	D	E	F	G	H	I
1	LineOfBusiness1	LineOfBusiness2	CostCenter	CenterName	SaleDate	ProductCategory	ProductName	Quantity	TotalCost
2	Retail	Storefront Locations	1	City Store	05-Jan-05	Beverage	Lemonade	1	$1.50
3	Retail	Storefront Locations	2	Country Store	08-Jan-05	Beverage	Lemonade	4	$6.00
4	Retail	Storefront Locations	1	City Store	08-Jan-05	Food	Hot Dog	3	$6.75
5	Retail	Storefront Locations	2	Country Store	08-Jan-05	Food	Hot Dog	4	$9.00
6	Retail	Satellite Locations	3	Kiosk Store	08-Jan-05	Food	Hot Dog	3	$6.75
7	Retail	Storefront Locations	1	City Store	12-Jan-05	Food	Hamburger	4	$18.00
8	Retail	Storefront Locations	2	Country Store	15-Jan-05	Beverage	Lemonade	1	$1.50
9	Retail	Satellite Locations	3	Kiosk Store	17-Jan-05	Beverage	Lemonade	1	$1.50
10	Retail	Storefront Locations	2	Country Store	10-Jan-05	Food	Hamburger	1	$4.50
11	Retail	Storefront Locations	1	City Store	15-Jan-05	Food	Hot Dog	1	$2.25
12	Retail	Storefront Locations	2	Country Store	19-Jan-05	Beverage	Lemonade	1	$1.50
13	Retail	Satellite Locations	3	Kiosk Store	21-Jan-05	Beverage	Fruit Punch	4	$7.00
14	Retail	Storefront Locations	1	City Store	21-Jan-05	Beverage	Fruit Punch	2	$3.50
15	Retail	Storefront Locations	1	City Store	21-Jan-05	Beverage	Lemonade	1	$1.50
16	Retail	Storefront Locations	1	City Store	21-Jan-05	Food	Hot Dog	1	$2.25
17	Retail	Storefront Locations	1	City Store	21-Jan-05	Food	Hamburger	1	$4.50
18	Retail	Storefront Locations	2	Country Store	22-Jan-05	Food	Hot Dog	3	$6.75
19	Retail	Storefront Locations	2	Country Store	22-Jan-05	Food	Hamburger	1	$4.50
20	Retail	Storefront Locations	2	Country Store	22-Jan-05	Beverage	Lemonade	1	$1.50
21	Retail	Storefront Locations	2	Country Store	22-Jan-05	Beverage	Fruit Punch	4	$7.00
22									
23	CenterName	ProductName	Quantity	TotalCost					
24	City Store	Lemonade	2	:$I$21,0),0))					
25	Country Store	Lemonade	7	$ 10.50					
26	City Store	Hot Dog	5	$ 11.25					
27	Country Store	Hot Dog	7	$ 15.75					
28	Kiosk Store	Hot Dog	3	$ 6.75					
29	City Store	Hamburger	5	$ 22.50					
30	Kiosk Store	Lemonade	1	$ 1.50					

Figure 6-7. The Array formula example, showing what it looks like when you edit the formula

While you can accomplish the same result by using a Group By query in Access, sometimes you want the results to update if the data is changed in Excel, say by a curious user without permissions to reach the original data.

To accomplish this by automation from Access, use the approach in Example 6-6.

Example 6-6. Array formula example

```
Public Sub ArrayFormulaExample()
Dim xlapp As Excel.Application
Dim xlwb As Excel.Workbook
Dim xlws As Excel.Worksheet
Dim xlrng As Excel.Range
Dim adors As ADODB.Recordset
Dim adofld As ADODB.Field
Dim w, x, y, z As Integer

Set xlapp = New Excel.Application
xlapp.Visible = True
Set xlwb = xlapp.Workbooks.Add
```

Example 6-6. Array formula example (continued)

```
Set xlws = xlwb.ActiveSheet
xlws.Name = "BaseData"

Set adors = New ADODB.Recordset
adors.Open "qry_BaseQuery", CurrentProject.Connection, adOpenStatic, adLockReadOnly

x = 1
For Each adofld In adors.Fields
  xlws.Cells(1, x).Value = adofld.Name
  x = x + 1
Next adofld

Set xlrng = xlws.Cells(2, 1)
xlrng.CopyFromRecordset adors
y = adors.RecordCount + 1
adors.Close

Set xlrng = xlws.Cells(y + 2, 1)
xlrng.Value = "Center Name"
Set xlrng = xlws.Cells(y + 2, 2)
xlrng.Value = "Product Name"
Set xlrng = xlws.Cells(y + 2, 3)
xlrng.Value = "Quantity"
Set xlrng = xlws.Cells(y + 2, 4)
xlrng.Value = "Cost"
Set xlrng = xlws.Cells(y + 3, 1)
adors.Open "Select CenterName, ProductName from qry_BaseQuery " & _
       "Group by CenterName, ProductName", CurrentProject.Connection, _
       adOpenStatic, adLockReadOnly
xlrng.CopyFromRecordset adors
w = y + 2 + adors.RecordCount

For z = (y + 3) To w
  Set xlrng = xlws.Cells(z, 3)
  xlrng.FormulaArray = _
  "=SUM( (RC1=R2C4:R" & y & "C4) * (RC2=R2C7:R" & y & "C7) * " & _
  "(R2C8:R" & y & "C8))"
  Set xlrng = xlws.Cells(z, 4)
  xlrng.FormulaArray = _
  "=SUM( (RC1=R2C4:R" & y & "C4) * (RC2=R2C7:R" & y & "C7) * " & _
  "(R2C9:R" & y & "C9))"
  xlrng.Style = "Currency"
Next z
xlws.Columns.AutoFit
adors.Close
Set adofld = Nothing
Set adors = Nothing
Set xlrng = Nothing
Set xlws = Nothing
Set xlwb = Nothing
Set xlapp = Nothing
End Sub
```

This method also can be used when you want to get pivot table-like results that update automatically, instead of when the user presses "Refresh data." Another way this method can be used is to multiply the Boolean results together using the SUM function, simulating the CountIf function but allowing you to use multiple criteria.

Graphing Variables in a Model

The next method is very useful if you build a model and want to see the results against various criteria. Let's assume you have multiple values in a table, and you want to input them into a model and store the result. This would normally be a very time-consuming process. However, by leveraging VBA, you can do it rather easily.

For this example, we use a table with three fields: sales, full-time equivalent (FTE), and contribution. The table uses an Excel workbook that uses the sales and FTE inputs to return a contribution profit number. This method is obviously more useful in a more complex model, but this simple example will demonstrate how it works. Note that in this example, the code opens a workbook that already exists; your path and filename will be different. Example 6-7 also uses a worksheet called "Model" in the workbook.

Example 6-7. Profit Model example

```
Public Sub ProfitModel()
Dim xlapp As Excel.Application
Dim xlwb As Excel.Workbook
Dim xlws As Excel.Worksheet
Dim adors As ADODB.Recordset

Set xlapp = New Excel.Application
xlapp.Visible = True
Set xlwb = xlapp.Workbooks.Open("C:\BookInformation\Chapter6\ProfitModel.xls")
Set xlws = xlwb.Sheets("Model")

Set adors = New ADODB.Recordset
adors.Open "tbl_ProfitModel", CurrentProject.Connection, _
        adOpenDynamic, adLockOptimistic

adors.MoveFirst
While Not adors.EOF
  xlws.Range("B10").Value = adors.Fields("Sales").Value
  xlws.Range("B6").Value = adors.Fields("FTE").Value
  adors.Fields("Contribution").Value = xlws.Range("B18").Value
  adors.MoveNext
Wend

adors.Close
xlwb.Close False
```

Example 6-7. Profit Model example (continued)

```
Set xlws = Nothing
Set xlwb = Nothing
xlapp.Quit
Set xlapp = Nothing
Set adors = Nothing
End Sub
```

This opens the Excel workbook shown in Figure 6-8.

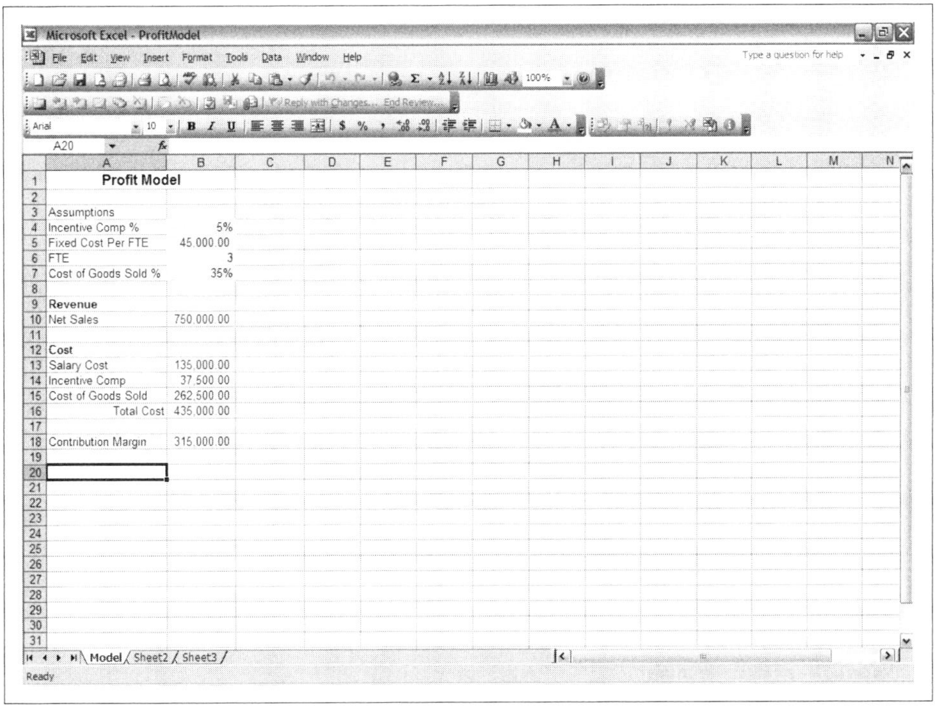

Figure 6-8. A very simplistic contribution profit model that takes various assumptions to come up with a result

For every record in the table, the code takes the sales and FTE assumption and places the values in the model. Then it takes the resulting contribution and stores the result in the table. You can use the data from this table with one of the graphing procedures we made earlier to graph the results. You can certainly store all of the variables in the table, or just change one variable at a time and hold all of the other variables constant. Your choice is driven by the reason for the modeling. However, you could use this code after changing only the Ranges and field names.

CHAPTER 7

Leveraging SQL Server Data with Microsoft Office

While the primary focus of this book is on using Access and Excel together to enable automation of reporting and analysis, it is difficult to ignore enterprise databases since in many cases they are the source data in a corporate setting. You don't need to know all about SQL Server to use it with Excel and Access. While you can read a SQL Server book if you need detail, this chapter introduces you to accessing data with tables, views, and stored procedures, accessing data through ADO, using temporary tables, and pushing and pulling data from SQL Server. As an additional topic, if you are familiar with Access, you know that crosstab queries are a very popular way to summarize data, so you may be surprised to find out that in SQL Server you cannot use them. I show how to build a stored procedure to get around this limitation, potentially simplifying your analysis of the data in Excel or Access substantially. Finally, I also cover using DTS to automate report production on a schedule.

 Stored procedures are similar to procedures that you create in any programming language. They may take input parameters, execute code, return values, or call other procedures. You gain a performance advantage when using a stored procedure versus running a query with parameters. In addition, using a stored procedure reduces network traffic, since a single statement can call a stored procedure instead of sending multiple (sometimes hundreds of) lines of code over the network.

Pass-Through Queries Versus Linked Tables

One of the easiest ways to access SQL Server data is to link to the table from Microsoft Access and write queries on the linked table. You can link to a table by right-clicking on whitespace anywhere in the database window and selecting Link Tables. The other way to access SQL Server data is through a pass-through query, where query instructions are sent over the network and the query is run on the server with results returned to the client. You choose between ease of use and performance. If you have written queries on Access tables, you know how to write a query on a linked SQL Server table. If the table is relatively small, you gain very little in performance by using a pass-through query. However, if you are dealing a table with several hundred thousand records and you want only records that meet certain criteria, you gain a tremendous advantage by using a pass-through query.

Why? If you write a query on a linked table and set up criteria, each record is brought from the server to the client to be evaluated, resulting in quite a bit of network traffic. If you write a pass-through query, the query instructions are passed to SQL Server and the query is evaluated on the server. Only data that meets the query criteria is passed to the client. The only problem with writing a pass-through query is that you will not get any help from Access in writing it. You need to know SQL Server's own Transact-SQL, though there are some ways around that.

When I have to write a pass-through query with multiple joins, I use a shortcut that helps me write it. First, link the SQL Server tables and use the query designer in Access to create the query. Microsoft Access uses the local table name; for example, a table called dbo.Table1 on SQL Server becomes dbo_Table1 in Access. Once you write your query, go to the top menu, select Query → SQL Specific → Pass-Through, and the query turns into SQL. Copy the SQL text into a word processor and replace "dbo_" with "dbo," using the Find and Replace function. Next, copy the query text from the word processor and paste it back into Access. Then, go to View → Properties, click on the ellipsis on the ODBC Connection String line, and Access takes you through dialog boxes to build the connection string for you.

I have found that even though this adds some steps, it ensures that the joins are correct and in the end is much easier than trying to write SQL by hand. Either method will give you the same results; the only difference will be in performance. The only other item that causes differences is that the wildcard character is "%" in SQL Server and "*" in Access, and there is a similar issue if you run a query from ADO instead of DAO.

There are times when your only option is to use a pass-through query. Let's assume that you want to standardize a parameterized query that you run on multiple occasions. You can do it easily by creating a stored procedure on SQL Server that accepts the arguments and returns the results. The problem with using a stored procedure is that Access cannot link to the table. The easiest way to access the data is to call the stored procedure from a pass-through query. The syntax is very easy. Assume the stored procedure is called GetData, and it needs two arguments, State and Zip Code. Also, assume that the State argument is a string, while Zip Code is numeric. In this case, the query text is Execute GetData 'PA', 17025; if you create a pass-through query and type in this text, you will get all the records in Pennsylvania with a zip code of 17025. Changing from queries to stored procedures allows you to standardize the method for getting the data and also eliminates errors. This is very helpful in trying to create "one version of the truth" when accessing enterprise data.

Companies often struggle with the decision of how much access to give individual users when accessing data from enterprise databases, provided they have not already bought a tool to do this. The dilemma is that if you allow users to write their own queries for everything, you run the risk of each user interpreting the logic of the data structures differently. For example, a company's Human Resources system gives a unique identifier that increments by 1 for each new record. An employee transfers from Job A (let's say record number 1200) to Job B (record 1250) and then back to Job A. When someone did the data entry, he just activated the Job A record and deactivated the Job B record, giving the employee's current job a lower ID number than her previous job. (It also caused problems with maintaining a history of jobs, but that is another issue.) The problem was identified when the employee did not show up on a query that gave active employees written by one user, but did appear on a different list written by another user. I was asked to look at it and found that one query writer looked at the status of the highest ID number for a particular employee to determine her status, and the other looked at open records. In this case, all we needed to do was standardize the way each report was run and write a business rule for how to handle job changes.

To combat problems like this, write standardized queries and put them into stored procedures that take the arguments needed to produce the desired results. That way, anytime someone needs that data, he can just run the stored procedure, and you can be certain that he is not making query logic errors. For example, you can have a stored procedure that returns active employees, which you can use to get the list anytime. If you need to, you can have the stored procedure create a temporary table that can be linked for other reports. In any case, using standardized views and stored procedures helps cut down on business logic problems.

Stored procedures also help with with security. If you are in charge of a database, you may not want people to have direct access to the tables. Or, if you want to make sure that you don't inadvertently change data, you may not want to access tables directly yourself. One way you can accomplish this is by only giving users access to stored procedures and views (a view is a query on SQL Server). This prevents the users from accessing the tables directly or making any changes to data, except as provided by the stored procedure. For example, you can give a user access to a stored procedure that takes as an argument a unique identifier for a record, and then another argument for the text or numeric data that you want to update a field. This gives the user the ability to update a record by using the stored procedure without giving her direct access to the table. In addition, you can create stored procedures that add new data or append records from one table into another. I certainly recommend this approach if you have multiple users of your database. Also, by using this approach, you can return records to Access without maintaining a constant connection to the database while you page through records. You can have code run anytime data is changed on the client that will fire the stored procedure to make the change on the server. In addition to the performance advantage, you also eliminate the possibility of two people trying to access the same record simultaneously.

Regardless of which method you use on SQL Server, you can accomplish most tasks using pass-through queries from Microsoft Access. If you need to simply page through records, using a linked table is a fine method, but in other cases, I recommend moving as much processing to the server as possible. I should also mention that if you make use of temporary tables (tables proceeded with a # or ##), using a pass-through query is a very easy way to access them.

Wildcards are tricky when you are dealing with Access and SQL Server or using ADO to use data in Microsoft Access. I first encountered a problem when I ran a query in Access that worked but would not return any results when the same query was opened with ADO. I soon found the problem was that the wildcard was * (Access/DAO wildcard) instead of % (ADO/SQL Server wildcard).

When fixing it, you run into the problem that if you set it up with % to run with ADO, you will not be able to open it in the Access GUI. You will run into the same problem if you write the query in the Access GUI and convert it into a pass-through query. Just keep in mind that if you are using wildcards to make sure that when you use DAO or the Access GUI, use * (even if the data is on SQL Server), and use % with ADO and SQL Server Pass-Through queries.

Creating a Connection Using VBA

Now that you understand a little about using the Access GUI to access data on SQL Server, I will show you how to do the same thing with VBA. In some cases it is easier to create a pass-through query with the Access GUI and then open the query with VBA. If you need to change the query, you can just change the query's SQL string with VBA. Also, in most cases, I recommend using ADO, rather than DAO, to access SQL Server. And finally, when you do development work with SQL Server, it is always best to use a test database before trying things on a production database.

There are some very good reasons to have a test database for your SQL Server production database. With Access, you can make a copy of a database to test something and scrap the copy if your code doesn't work or causes problems. When you are dealing with SQL Server, however, the process is not as simple, and you will most likely be contending with multiple users. Running your code on a test database reduces potential issues. It is even useful if you are just running queries, as you don't want to run a query that takes a long time to run during the middle of the day with 50 users on the database. Often, you won't know how long something takes to run until you test it.

Let's say that you have data in SQL Server that you need to put into an Excel report. Three viable alternatives are using:

- Access and VBA to pull the data and automate Excel
- Excel VBA to pull the data directly into Excel
- ActiveX script in Data Transformation Services (DTS) on SQL Server to build the report

I show the VBA options in this section and the DTS option in the next section. I do not get into the actual building of the report, simply the movement of data. Once you have the data in Excel, you can use the same techniques used throughout the rest of the book to automate Excel.

Building the Connection in Access

When using Access, decide whether you will use DAO or ADO, and whether you will build the connection string with VBA or create a DSN. There is no one right answer. I prefer to create an XML file that can be opened as an ADO recordset to hold the connection string information and have Access open that file to build the connection. As long as the end user has access to the XML file on their machine, she can use the application. If you use a DSN, you will have to make changes on everyone's PC to use the application. A second convenience is that you can have the XML file on a network drive. This comes in handy if you need to change server information in the future. It also allows you to test the application on the test server and the production server by just changing one line in the XML file.

The easiest way to create the XML file is to create a table in Access with the required information, open up that table with ADO, and save the recordset as XML. Here are the steps to do that—I should also mention that I use multiple rows of data for each part of the connection, rather than multiple columns.

First, go into the Access GUI and create a new table in Design View with two columns. Call the first column ADO_Argument (Text—20 characters) and the second column Argument_Text (Text—50 characters). Next, save the table as tbl_SQLConnection and select No when asked whether you want to create a primary key. Now you are ready to fill in the information. The following information can be filled in for the connection string:

- Provider
- Data source
- Initial catalog
- Integrated security

You can also enter a username and password, but I do not recommend it unless you use some type of public username for very limited reporting. I suggest having a dialog box pop up asking for the username and password. For this example, we will pass username and password as parameters to the VBA procedure. Also note that if you use integrated security, you do not need to pass a username and password. I show Integrated Security in the XML file, but you should omit that line if you want to use a username and password.

Now, open your table and enter **sqloledb** for Provider, the name of your SQL Server or the IP address of your SQL Server for Data Source, the database name for Initial Catalog, and **SSPI** for Integrated Security. If you are building this on a network where everyone can use the server name for Data Source, then using the server name would be fine. However, in most cases, I recommend using the IP address, particularly if you are building this application for use in multiple locations. Once this is entered, the procedure in Example 7-1 will save it as an XML file.

Example 7-1. Sample procedure to save a recordset as XML

```
Public Sub MakeXML()
Dim adors As ADODB.Recordset

Set adors = New ADODB.Recordset

adors.Open "tbl_SQLConnection", CurrentProject.Connection
adors.Save "C:\Documents and Settings\All Users\" & _
          "Documents\SQLConn.XML", adPersistXML
adors.Close
Set adors = Nothing

End Sub
```

This code puts the file in a folder that should exist on most Windows XP systems. You might notice that the folder shows as "Shared Documents" on the screen, but if you go into the properties of a file in the folder, you see the folder needs to be referred to as "Documents" in a path; this is similar to the "My Documents" folder showing up as "Michael Schmalz's Documents," which you can't refer to in a path. While the code uses a location that should exist on most Windows XP systems, you can select whatever location you would like. Find the XML file and open it up with Notepad, and you see the following if you use ADO 2.8. You may see something a little different if you use prior versions of ADO. However, as long as you use the same version as your other users, it will work on their machines.

```
<xml xmlns:s='uuid:BDC6E3F0-6DA3-11d1-A2A3-00AA00C14882'
    xmlns:dt='uuid:C2F41010-65B3-11d1-A29F-00AA00C14882'
    xmlns:rs='urn:schemas-microsoft-com:rowset'
    xmlns:z='#RowsetSchema'>
<s:Schema id='RowsetSchema'>
    <s:ElementType name='row' content='eltOnly'>
        <s:AttributeType name='ADO_Argument' rs:number='1' rs:nullable='true' rs:
maydefer='true' rs:writeunknown='true'>
```

```
            <s:datatype dt:type='string' dt:maxLength='20'/>
        </s:AttributeType>
        <s:AttributeType name='Argument_Text' rs:number='2' rs:nullable='true' rs:
maydefer='true' rs:writeunknown='true'>
            <s:datatype dt:type='string' dt:maxLength='50'/>
        </s:AttributeType>
        <s:extends type='rs:rowbase'/>
    </s:ElementType>
</s:Schema>
<rs:data>
    <z:row ADO_Argument='Provider' Argument_Text='sqloledb'/>
    <z:row ADO_Argument='Data Source' Argument_Text='MJS_Home'/>
    <z:row ADO_Argument='Initial Catalog' Argument_Text='Pubs'/>
    <z:row ADO_Argument='Integrated Security' Argument_Text='SSPI'/>
</rs:data>
</xml>
```

As you can see, this is a much easier way to write the XML file than trying to do it yourself, though it is certainly possible to write it by hand. In many cases, when I use this method with a VB file, I put in many more pieces of information. I use this technique instead of using an .INI file because I find it is much more flexible. It is very easy to edit this file to add more records; copy a row that begins with <z:row and ends with />, paste it on the line below, and change the data inside the single quotes. Again, this method fills in four pieces of information. If you are building an application to run on your computer with no other users, it is probably overkill. However, you never know when you will have additional users, and you can use this same XML file over and over, even among multiple Access and Excel applications that need to access the same SQL Server.

To open the XML file as an ADO recordset, use the Open method of the ADO recordset object and use the path and filename. Example 7-2 shows a procedure that opens up an XML file and puts the information from the file into the Immediate Window.

Example 7-2. Procedure to read an XML file as a recordset

```
Public Sub ReadXML( )
Dim adors As ADODB.Recordset

Set adors = New ADODB.Recordset

adors.Open "C:\Documents and Settings\All Users\" & _
           "Documents\SQLConn.XML"

adors.MoveFirst
While Not adors.EOF
  Debug.Print adors.Fields(0).Value & " - " & _
              adors.Fields(1).Value
  adors.MoveNext
Wend

adors.Close

End Sub
```

Now that you understand how to open the XML file, Example 7-3 shows a procedure to open the recordset by pulling the data from SQL Server and pushing that data into a new Excel workbook. To use this, you need a reference to the same version of ADO that you used to build the XML file, as well as a reference to Microsoft Excel. You do this by going to Tools → References in the Design Mode of the module. Note that in this procedure, Excel stays open; you could also set it up to save the Workbook using the SaveAs method of the Workbook object. If you do that, also use the Quit method of the Excel Application object to close Excel.

Example 7-3. Push data from SQL Server to Excel

```
Public Sub OpenSQLWriteExcel(UserName As String, Password As String)
Dim adocn As ADODB.Connection
Dim adoconnrs As ADODB.Recordset
Dim adors As ADODB.Recordset
Dim adofld As ADODB.Field
Dim ConnString As String
Dim xlapp As Excel.Application
Dim xlwb As Excel.Workbook
Dim xlws As Excel.Worksheet
Dim xlrng As Excel.Range
Dim x As Integer

Set adoconnrs = New ADODB.Recordset
adoconnrs.Open "C:\Documents and Settings\All Users\" & _
               "Documents\SQLConn.XML"

adoconnrs.MoveFirst
While Not adoconnrs.EOF
  ConnString = ConnString & _
      adoconnrs.Fields(0).Value & " = '" & adoconnrs.Fields(1).Value & "';"
  adoconnrs.MoveNext
Wend

adoconnrs.Close

ConnString = ConnString & "User ID = '" & UserName & "';"
ConnString = ConnString & "Password = '" & Password & "';"

Set adocn = New ADODB.Connection
adocn.ConnectionString = ConnString
adocn.Open

Set adors = New ADODB.Recordset

adors.Open "pubs.dbo.Authors", adocn
adors.MoveFirst

Set xlapp = New Excel.Application
xlapp.Visible = True
Set xlwb = xlapp.Workbooks.Add
Set xlws = xlwb.ActiveSheet
```

Example 7-3. Push data from SQL Server to Excel (continued)

```
x = 1
For Each adofld In adors.Fields
  xlws.Cells(1, x).Value = adofld.Name
  x = x + 1
Next adofld
Set xlrng = xlws.Range("A2")
xlrng.CopyFromRecordset adors
xlws.Columns.AutoFit

adors.Close
adocn.Close

Set xlrng = Nothing
Set xlws = Nothing
Set xlwb = Nothing
Set xlapp = Nothing
Set adoconnrs = Nothing
Set adocn = Nothing
Set adors = Nothing
End Sub
```

This is a lot of code to open up a recordset that is doing very little. The code is cut by quite a bit if you open the authors table as a linked table, but the time you lose in writing this procedure will be saved many times over if you have to make changes to the connection information or if you use this application on multiple machines.

Once you have the data in Excel, automate Excel to put in subtotals or make a pivot table out of the data. The authors table of the Pubs database doesn't really lend itself to that type of analysis, but you can see how to get the information. Also note that Access is not involved at all in this code other than being the automation engine. It makes sense to do things like this in Access because you can build a nice frontend that looks very similar to a VB application. An Access frontend that builds many reports in Excel will be much easier for your end users than navigating multiple Excel documents to find their file. Also, in many cases you will do some additional automation and possibly even link to other data in the Access database. For this very simplistic example, the code will be virtually the same in Excel.

Pulling Data in with Excel Alone

This next example shows how to do the same thing without involving Microsoft Access. It will look similar to the Access version, though. Open Excel and get into a new Workbook. Rename Sheet1 to Connection Info by double-clicking on the Sheet Name tab, right-click on Sheet2, select Delete, and do the same for Sheet3.

Next, in cell A1 type **username**, and in cell A2 type **password**. For cell B1, go to Format → Cells, go to the Protection tab, and uncheck the box for Locked. For cell B2 go to Format → Cells, and on the Protection tab, uncheck the box for Locked, but check

---

the box for Hidden. Still for Cell B2, go to the Font tab, and for Color select White (or whatever background color you are using on your worksheet). Go to Tools → Macros → Visual Basic Editor, or press Alt+F11. Right-click on the VBAProject of your workbook and select Insert → Module. It defaults to Module1; select Insert → Procedure, and enter the code in Example 7-4.

Example 7-4. Procedure to pull data from SQL Server into Excel

```
Public Sub OpenSQLWriteExcel()
Dim adocn As ADODB.Connection
Dim adoconnrs As ADODB.Recordset
Dim adors As ADODB.Recordset
Dim adofld As ADODB.Field
Dim ConnString As String
Dim xlwb As Excel.Workbook
Dim xlws As Excel.Worksheet
Dim xlrng As Excel.Range
Dim x As Integer
Dim UserName As String
Dim Password As String

UserName = Sheets("Connection Info").Range("B1").Value
Password = Sheets("Connection Info").Range("B2").Value

Set adoconnrs = New ADODB.Recordset
adoconnrs.Open "C:\Documents and Settings\All Users\" & _
               "Documents\SQLConn.XML"

adoconnrs.MoveFirst
While Not adoconnrs.EOF
  ConnString = ConnString & _
      adoconnrs.Fields(0).Value & " = '" & adoconnrs.Fields(1).Value & "';"
  adoconnrs.MoveNext
Wend

adoconnrs.Close

ConnString = ConnString & "User ID = '" & UserName & "';"
ConnString = ConnString & "Password = '" & Password & "';"

Set adocn = New ADODB.Connection
adocn.ConnectionString = ConnString
adocn.Open

Set adors = New ADODB.Recordset

adors.Open "pubs.dbo.Authors", adocn
adors.MoveFirst

Set xlwb = ActiveWorkbook
Set xlws = xlwb.Worksheets.Add
xlws.Name = "Data"
x = 1
```

Example 7-4. Procedure to pull data from SQL Server into Excel (continued)

```
For Each adofld In adors.Fields
  xlws.Cells(1, x).Value = adofld.Name
  x = x + 1
Next adofld
Set xlrng = xlws.Range("A2")
xlrng.CopyFromRecordset adors
xlws.Columns.AutoFit

adors.Close
adocn.Close

Set xlrng = Nothing
Set xlws = Nothing
Set xlwb = Nothing
Set adoconnrs = Nothing
Set adocn = Nothing
Set adors = Nothing
End Sub
```

This doesn't use the Excel Application object, nor does it pass the username and password as parameters. Instead, that information comes from the worksheet. Keep in mind that if you put a username and password into the worksheet, you should take adequate precautions to protect it. One way to do this is to go to View → Toolbars → Visual Basic and click on the Toolbox button to bring up the list of controls that you can put on the worksheet. Next, click on the Command button and drag it onto the worksheet. Go to the properties of the button and make the caption Get SQL Data.

You also have to make the button work after the sheet is protected. Right-click on the button, go to Format Control, select the Protection tab, and uncheck the box for Locked. Next, right-click the button again and select View Code. Enter the following code:

```
Private Sub CommandButton1_Click()
Call Module1.OpenSQLWriteExcel
Sheets("Connection Info").Range("B2").Value = ""
End Sub
```

This code calls the procedure that you put in Module1, and after it runs, it erases the password that you entered. The final step is to click on the button that says Exit Design Mode on the Visual Basic toolbar. Close both the Toolbox dialog and the Visual Basic dialog, click off of the button, and go to Tools → Protection → Protect Sheet. Enter a password and validate it on the next dialog box.

Once these steps are complete, the spreadsheet ensures that no one else can see the password that you typed. It is the same color as the background and is hidden in the formula bar. Notice that when you click the button it clears out the password after it runs. This ensures that you don't save the workbook with the password in it. The workbook should look similar to Figure 7-1, and after you type in your username and password and click the button, you should get a worksheet that looks like Figure 7-2.

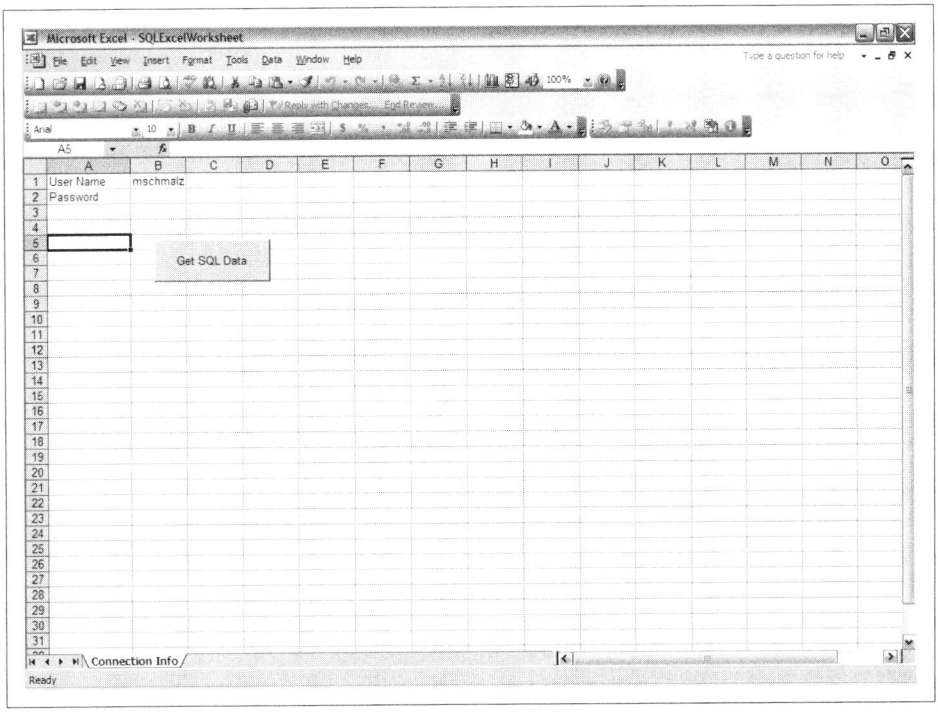

Figure 7-1. *The Excel worksheet used to run the code to pull the data from SQL Server and place it in a new worksheet*

If you attempt to press the button again, you receive an error message saying that you cannot rename a worksheet the same name as an existing sheet. If you delete the data sheet and press the button again, you receive another error message because the code deletes the password each time it is called.

The last line of the XML file tells SQL Server to use integrated security, which means that if you have your SQL Server set up to allow you to use your Windows login instead of using SQL Server Security, it ignores the username and password that you entered. This is important because if you leave this line in and test the worksheet, you will not receive the errors noted above. I suggest leaving this line in if you are using integrated security because you can avoid having to put a place for username and password. However, if you want to force a user to put in her username and password, go into the XML file, delete the entire line that sets Integrated Security to SSPI, and save the file.

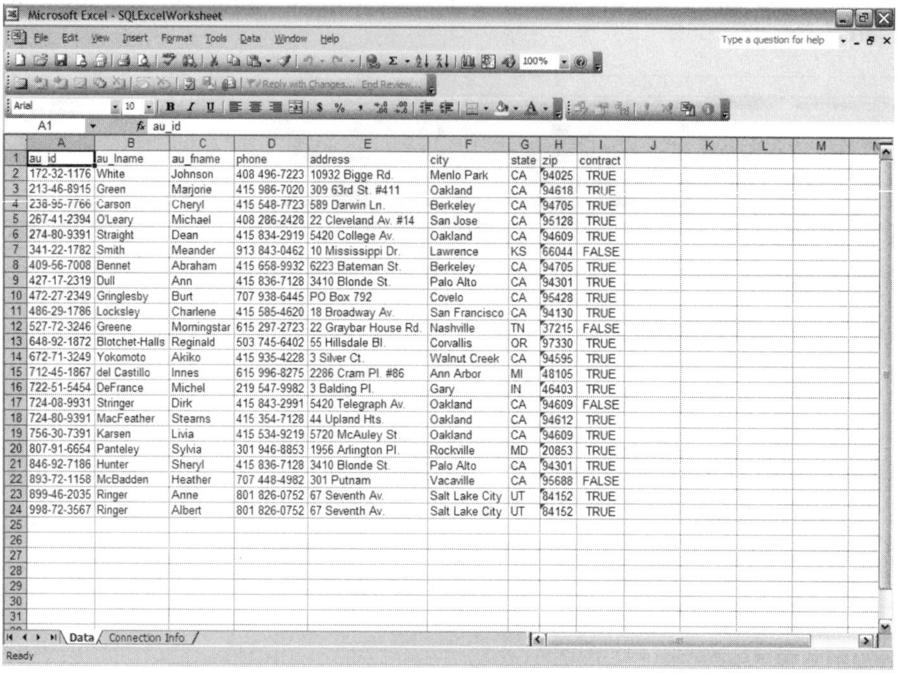

au_id	au_lname	au_fname	phone	address	city	state	zip	contract
172-32-1176	White	Johnson	408 496-7223	10932 Bigge Rd.	Menlo Park	CA	94025	TRUE
213-46-8915	Green	Marjorie	415 986-7020	309 63rd St. #411	Oakland	CA	94618	TRUE
238-95-7766	Carson	Cheryl	415 548-7723	589 Darwin Ln.	Berkeley	CA	94705	TRUE
267-41-2394	O'Leary	Michael	408 286-2428	22 Cleveland Av. #14	San Jose	CA	95128	TRUE
274-80-9391	Straight	Dean	415 834-2919	5420 College Av.	Oakland	CA	94609	TRUE
341-22-1782	Smith	Meander	913 843-0462	10 Mississippi Dr.	Lawrence	KS	66044	FALSE
409-56-7008	Bennet	Abraham	415 658-9932	6223 Bateman St.	Berkeley	CA	94705	TRUE
427-17-2319	Dull	Ann	415 836-7128	3410 Blonde St.	Palo Alto	CA	94301	TRUE
472-27-2349	Gringlesby	Burt	707 938-6445	PO Box 792	Covelo	CA	95428	TRUE
486-29-1786	Locksley	Charlene	415 585-4620	18 Broadway Av.	San Francisco	CA	94130	TRUE
527-72-3246	Greene	Morningstar	615 297-2723	22 Graybar House Rd.	Nashville	TN	37215	FALSE
648-92-1872	Blotchet-Halls	Reginald	503 745-6402	55 Hillsdale Bl.	Corvallis	OR	97330	TRUE
672-71-3249	Yokomoto	Akiko	415 935-4228	3 Silver Ct.	Walnut Creek	CA	94595	TRUE
712-45-1867	del Castillo	Innes	615 996-8275	2286 Cram Pl. #86	Ann Arbor	MI	48105	TRUE
722-51-5454	DeFrance	Michel	219 547-9982	3 Balding Pl.	Gary	IN	46403	TRUE
724-08-9931	Stringer	Dirk	415 843-2991	5420 Telegraph Av.	Oakland	CA	94609	FALSE
724-80-9391	MacFeather	Stearns	415 354-7128	44 Upland Hts.	Oakland	CA	94612	TRUE
756-30-7391	Karsen	Livia	415 534-9219	5720 McAuley St.	Oakland	CA	94609	TRUE
807-91-6654	Panteley	Sylvia	301 946-8853	1956 Arlington Pl.	Rockville	MD	20853	TRUE
846-92-7186	Hunter	Sheryl	415 836-7128	3410 Blonde St.	Palo Alto	CA	94301	TRUE
893-72-1158	McBadden	Heather	707 448-4982	301 Putnam	Vacaville	CA	95688	FALSE
899-46-2035	Ringer	Anne	801 826-0752	67 Seventh Av.	Salt Lake City	UT	84152	TRUE
998-72-3567	Ringer	Albert	801 826-0752	67 Seventh Av.	Salt Lake City	UT	84152	TRUE

Figure 7-2. The resulting worksheet when you press the button

Using DTS to Automate Excel

This section will only be useful for you if you have SQL Server Enterprise Manager. If you don't have Enterprise Manager, ask your database administrator to do this for you if it would be useful for you. First, let's discuss what Data Transformation Services (DTS) is all about. In SQL Server 2000, you can create packages that work with data in SQL Server or other applications, run scripts, execute stored procedures, etc. DTS lets you build export systems that run on a schedule right in SQL Server. If you normally run several queries from SQL Server daily to build reports, you can set them up to run on a schedule and automate Excel right from DTS. You can then save the reports in a common location, or even have DTS email the reports to you when they are done. There are several ways this can be done, but I am going to show you how to use ActiveX and VBScript.

In Enterprise Manager, right-click on Data Transformation Services and select New Package from the drop-down menu. This gives you a new package that, at this point, does nothing. On the package menu, select Task → ActiveX Script Task. This brings up a code window. Type the code from Example 7-5 in the code window.

Example 7-5. SQL Server ActiveX script example to automate Excel

```
'***********************************************************************
'  Visual Basic ActiveX Script
'***********************************************************************

Function Main( )

dim xlapp
dim xlwb
dim xlws
dim xlrng
dim adoconn
dim adors
dim x
dim y

set adoconn = createobject("ADODB.Connection")
adoconn.connectionstring = "driver={SQL Server};" & _
    "server=MJS_HOME;uid=Michael Schmalz;trusted_connection=True;database=Northwind"
adoconn.open

set adors = createobject("ADODB.Recordset")
adors.open "Select [Products by Category].* from [Products by Category]", adoconn

set xlapp = createobject("Excel.Application")
set xlwb = xlapp.workbooks.add
set xlws = xlwb.activesheet
xlapp.visible = true

set xlrng = xlws.cells(2,1)


y = adors.fields.count -1

for x = 0 to y
    xlws.cells(x+1).value = adors.fields(x).name
next

xlrng.copyfromrecordset adors
xlws.columns.autofit

set xlrng = xlws.range(xlws.cells(2,1),xlapp.activecell.specialcells(11))
xlrng.Sort xlws.Range("A2"), 1

set xlrng = xlws.range(xlws.cells(1,1),xlapp.activecell.specialcells(11))
xlrng.subtotal 1, -4157, 4, -1, 0, -1

set xlrng = xlws.columns("D:D")
xlrng.style = "Comma"
xlrng.numberformat = "0"

xlws.Outline.ShowLevels 2
```

Example 7-5. SQL Server ActiveX script example to automate Excel (continued)

```
xlwb.saveas ("c:\sampleDTSexcelworkbook.xls")
xlwb.close
xlapp.quit


Main = DTSTaskExecResult_Success
End Function
```

There are a couple of things that make this code tricky to write. First, because we are using VBScript instead of VBA or VB, we do not have access to the object properties, which means you will not get help as you write the code. Second, you cannot use the constants that are available when you use VBA or VB. For example, in the part of the line that says xlapp.activecell.specialcells(11), the 11 refers to a constant called Excel.xlCellTypeLastCell. If you do not know that xlCellTypeLastCell equals 11, go into the Immediate Window in Excel, type in ? Excel.xlCellTypeLastCell, and press Enter. Excel tells you what the constant is. You can do this for constants related to any object by typing in the object name, the period, and the name of the constant.

This example is a little different from anything you have read in this book so far. First, notice that the variables are declared with no type. Each of them has the type Variant. Since we do not have access to the objects' properties, you have to use the CreateObject method to create the ADO Connection and Excel Application (this is called *late binding*). The query is called "Products by Category," and for unknown reasons, the Northwind database has spaces in the names of the views. I don't recommend this when you develop databases because you then have to put the name of the view or table in brackets. So, you will notice the brackets when you see the line opening the recordset in the code.

Now that the recordset is open, you see the lines of code that create the Excel application, make it visible, and create the other necessary Excel objects. Also, notice that instead of going through the field names using For...Each and going through the ADO fields, I use For x = 0 to y, where y is set to the number of fields in the query minus 1. You could use this method in other places, but I generally prefer to cycle through the fields. The one tricky thing about this method is that Field(0) goes in the first column. This is why you see xlws.cells(x+1).value = adors.fields(x).name, where in the code in Example 7-4, we started with x = 1 and ended with x = x + 1 after each field. This section of code puts all of the field names in the top row.

The next section uses the CopyFromRecordset method to put the data into the Excel worksheet and uses AutoFit to resize the columns. The code sorts by the Product Category, which is the first column, and does a subtotal on the fourth column, the Quantity. In the subtotal method, the first argument is the Group By field. In this case, we want to group by the first column, so we enter **1**. The next argument asks which function to use. Since I want a sum, I find out the constant for xlSum by going into the Immediate Window in Excel and typing in ? Excel.xlSum—the result is -4157.

The next argument is the column(s) that you want totaled. In this case, we are totaling only one column (the fourth), so we type in **4**. The next argument asks whether to replace the current subtotals. Use the value -1, which is TRUE in VBA. The next argument asks whether you want page breaks. In this case, a 0 is FALSE, meaning that you do not want page breaks. The final argument asks whether you want the summary to be above or below the numbers. The choices are xlSummaryAbove or xlSummaryBelow. I chose xlSummaryBelow, which is 1; xlSummaryAbove is 0.

After this, the code sets the number format to have commas with no decimal places. Then, since this report shows subtotals, I use the ShowLevels method of the Outline property of the Worksheet—the Outline property refers to the Outline object on the worksheet. After the first level, the default view, the second level is the level category name, which you can see by going into the Excel worksheet created by this DTS package. Click on 1, 2, or 3 on the upper-left section of the worksheet (below the menus and toolbars) to change the level. Figure 7-3 shows what the resulting workbook looks like.

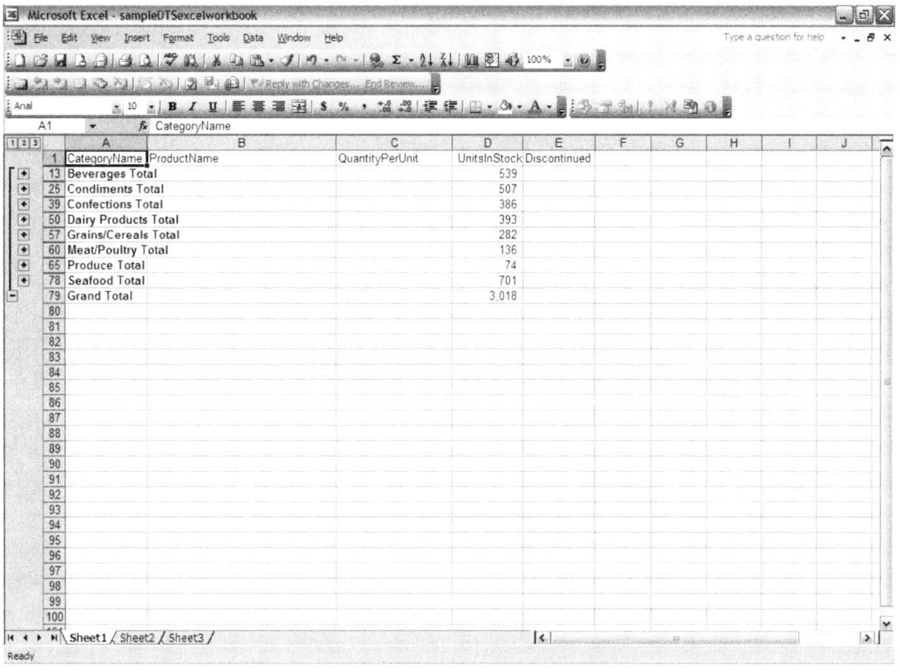

Figure 7-3. The Excel workbook created by the DTS package

For easier Excel reporting (subtotals, sorting, pivot tables, etc.), if you report from SQL Server, look into having the reports done on a schedule with DTS. Once you have all of this information typed in and have saved the package, you will see a green arrow pointing to the right in the toolbar that says Execute when you hover over it. Press that button to create your Excel workbook.

To run this code on a schedule, right-click on the package in Enterprise Manager and select Schedule Package. You can set it up to run on the schedule that you want at the time that you want. If you have a nightly process that is done at 2 a.m. and people come into work at 7 a.m., you can set your packages to run at 5 a.m. and save them into a public folder so that they are available first thing, or you can add an Email task and have the file emailed to the appropriate people. If you are interested in going into depth into these types of automation, it's well worth getting a book specifically on SQL Server.

Crosstab Queries on SQL Server

If you have been using Access, you may be quite familiar with using Crosstab queries. However, you may be surprised to find out that SQL Server does not support this type of query. I'm not sure why not, but I had a client who wanted to do a crosstab out of SQL Server, and I had to find a way to do it. I looked at bringing the table into Access and then just running the crosstab from Access. That would have been a viable method, but we were calling the query from a VB application that was not using an Access database at all. What resulted was a generic Stored Procedure that returned a crosstab query. However, there were some stumbling blocks along the way that deserve careful attention.

I looked in Books Online for SQL Server (the help file that comes with SQL Server) and found that you could use the Case...When statement to simulate a crosstab query. There is an example of how to do it by pivoting quarterly sales data in Books Online. However, this is very limited, and in that case, you know the exact number of columns that you need. The bigger question was: how can I create a list of the columns that I need dynamically from arguments passed to a stored procedure? The solution was to create a temporary table by using the sp_executesql system-stored procedure. Doing this enabled me to not use dynamic text to open the list of columns. I was able to declare the cursor with a line of text that did not change even if the underlying temporary table was very different.

A cursor can be compared to a recordset in ADO. The biggest difference is how you cycle through the records. In ADO, you use the MoveNext method to go through each record. When you write Stored Procedures, use the FETCH method, and instead of testing for EOF, test to make sure that the @@FETCH_STATUS equals 0. When the @@FETCH_STATUS does not equal 0, you have reached the end of the records, and you should exit your loop.

In the stored procedure listed below, I use While @@FETCH_STATUS = 0; you will find many examples on the Internet where people use @@FETCH_STATUS <> -1. Either method works, but I prefer to test for 0 because there is also a status of -2 that means that the record is missing. While this would be next to impossible in the example used here, it can come up in other cases. So, if I only want to work on successful fetches, I think testing for 0 is the way to go. To summarize, 0 means that the fetch was successful, -1 means that the fetch failed or it has reached the end of the records, and -2 means that the row fetched is missing.

Now, to actually build the stored procedure, go into the Northwind Database in SQL Server Enterprise Manager, right-click on Stored Procedures, and select New Stored Procedure. Enter the code in Example 7-6, and save the procedure.

Example 7-6. SQL Server simple crosstab stored procedure

```
CREATE PROCEDURE [dbo].[SimpleXTab] @XField varChar(20), @XTable varChar(20),
@XWhereString varChar(250), @XFunction varChar(10), @XFunctionField varChar(20), @XRow
varchar(40)
 AS
Declare @SqlStr nvarchar(4000)
Declare @tempsql nvarchar(4000)
Declare @SqlStrCur nvarchar(4000)
Declare @col nvarchar(100)

set @SqlStrCur = N'Select [' + @XField + '] into ##temptbl_Cursor from
            [' + @XTable + ']  ' + @XWhereString + ' Group By [' + @XField + ']'

/* select @sqlstrcur */
exec sp_executesql @sqlstrcur

 declare xcursor Cursor  for  Select * from ##temptbl_Cursor

 open xcursor

 Fetch next from  xcursor
 into @Col

While @@Fetch_Status = 0
Begin
  set @Sqlstr = @Sqlstr + ", "
  set @tempsql = isnull(@sqlstr,'') + isnull(@XFunction + '( Case When ' +
     @XField + " = '" +@Col + "' then [" + @XFunctionField +
     "] Else 0 End) As [" + @XFunction + @Col + "]" ,'')
  set @Sqlstr = @tempsql
  Fetch next from xcursor into @Col

End

 /* Select @Sqlstr as [mk], len(@sqlstr) as [leng] */
```

Example 7-6. SQL Server simple crosstab stored procedure (continued)

```
set @tempsql = 'Select '  + @XRow + ', ' + @Sqlstr + ' From ' + @XTable +
                          @XWhereString +  ' Group by ' + @XRow
set @Sqlstr = @tempsql

Close xcursor
Deallocate xcursor

  set @tempsql = N'Drop Table ##temptbl_Cursor'
  exec sp_executesql @tempsql

 /*  Select @Sqlstr as [mk], len(@sqlstr) as [leng] */

   exec sp_executesql @Sqlstr
GO
```

I have created a view used to test the crosstab query stored procedure, but you can
use this view in any SQL Server Database and on any table. It was written to take
generic arguments and be reusable. The view can be created by right-clicking on the
Views list item in Enterprise Manager on the Northwind database and selecting New
View. You can also use a Create View statement and run it in Query Analyzer. If you
use Query Analyzer, put the following code in for the view and run it. If you use the
New View method from Enterprise Manager, skip the Create View statement by typing in everything starting at Select.

```
CREATE VIEW dbo.vw_SampleQuery
AS
SELECT      dbo.Orders.ShipName, dbo.Categories.CategoryName,
            dbo.Orders.ShipCountry,
            (dbo.[Order Details].UnitPrice * dbo.[Order Details].Quantity)
            * (1 - dbo.[Order Details].Discount) AS OrderAmt
FROM        dbo.Orders INNER JOIN
            dbo.[Order Details] ON dbo.Orders.OrderID =
            dbo.[Order Details].OrderID INNER JOIN
            dbo.Products ON dbo.[Order Details].ProductID =
            dbo.Products.ProductID INNER JOIN
            dbo.Categories ON dbo.Products.CategoryID = dbo.Categories.CategoryID
```

This creates a view called vw_SampleQuery that returns the columns I wanted for my
crosstab query. To test the procedure, you can either create a pass-through query in
Access or use Query Analyzer in SQL Server. To use the pass-through query in
Access, create a pass-through query, using Northwind on SQL Server as the ODBC
connection, and use the following code to run the procedure:

```
Execute SimpleXTab 'CategoryName', 'vw_SampleQuery', '', 'Sum', 'OrderAmt',
'ShipCountry'
```

These arguments tell SQL Server that we want to have CategoryName from vw_
SampleQuery as the columns. The empty string is the Where clause. In this case, I
want all records. Type in **Where** and then the expression to restrict the number of
records. It could be anything from a date range to a range of sale amounts, etc. The

next argument asks what function you want to summarize by. Here we use `Sum`. Be careful if you use other functions because the stored procedure fills in 0 for the value when the match does not occur, so if you use min or max, these zeros could skew the results. If you want to use them, adjust the code. In any case, when you run the results from Access, you get the result that you see in Figure 7-4.

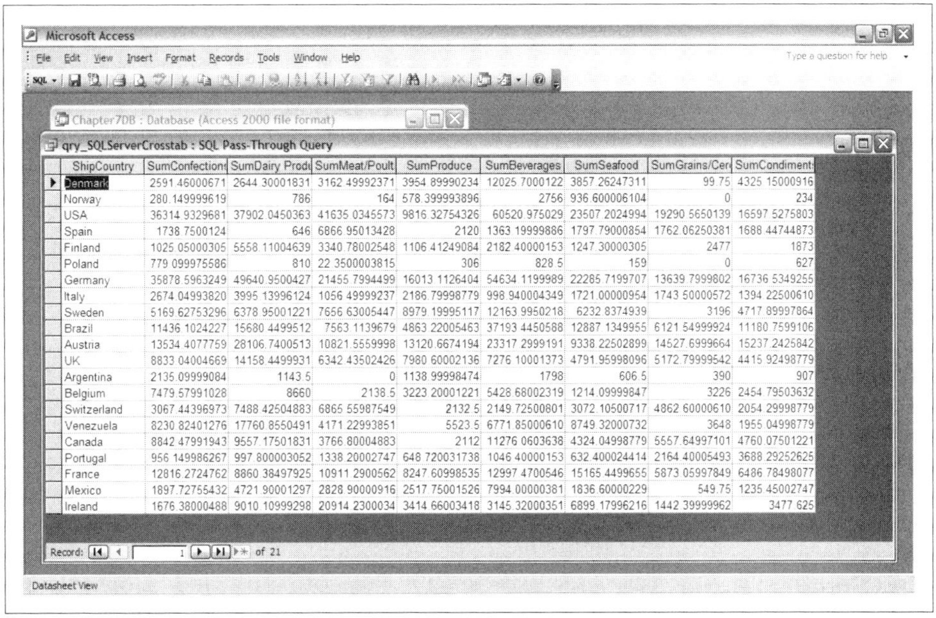

ShipCountry	SumConfection	SumDairy Produ	SumMeat/Poult	SumProduce	SumBeverages	SumSeafood	SumGrains/Cer	SumCondiment
Denmark	2591.46000671	2644.30001831	3162.49992371	3954.89990234	12025.7000122	3857.26247311	99.75	4325.15000916
Norway	280.149999619	786	164	578.399993896	2756	936.600006104	0	234
USA	36314.9329681	37902.0450363	41635.0345573	9816.32754326	60520.975029	23507.2024994	19290.5650139	16597.5275803
Spain	1738.7500124	646	6866.95013428	2120	1363.19999886	1797.79000854	1762.06250381	1688.44744873
Finland	1025.05000305	5558.11004639	3340.78002548	1106.41249084	2182.40000153	1247.30000305	2477	1873
Poland	779.099975586	810	22.3500003815	306	828.5	159	0	627
Germany	35878.5963249	49640.9500427	21455.7994499	16013.1126404	54634.1199989	22285.7199707	13639.7999802	16736.5349255
Italy	2674.04993820	3995.13996124	1056.49999237	2186.79998779	998.940004349	1721.00000954	1743.50000572	1394.22500610
Sweden	5169.62753296	6378.95001221	7656.63005447	8979.19995117	12163.9950218	6232.8374939	3196	4717.89997864
Brazil	11436.1024227	15680.4499512	7563.1139679	4863.22005463	37193.4450588	12887.1349955	6121.54999924	11180.7599106
Austria	13534.4077759	28106.7400513	10821.5559998	13120.6674194	23317.2999191	9338.22502899	14527.6999664	15237.2425842
UK	8833.04004669	14158.4499931	6342.43502426	7980.60002136	7276.10001373	4791.95998096	5172.79999542	4415.92498779
Argentina	2135.09999084	1143.5	0	1138.99998474	1798	606.5	390	907
Belgium	7479.57991028	8660	2138.5	3223.20001221	5428.68002319	1214.09999847	3226	2454.79503632
Switzerland	3067.44396973	7488.42504883	6865.55987549	2132.5	2149.72500801	3072.10500717	4862.60000610	2054.29998779
Venezuela	8230.82401276	17760.8550491	4171.22993851	5523.5	6771.85000610	8749.32000732	3648	1955.04998779
Canada	8842.47991943	9557.17501831	3766.80004883	2112	11276.0603638	4324.04998779	5557.64997101	4760.07501221
Portugal	956.149986267	997.800003052	1338.20002747	648.720031738	1046.40000153	632.400024414	2164.40005493	3688.29252625
France	12816.2724762	8860.38497925	10911.2900562	8247.60998535	12997.4700546	15165.4499655	5873.05997849	6486.78498077
Mexico	1897.72755432	4721.90001297	2828.90000916	2517.75001526	7994.00000381	1836.60000229	549.75	1235.45002747
Ireland	1676.38000488	9010.10999298	20914.2300034	3414.66003418	3145.32000351	6899.17996216	1442.39999962	3477.625

Figure 7-4. The result of the crosstab query example that summarizes OrderAmt by ShipCountry, run from Access as a pass-through query

I purposely did not go into great detail as to how this stored procedure works. If you read through it, you see that it is very similar to the created crosstab that we did in Chapter 5, except that this procedure uses just one column. I have also created a stored procedure that uses multiple columns in SQL Server, but it is beyond the scope of this book.

A few items that I want to cover are how the temporary table is declared and the limitation on the size of the query string. The temporary table is created with two number/pound signs (##) in front of the temporary table name; this creates a global temporary table. This table is subsequently dropped. The creation and the dropping of the table are enabled by a system-stored procedure that executes an SQL String. You will notice the N' in front of the SQL String, signifying that it is a Unicode string. This is important because a Unicode string is limited to 4,000 characters. A regular string is limited to 8,000 characters. The reason why a Unicode string can only have half the number of characters is that it uses 2 bytes per character, while a regular string uses 1 byte per string. This limitation will come up if you have a lot of columns and/or a long view name.

I have two lines of code in the stored procedure that are remarked out. To make a remark in a stored procedure, enter /* remark */. If you get an error when running the stored procedure, you can edit the procedure to put the remarks on the line that executes the SQL and takes the remarks off of the line that is getting the length of the string. If the string is too long, you either need to restrict your data with a where clause, use a shorter view name, or do something else to reduce the number of columns. I have created a stored procedure that gets around this limitation, but never used it in production because the necessary checking makes it run slowly.

There are also some third-party controls that you can purchase to produce crosstab queries on SQL Server, but the method I outline should be sufficient for most basic crosstab queries. It is also nice because you only need one stored procedure, and you can call it multiple times with different tables and other criteria. If you want more row headers than ShipCountry, you can put them in the same string and separate the field names by commas. (Do not place a comma at the end.)

SQL Server Summary

This chapter went into some intermediate-level topics on SQL Server that you may not already be familiar with. I could write several chapters on the topics covered, but I just wanted to introduce them in this chapter. If you type in the examples as shown, you can see how they work. I find that by following examples and tweaking code, I learn a lot about how things work. I encourage you to follow these examples, and I strongly suggest that you test everything in Pubs or Northwind before trying it on a production database if you are not completely familiar with SQL Server.

If you are already familiar with SQL Server, I hope that the topics on DTS introduced you to some additional functionality. When I work with clients using SQL Server, I find that very few take advantage of the ActiveX script tasks, Email tasks, and scheduling functionality, except in the case of administrative tasks. There are so many ways to use the scheduling tool that I even use it when it doesn't involve SQL Server. You can create connections to Access databases with DTS and drop and create tables on a daily basis for different types of reporting, even if none of the data is on SQL Server. In addition, you can find a lot of good examples in the *SQL Server Books Online* if you get stumped trying to figure something out.

It is going to be increasingly difficult to ignore SQL Server and other enterprise databases as these databases are used at more companies. Even though it is unlikely that you want or need to become an expert in SQL Server, just understanding the basics will be very helpful. I encourage you to look at the online resources offered by Microsoft, O'Reilly, and other user groups to gain additional knowledge. For the most part, when you use SQL Server, you will work with a database that is already created, and you may not be in an administrative role. This differs from typical Excel and Access practice, but your Access and Excel skills will be relevant to processing information you've extracted from SQL Server.

CHAPTER 8

Advanced Excel Reporting Techniques

You should now be familiar enough with moving data between Access and Excel that you think of ways to automate reporting and analysis traditionally done in Excel. When considering report automation, I break it into three categories:

- Changing data in an existing report
- Creating a report from scratch including all data, formulas, and formatting
- Using a report template built in a database table

In order to take advantage of these options, you need to become very familiar with the Excel Worksheet and Range objects. You also need to work effectively with multiple worksheets in the same workbook and work step by step through the reporting process. Even for the most complicated reports, you will most likely be able to walk through the steps manually and put in logic checks for each thought process. Then it's a matter of getting the data, writing the formulas, and formatting the worksheet.

Writing Flexible Formulas

In addition to dealing with the Excel objects, understanding how to use R1C1 format to write formulas makes coding much easier. For example, subtracting the cell one row above from the cell two rows above is very straightforward when using R1C1 notation. If you use A1 notation, you have to go through multiple steps to write the string. First, figure out what column and row you are in, and then turn the column number into a letter. Next, create strings by concatenating the column letter with the row numbers needed for your formula. Doing this for several columns would get tiresome, not to mention difficult to follow. You could also perform the calculation in VBA by using the row and column numbers with the Cells object, resulting in a fixed value instead of a formula. This is likely not what you want for most reporting because it can lead to inconsistent information if the original numbers are changed. Using the R1C1 format, you refer to the other cells by the number of rows or columns in relation to the current cell. In the previous example, the formula in R1C1 notation would be = R[-2]C - R[-1]C, which calculates the cell.

Excel uses R1C1 notation to refer to a cell by the row and column numbers. For example, cell B10 is in column 2 and row 10; refer to this as R10C2 by using R1C1 notation. R1C1 notation also allows you to refer to a cell in relation to the current cell when writing a formula. Instead of placing a number for the row or column, you can place a number in brackets after R or C to move the specified number of columns or rows to refer to the cell you want.

When you use a number for the row or column, Excel shows it as a fixed reference by using a $ in the formula. You can also refer to the row and column with a fixed reference for one and a relative reference for the other. R2C[-1] would refer to the second row of the column to the left of the current cell.

When you write formulas, there are several properties that you can set to write the formula or value (see Table 8-1). This chapter covers Formula, FormulaR1C1, and FormulaArray, which provide most of the functionality that you need.

Table 8-1. Excel formula properties of the range object

Property	Description
Formula	Returns or sets a formula using A1-style notation
FormulaArray	Returns or sets an array formula using R1C1-style notation
FormulaLocal	Returns or sets a formula using A1-style notation in the language of the user
FormulaR1C1	Returns or sets a formula using R1C1-style notation
FormulaR1C1Local	Returns or sets a formula using R1C1-style notation in the language of the user
Value	Returns or sets a fixed value

Let's look at returning R1C1 formula values so that you can get a feel for how to write them. Specifically, you need to understand how to set fixed and relative references. Look at the formulas in Figure 8-1, shown in A1-style notation below each result. Create a workbook similar to this one and press Alt+F11 to go to the Visual Basic Editor. Then, press Ctrl-G to go to Immediate Window.

The first formula to look at is cell B5, also shown as text in cell B6 in Figure 8-1. In this formula, use relative references so that if you copy them from left to right, they update to the correct formula. If you copy them down, this formula will not yield the correct result. Type the following line in the immediate window, and it shows you how to write this formula in R1C1-style notation:

```
? sheets("Sheet1").Range("B5").FormulaR1C1
```

The result comes back =R[-3]C-R[-2]C for the A1-style formula of =B2-B3. This R1C1-style formula works in any of the cells in row 5. Breaking down this formula, it tells Excel to subtract the cell two rows up in the current column from the cell three rows

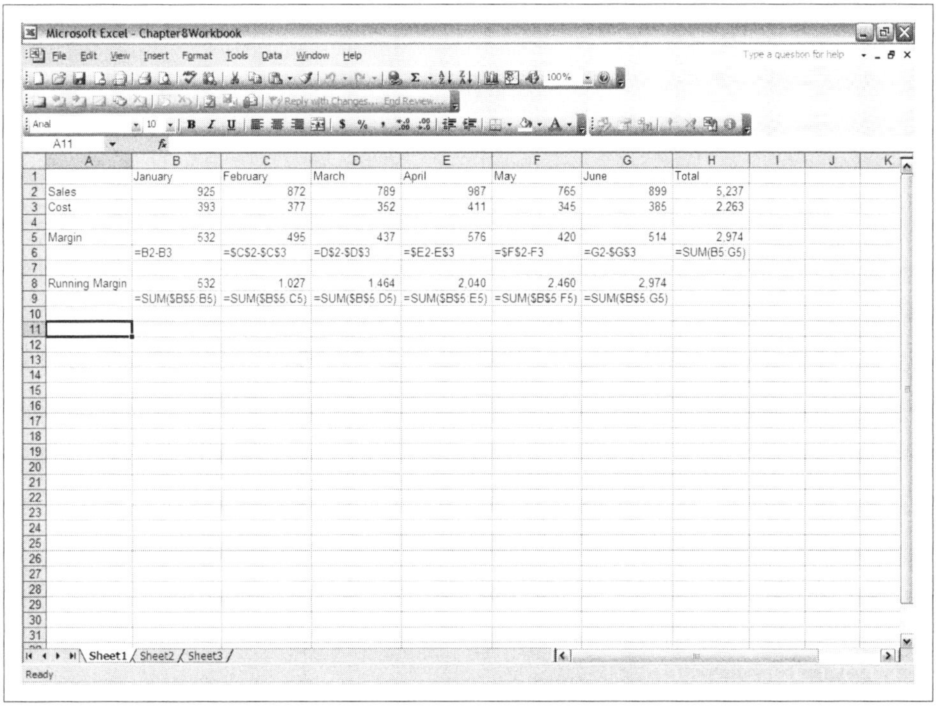

Figure 8-1. The worksheet showing similar formulas written a variety of different ways

	A	B	C	D	E	F	G	H
1		January	February	March	April	May	June	Total
2	Sales	925	872	789	987	765	899	5,237
3	Cost	393	377	352	411	345	385	2,263
4								
5	Margin	532	495	437	576	420	514	2,974
6		=B2-B3	=$C$2-$C$3	=D$2-$D$3	=$E2-E$3	=$F$2-F3	=G2-$G$3	=SUM(B5 G5)
7								
8	Running Margin	532	1,027	1,464	2,040	2,460	2,974	
9		=SUM($B$5 B5)	=SUM($B$5 C5)	=SUM($B$5 D5)	=SUM($B$5 E5)	=SUM($B$5 F5)	=SUM($B$5 G5)	

up in the current column. Next, look at the formula in cell C5. Type the following line in the immediate window:

```
? sheets("Sheet1").Range("C5").FormulaR1C1
```

This formula result comes back =R2C3-R3C3 for the A1-style formula of =$C$2-$C$3. For this formula, the exact same A1-style formula result comes back regardless of the cell being because the formula tells Excel to subtract row 3 column 3 (C3) from row 2 column 3 (C2). When using R1C1 notation, whenever you use a row or column number and do not put it in brackets, it results in the row or column being preceded by a $ in the formula. When a $ is used in A1-style notation, Excel creates a fixed reference. If you copy a formula with fixed references, the portion with the $ will not change, regardless of where you copy it. This is important to keep in mind as you decide how to write the formula. Type the following line in the immediate window:

```
? sheets("Sheet1").Range("D5").FormulaR1C1
```

The formula result comes back =R2C-R3C4 for the A1-style formula of =D$2-$D$3. Notice that in this formula, dollar signs precede everything except the D in the first cell reference in the formula. Looking at the R1C1-style notation, you see that the column reference uses the current column C. If you put a number after the column reference, it returns the column with a dollar sign. Look at the others as well, but for the next formula, look at B8. Type the following line in the immediate window:

```
? sheets("Sheet1").Range("B8").FormulaR1C1
```

The formula results come back `=SUM(R5C2:R[-3]C)` for the A1-style formula of `=SUM($B$5:B5)`. This formula is important because same R1C1-style formula comes back for the entire row. This is the easiest way to write a running sum—using a fixed reference for the beginning of the sum range and a relative reference for the end of the range. If you copy the formula across, it returns the correct formula for the running sum for each column.

Certainly look at the other formulas; looking at the resulting R1C1 formulas should help you write them yourself. I strongly encourage you to use this technique to write more complex formulas, since it is much easier to create the formula in the Excel GUI than to write it yourself.

Changing Data in an Existing Report

When changing data in an existing Excel report from Access, you have a few different scenarios to consider. In the first scenario, you fill in a few pieces of data in different places on the worksheet. In the second scenario, you replace data that resembles a recordset. In the final scenario, you do a combination of the two. A combination could be a situating in which you change certain variables based on the number of records in a recordset, or possibly a situation in which you bring in a recordset and take other values from the database. A good example of the combination scenario is a profitability model, where sales are loaded from a recordset and specific pricing is entered as separate data points.

Regardless of the scenario, the first few steps are the same when using VBA from Access. Just to open the existing Excel worksheet, you need an Excel `Application` object and a `Workbook` object, and I suggest using a string variable to hold the file name. You also need a reference to Excel using Tools → References from Design View in the Access module. The code in Example 8-1 opens an existing workbook. Example 8-2 is designed as a procedure called from another procedure. I pass the variables `ByRef`, so this assumes that I have Excel `Application` and `Workbook` objects declared in the calling procedure. I would just use the code without calling a different procedure in a production environment, but this is just to demonstrate the concept of opening a workbook. See the calling procedure in Example 8-2 and note that the filename and path used in the `GetXLWB` call will be different on your computer.

Example 8-1. Generic procedure to open an existing workbook

```
Public Sub GetXLWB(fname As String, ByRef xlapp As Excel.Application, _
                   ByRef xlwb As Excel.Workbook)
Set xlapp = New Excel.Application
```

Example 8-1. Generic procedure to open an existing workbook (continued)

```
Set xlwb = xlapp.Workbooks.Open(fname)
End Sub
```

Example 8-2. Procedure that calls the procedure in 8-1 and returns a result

```
Public Sub xlCallingProc( )
Dim xlapp As Excel.Application
Dim xlwb As Excel.Workbook
Dim xlws As Excel.Worksheet

Call GetXLWB("C:\Devwork\Chapter8workbook.xls", xlapp, xlwb)

Set xlws = xlwb.Sheets("Sheet1")

MsgBox "The value in cell H5 is " & xlws.Range("H5").Value, vbInformation

xlwb.Close
xlapp.Quit

Set xlws = Nothing
Set xlwb = Nothing
Set xlapp = Nothing
End Sub
```

If you look back at Figure 8-1, it shows a worksheet that calculates a total margin housed in cell H5. The procedure in Example 8-2 opens this workbook and returns the value in cell H5 in a message box.

At this point, you know how to open a workbook and read a value from a worksheet. Let's look at a case, using the code in Example 8-3, where you want to open up each workbook in a directory of several workbooks and pull a recordset from the database based on the information in a cell. Then print the report if the PrintOpt variable's value is TRUE.

Example 8-3. Processing multiple workbooks

```
Public Sub MultiProc(pname As String, printopt As Boolean)
  ' passes a parameter to a recordset to build a report
Dim xlapp As Excel.Application
Dim xlwb As Excel.Workbook
Dim xlws As Excel.Worksheet
Dim xlrng As Excel.Range
Dim fname As String
Dim param As String
Dim x, y, z, a, b, c As Integer
Dim db As DAO.Database
Dim qry As DAO.QueryDef
Dim rs As DAO.Recordset

Set db = CurrentDb
```

Example 8-3. Processing multiple workbooks (continued)

```
Set xlapp = New Excel.Application
xlapp.Visible = True

fname = Dir(pname & "*.xls")

While fname <> ""
  Set xlwb = xlapp.Workbooks.Open(pname & fname)
  Set xlws = xlwb.Sheets("ReportParameters")
  Set qry = db.QueryDefs("qry_ExcelReport")
  param = xlws.Range("B2").Value
  qry.Parameters(0).Value = param
  Set rs = qry.OpenRecordset
  Set xlrng = xlwb.Sheets("ReportData").Range("A2")
  xlrng.CopyFromRecordset rs
  x = rs.RecordCount
  rs.Close
  Set xlws = xlwb.Sheets("Report")
  xlws.Cells(3, 1).Value = "Category"
  xlws.Cells(3, 2).Value = "Units"
  xlws.Cells(3, 3).Value = "Sales"
  Set xlrng = xlws.Range(xlws.Cells(3, 1), xlws.Cells(3, 3))
  xlrng.Font.Bold = True
  Set qry = db.QueryDefs("qry_ExcelProducts")
  qry.Parameters(0).Value = param
  Set rs = qry.OpenRecordset
  Set xlrng = xlws.Range("A4")
  xlrng.CopyFromRecordset rs
  y = rs.RecordCount
  For b = 4 To y + 3
    Set xlrng = xlws.Cells(b, 2)
    xlrng.FormulaArray = "=Sum((ReportData!R2C2:R" & x + 1 & _
                    "C2=Report!R" & b & "C1)*ReportData!R2C4:R" & _
                    x + 1 & "C4)"
    Set xlrng = xlws.Cells(b, 3)
    xlrng.FormulaArray = "=Sum((ReportData!R2C2:R" & x + 1 & _
                    "C2=Report!R" & b & "C1)*ReportData!R2C5:R" & _
                    x + 1 & "C5)"
  Next b
  Set xlrng = xlws.Range(xlws.Cells(4, 2), xlws.Cells(y + 3, 2))
  xlrng.NumberFormat = "#,##0"
  Set xlrng = xlws.Range(xlws.Cells(4, 3), xlws.Cells(y + 3, 3))
  xlrng.NumberFormat = "$0.00"
  rs.Close
  z = y + 5
  xlws.Cells(z, 1).Value = "Center"
  xlws.Cells(z, 2).Value = "Units"
  xlws.Cells(z, 3).Value = "Sales"
  Set xlrng = xlws.Range(xlws.Cells(z, 1), xlws.Cells(z, 3))
  xlrng.Font.Bold = True
  z = z + 1
  Set qry = db.QueryDefs("qry_ExcelCenters")
  qry.Parameters(0).Value = param
```

Example 8-3. Processing multiple workbooks (continued)

```
    Set rs = qry.OpenRecordset
    Set xlrng = xlws.Cells(z, 1)
    xlrng.CopyFromRecordset rs
    a = z + rs.RecordCount
    For b = z To a - 1
      Set xlrng = xlws.Cells(b, 2)
      xlrng.FormulaArray = "=Sum((ReportData!R2C1:R" & x + 1 & _
                    "C1=Report!R" & b & "C1)*ReportData!R2C4:R" & _
                    x + 1 & "C4)"
      Set xlrng = xlws.Cells(b, 3)
      xlrng.FormulaArray = "=Sum((ReportData!R2C1:R" & x + 1 & _
                    "C1=Report!R" & b & "C1)*ReportData!R2C5:R" & _
                    x + 1 & "C5)"
    Next b

    Set xlrng = xlws.Range(xlws.Cells(z, 2), xlws.Cells(a - 1, 2))
    xlrng.NumberFormat = "#,##0"
    Set xlrng = xlws.Range(xlws.Cells(z, 3), xlws.Cells(a - 1, 3))
    xlrng.NumberFormat = "$0.00"

    xlws.Columns.AutoFit
    If printopt Then xlws.PrintOut
    xlwb.SaveAs "C:\Reports\" & fname
    xlwb.Close
    Set xlwb = Nothing

    fname = Dir
Wend

Set xlrng = Nothing
Set xlws = Nothing
xlapp.Quit
Set xlapp = Nothing
rs.Close
qry.Close
Set rs = Nothing
Set qry = Nothing
Set db = Nothing

End Sub
```

I should point out a few things here. First, I use an array function instead of the SumIf function. This technique was shown in Chapter 6. This example checks for only one criterion, so I could have easily used SumIf. However, by using Sum in an array function, you can check for multiple criteria by multiplying each Boolean result together and then multiplying by the range of values. For each row, if the Boolean result is FALSE, the row nets to zero because anything multiplied by zero is zero. If the value is TRUE, it multiplies the result by 1, which doesn't change the result. If this seems difficult to follow, refer to Figure 6-7 and Example 6-6 to see how it works in more detail. It is important to note that in VBA, the value of vbTrue is -1, so you can't use this logic in VBA as you can in the Excel GUI. Also note that I use several Integer variables to keep track of where I am on the worksheet after pasting each recordset.

Here is how the procedure works. By passing a path name, the DIR function brings up a filename that matches the criterion. Move to the next result by calling the DIR function again without any parameters. So, this procedure loops through each Excel workbook in a directory and looks in a cell to determine which report needs to be run. It then passes this value as a parameter to several queries, the results of which are placed in one worksheet that houses data and another worksheet that is the actual report. Next, it builds the array formulas and formats the cells. Finally, if you said TRUE to the print option, it prints the worksheet and saves the report in a directory called *C:\Reports*. If you do not have this directory, you have to update it to one on your system. I show how to build a GUI to run a procedure like this in Access (Chapter 11) or Excel (Chapter 10), but for now, to check out how this works, type in the following line in the Immediate Window in the Visual Basic Editor in Access:

```
Call multiproc("C:\DevWork\Chapter8\",TRUE)
```

Again, this assumes that you have Excel documents in a directory called *C:\DevWork\Chapter8*. If there are no Excel files in that directory, it fails to do anything. It also assumes that the Excel workbooks have a sheet called "ReportParameters."

Note that I have reused the xlws variable several times; I have also referred to other sheets directly without setting the worksheet variable equal to the other worksheet. I could have just as easily created three separate worksheet variables, but it was unnecessary for this explanation. The result of this procedure is shown in Figure 8-2.

Because of the way this workbook is set up, you could pull the line of business names from the database and open one Excel Workbook as a template. Then just update the line of business names on the ReportParameters worksheet and run the rest of the code. I actually suggest using one Excel file as a template, but I wanted to introduce the DIR function. I use the DIR function to process Excel documents and load hundreds of lines of data in Access databases for budgeting and other business purposes. If you have a consistent set of workbooks to process, being able to cycle through all of the Excel files in a folder is very helpful.

You may also notice that while Example 8-2 uses a report template, the formulas are still created by Access. You can just as easily have a template where you only update data and do not create formulas. In this case, it is necessary to rewrite the formulas because the number of categories can change between each workbook.

Creating a Report from Scratch

When creating a report from scratch, you need to take care of some items beyond formulas and number formatting. You may need to add a worksheet header and footer, work with fonts, and use the page setup options to affect how the worksheet

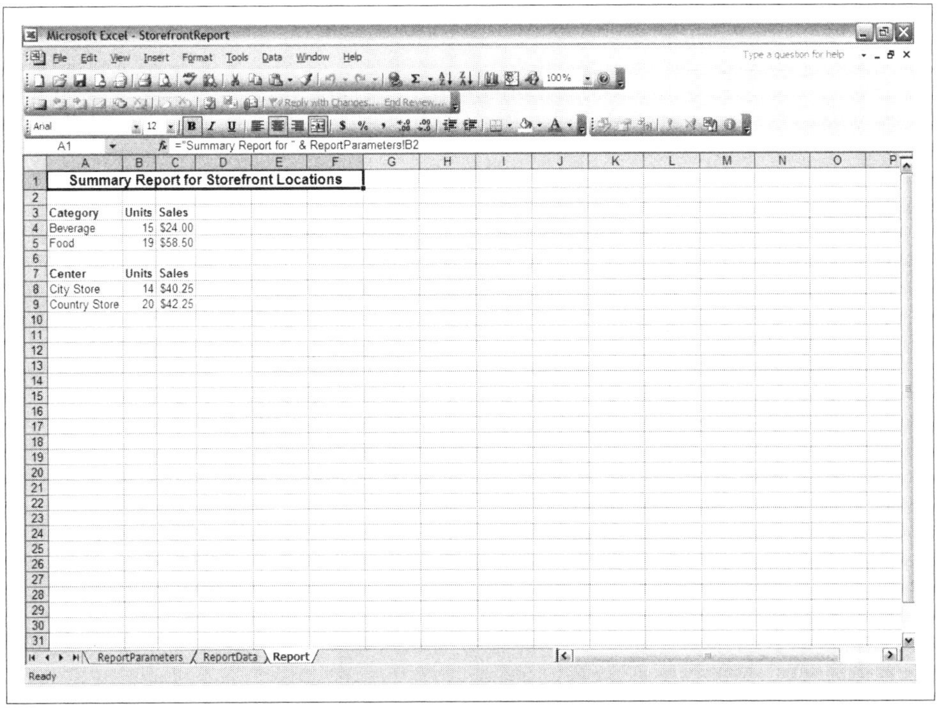

Figure 8-2. Worksheet resulting from the code in Example 8-3, with a formula in the formula bar that allows the same report template to be used regardless of the line of business

prints. Because we have already worked with a procedure that built the formulas and number formatting from scratch, I modify that procedure to create Example 8-4. For this example, I create a new workbook and add two worksheets. The first worksheet houses the data, and the second worksheet houses the report. I place a title in the worksheet header and format the worksheet to print landscape on one page. The procedure cycles through a recordset to run each report and saves the workbook in a folder on the C drive.

Example 8-4. Report from scratch module

```
Public Sub MultiProcRS( )
Dim xlapp As Excel.Application
Dim xlwb As Excel.Workbook
Dim xlws As Excel.Worksheet
Dim xlrng As Excel.Range
Dim param As String
Dim x, y, z, a, b, c As Integer
Dim db As DAO.Database
Dim qry As DAO.QueryDef
Dim rs As DAO.Recordset
Dim fld As DAO.Field
Dim fldcol As Integer
```

Example 8-4. Report from scratch module (continued)

```
Dim cyclers As DAO.Recordset

Set db = CurrentDb

Set cyclers = db.OpenRecordset("SELECT tbl_CostCenters.LineOfBusiness2, " & _
  "tbl_CostCenters.LineOfBusiness3 " & _
  "FROM tbl_CostCenters " & _
  "GROUP BY tbl_CostCenters.LineOfBusiness2, tbl_CostCenters.LineOfBusiness3 " & _
  "HAVING (((tbl_CostCenters.LineOfBusiness3)=""Profit Centers""));")

Set xlapp = New Excel.Application
xlapp.Visible = True

cyclers.MoveFirst
While Not cyclers.EOF
  Set xlwb = xlapp.Workbooks.Add
  Set xlws = xlwb.Sheets.Add
  xlws.Name = "ReportData"
  Set qry = db.QueryDefs("qry_ExcelReport")
  param = cyclers.Fields(0).Value
  qry.Parameters(0).Value = param
  Set rs = qry.OpenRecordset
  fldcol = 1

  For Each fld In rs.Fields
    xlws.Cells(1, fldcol).Value = fld.Name
    fldcol = fldcol + 1
  Next fld

  Set xlrng = xlws.Range("A2")
  xlrng.CopyFromRecordset rs
  x = rs.RecordCount
  rs.Close
  Set xlws = xlwb.Sheets.Add
  xlws.Name = "Report"
  xlws.Cells(3, 1).Value = "Category"
  xlws.Cells(3, 2).Value = "Units"
  xlws.Cells(3, 3).Value = "Sales"
  Set xlrng = xlws.Range(xlws.Cells(3, 1), xlws.Cells(3, 3))
  xlrng.Font.Bold = True
  Set qry = db.QueryDefs("qry_ExcelProducts")
  qry.Parameters(0).Value = param
  Set rs = qry.OpenRecordset
  Set xlrng = xlws.Range("A4")
  xlrng.CopyFromRecordset rs
  y = rs.RecordCount
  For b = 4 To y + 3
    Set xlrng = xlws.Cells(b, 2)
    xlrng.FormulaArray = "=Sum((ReportData!R2C2:R" & x + 1 & _
                  "C2=Report!R" & b & "C1)*ReportData!R2C4:R" & _
                  x + 1 & "C4)"
    Set xlrng = xlws.Cells(b, 3)
```

Example 8-4. Report from scratch module (continued)

```
      xlrng.FormulaArray = "=Sum((ReportData!R2C2:R" & x + 1 & _
                      "C2=Report!R" & b & "C1)*ReportData!R2C5:R" & _
                      x + 1 & "C5)"
   Next b
   Set xlrng = xlws.Range(xlws.Cells(4, 2), xlws.Cells(y + 3, 2))
   xlrng.NumberFormat = "#,##0"
   Set xlrng = xlws.Range(xlws.Cells(4, 3), xlws.Cells(y + 3, 3))
   xlrng.NumberFormat = "$0.00"
   rs.Close
   z = y + 5
   xlws.Cells(z, 1).Value = "Center"
   xlws.Cells(z, 2).Value = "Units"
   xlws.Cells(z, 3).Value = "Sales"
   Set xlrng = xlws.Range(xlws.Cells(z, 1), xlws.Cells(z, 3))
   xlrng.Font.Bold = True
   z = z + 1
   Set qry = db.QueryDefs("qry_ExcelCenters")
   qry.Parameters(0).Value = param
   Set rs = qry.OpenRecordset
   Set xlrng = xlws.Cells(z, 1)
   xlrng.CopyFromRecordset rs
   a = z + rs.RecordCount
   For b = z To a - 1
      Set xlrng = xlws.Cells(b, 2)
      xlrng.FormulaArray = "=Sum((ReportData!R2C1:R" & x + 1 & _
                      "C1=Report!R" & b & "C1)*ReportData!R2C4:R" & _
                      x + 1 & "C4)"
      Set xlrng = xlws.Cells(b, 3)
      xlrng.FormulaArray = "=Sum((ReportData!R2C1:R" & x + 1 & _
                      "C1=Report!R" & b & "C1)*ReportData!R2C5:R" & _
                      x + 1 & "C5)"
   Next b

   Set xlrng = xlws.Range(xlws.Cells(z, 2), xlws.Cells(a - 1, 2))
   xlrng.NumberFormat = "#,##0"
   Set xlrng = xlws.Range(xlws.Cells(z, 3), xlws.Cells(a - 1, 3))
   xlrng.NumberFormat = "$0.00"

   xlws.Columns.AutoFit

   With xlws.PageSetup
      .CenterHeader = "&16Summary Report for " & param & vbCr & _
        "&10As of " & Now( )
      .LeftMargin = Excel.Application.InchesToPoints(0.75)
      .RightMargin = Excel.Application.InchesToPoints(0.75)
      .TopMargin = Excel.Application.InchesToPoints(1)
      .BottomMargin = Excel.Application.InchesToPoints(1)
      .HeaderMargin = Excel.Application.InchesToPoints(0.5)
      .FooterMargin = Excel.Application.InchesToPoints(0.5)
      .Orientation = Excel.xlLandscape
      .FitToPagesTall = 1
      .FitToPagesWide = 1
```

Example 8-4. Report from scratch module (continued)

```
    .PrintErrors = Excel.xlPrintErrorsDisplayed
  End With
  xlwb.SaveAs "C:\Reports\" & param & ".xls"
  xlwb.Close
  Set xlwb = Nothing

  cyclers.MoveNext
Wend

Set fld = Nothing
cyclers.Close
Set cyclers = Nothing
Set xlrng = Nothing
Set xlws = Nothing
xlapp.Quit
Set xlapp = Nothing
rs.Close
qry.Close
Set rs = Nothing
Set qry = Nothing
Set db = Nothing

End Sub
```

An SQL string creates the recordset called `cyclers`. As you look at the string, notice the two sets of double quotes around `Profit Centers`. I could have used a query with a parameter and simply passed the parameter to the query, but it is often useful to place the criteria directly in the SQL. If you pass numeric values, it is very easy to do. However, when you get to string values, you must place quotes inside your string. Using single quotes sometimes causes problems if you have an apostrophe in your variable. By placing two double quotes on both sides, the string is built with the appropriate double-quote around the text. This avoids problems with single quotes noted above.

Because this procedure is not called with parameters, you can just press F5 while inside the procedure to run it. You get two Excel files that are nearly identical to the ones produced in Example 8-3. The main difference is that a parameter worksheet isn't needed, and the title is used in the header of the worksheet instead of placing it in the first row.

Also, pay particular attention to the `PageSetup` section of the code. When the header string is being set, you will see `&16` at the beginning of the string, and `vbCr` and `&10` at the beginning of the next line. The ampersand, along with a number, sets the font size for the string. The `vbCr` places a carriage return (like pressing enter in the header) between the lines. Next, look at the `InchesToPoints` method of the Excel `Application` object. Because the margins are set in `points`, Excel provides this handy method to allow you to set the margin with Inches. For reference, 1 inch is 72 points, but it is much easier to use the method.

If you use the macro recorder to set the page setup, add `Excel.` in front of each instance of `Application.InchesToPoints`. This is necessary because this method is part of the Excel `Application` object, and if you just reference the application while in Access, it attempts to use Access objects and it will not find this method in Access. When you open the created Excel workbook and do a Print Preview of the report, notice that there are two different font sizes in the header, and it is formatted to print on one page. You can also set up a page to print with print titles, with a different orientation, or on multiple pages. The easiest way to set it up is to just use the macro recorder in Excel and edit the code to add the Excel references where needed.

Using an Access Table for Reporting

While you can do all of this reporting without putting it into a table, I have found that by using a table to house report formats, you can make changes without touching the code. This makes it easier to develop reporting applications and allow others to maintain them. How much you put into the report formats is up to you. I suggest having fields available for font parameters, number formats, formulas, and a true/false field to allow you to hide the row. Let's look at the merits of using a table.

Assume that you wrote code that builds an income statement report with about 30 lines and several sums. At the bottom, to come up with net income, add income subtotals together and subtract expense subtotals. Of course there are underlines, double-underlines, and other formatting, as well as formulas. This report works well for a while but after five or six months in production, someone wants to add a few lines to the report to break out some expenses. If you did all of this formatting in code, you would have to edit just about every line that has to do with formatting, formulas, etc.

Now, if you have a table that holds all of the instructions, you would just need to put in the lines that you need, which would hold the formatting that you wanted for those rows. You then might have to update the formulas in the table to account for the number of new rows. I have found that it is much easier to teach someone how to update a formula in R1C1-style notation than it is to teach someone who has never done programming how to update a reporting module. Your choice depends largely on the role that you want to play. Many consultants make a nice living by maintaining their own applications for clients, and there is nothing wrong with writing the report with code alone. However, I would seriously consider putting the reporting formats in a table to make your application easier to modify.

With that said, let's take a look at this method from the top. First, look at the table design. Go into Access and create a new table. The first column is a line number. Having line numbers, even if you don't print them, ensures that your report shows up in the expected order. Next, decide whether to force the user to put in the exact formatting strings that Excel requires, or whether to use descriptive text, and either have it look up the Excel string in a table or add it to your code. Once you have figured that out, determine the number of columns that you need and give them names that are descriptive enough to make it easy for the user. I suggest using a table of lookup values, as this both makes the programming side much easier and is easier for the user. In addition, you can eliminate or add options to the table without having to touch the code. You won't be able to do that for the formula strings, but for anything where you set Excel constants, I suggest having a table of values (see Figure 8-3).

Let's say that in your report you want to allow users to choose whether to place a border in any given row on the report. There are many ways to make these options available to your users. As previously stated, the easiest way is to have a table with the different options and a lookup value to the value of the Excel constant. To accomplish the border on the row, create a table with two columns called tbl_Border. If the user doesn't want a border, she can leave the field blank. See the values in Table 8-2; you can look up these values in the Immediate Window in Excel as you looked up the formulas earlier in this chapter and the Excel constants in Chapter 7.

Table 8-2. Excel constant lookup values for borders

Description	Excel_Border_Constant_Value
Diagonal Down	5
Diagonal Up	6
Edge Bottom	9
Edge Left	7
Edge Right	10
Edge Top	8
Inside Horizontal	12
Inside Vertical	11

Now that you have the values for the placement of the border, you need a second table with the values of the types of lines that you want on the border. Call this table tbl_LineTypes. See the values in Table 8-3.

Table 8-3. Excel constant lookup values for border line styles

Description	Excel_Line_Constant_Value
Continuous	1
Dash	-4115
Dash Dot	4
Dash Dot Dot	5

Table 8-3. Excel constant lookup values for border line styles (continued)

Description	Excel_Line_Constant_Value
Dot	-4118
Double	-4119
Slant Dash Dot	13
No Line	-4142

Once you have the values, the code is very simple. Assume you store the constant values in a variables declared as Long, and use `Blocation` and `Bstyle`. To find out whether the code needs to run, first to make sure that the user selected a style. There are a number of ways to check, but I suggest setting the value to 0 right after declaring it; if there is no selection, there will be no value put in, and the code will be skipped. Here is the small section of code:

```
If Blocation <> 0 Then
With xlrng.Borders(Blocation)
  .LineStyle = Bstyle
End With
End If
```

You could also add options for line weight, line color, etc., but for now, keep it simple and allow these two options for borders. Also, put in a formula column, a font size, a Yes/No field for bold, and a number format column. The formula and number format will most likely be freeform text and the font size will just take a number. However, you could offer some styles as options for the number format. Table 8-4 defines what your table will look like. Call the table `tbl_ReportFormat`.

Table 8-4. Access table setup

Field name	Data type
Line_Number	Long Integer
Link_Field	Long Integer
Print_Description	Text
Excel_R1C1_Formula	Text
Excel_Number_Format	Text
Font_Bold	Yes/No
Border_Location	Text
Border_Style	Text
Font_Size	Long Integer

This gives you a good start to see the possibilities. Keep in mind that any other formatting or formula options that you want to set can be done with a table like this.

Now, let's put this to use. The first thing that you need to know is what to link to with the `Link_Field`. In this case, I use the product number for the rows where I pull data. Look at Figure 8-3 to see what the table looks like filled in.

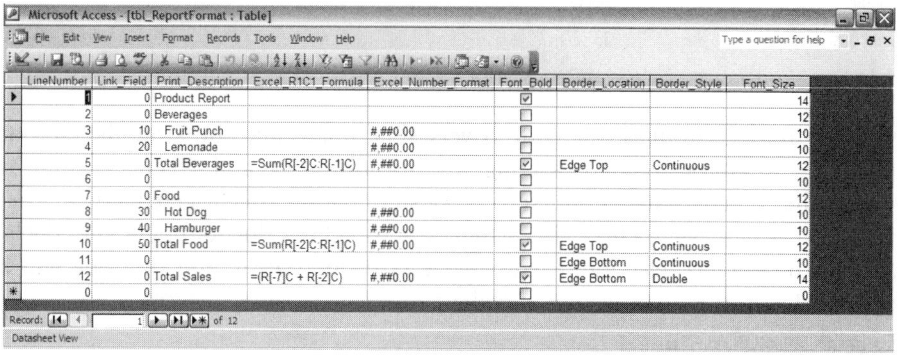

Microsoft Access - [tbl_ReportFormat : Table]

LineNumber	Link_Field	Print_Description	Excel_R1C1_Formula	Excel_Number_Format	Font_Bold	Border_Location	Border_Style	Font_Size
1	0	Product Report			☑			14
2	0	Beverages			☐			12
3	10	Fruit Punch		#,##0.00	☐			10
4	20	Lemonade		#,##0.00	☐			10
5	0	Total Beverages	=Sum(R[-2]C:R[-1]C)	#,##0.00	☑	Edge Top	Continuous	12
6	0				☐			10
7	0	Food			☐			12
8	30	Hot Dog		#,##0.00	☐			10
9	40	Hamburger		#,##0.00	☐			10
10	50	Total Food	=Sum(R[-2]C:R[-1]C)	#,##0.00	☑	Edge Top	Continuous	12
11	0				☐	Edge Bottom	Continuous	10
12	0	Total Sales	=(R[-7]C + R[-2]C)	#,##0.00	☑	Edge Bottom	Double	14
0	0				☐			0

Record: 1 of 12

Datasheet View

Figure 8-3. The resulting table to produce a report format using the same data used in previous examples

In the previous examples, we used a query called `qry_BaseQuery`. I modify it in this example to be `qry_BaseQuery_ReportFormat`. The only difference is that I added the `ProductNum` field, since that is what we are using to link to the report format table. In these reports, I want every row to show up—even if there are no values—I have to be very careful about the order in which I run the queries. First, run `qry_BaseQuery_ReportFormat`. Next, run `qry_ReportStep1`, which takes a parameter for the line of business that we want to report on. The final query uses a left join because we want all rows in the report format table and only the rows that match in the `qry_ReportStep1` query. See Example 8-5 for the SQL of `qry_BaseQuery_ReportFormat`, Example 8-6 for the SQL of `qry_ReportStep1`, and Example 8-7 for the SQL of `qry_ReportStep2`.

Example 8-5. qry_BaseQuery_ReportFormat

```
SELECT tbl_CostCenters.LineOfBusiness1, tbl_Products.ProductNum, tbl_CostCenters.
LineOfBusiness2, tbl_CostCenters.CostCenter, tbl_CostCenters.CenterName, tbl_Sales.
SaleDate, tbl_Products.ProductCategory, tbl_Products.ProductName, tbl_Sales.Quantity, tbl_
Sales.TotalCost
FROM tbl_Products INNER JOIN (tbl_CostCenters INNER JOIN tbl_Sales ON tbl_CostCenters.
CostCenter = tbl_Sales.CostCenter) ON tbl_Products.ProductNum = tbl_Sales.ProductNum;
```

Example 8-6. qry_ReportStep1

```
PARAMETERS StoreType Text ( 255 );
SELECT qry_BaseQuery_ReportFormat.LineOfBusiness2, qry_BaseQuery_ReportFormat.ProductNum,
Sum(qry_BaseQuery_ReportFormat.Quantity) AS SumOfQuantity, Sum(qry_BaseQuery_ReportFormat.
TotalCost) AS SumOfTotalCost
FROM qry_BaseQuery_ReportFormat
```

Example 8-6. qry_ReportStep1 (continued)

```
GROUP BY qry_BaseQuery_ReportFormat.LineOfBusiness2, qry_BaseQuery_ReportFormat.ProductNum
HAVING (((qry_BaseQuery_ReportFormat.LineOfBusiness2)=[StoreType]));
```

Example 8-7. qry_ReportStep2

```
SELECT tbl_ReportFormat.LineNumber, tbl_ReportFormat.Print_Description, tbl_ReportFormat.
Excel_R1C1_Formula, tbl_ReportFormat.Excel_Number_Format, tbl_ReportFormat.Font_Bold, tbl_
Border.Excel_Border_Constant_Value, tbl_LineTypes.Excel_Line_Constant_Value, tbl_
ReportFormat.Font_Size, Sum(qry_ReportStep1.SumOfQuantity) AS Quantity,
Sum(qry_ReportStep1.SumOfTotalCost) AS Sales
FROM ((tbl_ReportFormat LEFT JOIN qry_ReportStep1
ON tbl_ReportFormat.Link_Field = qry_ReportStep1.ProductNum)
LEFT JOIN tbl_Border
ON tbl_ReportFormat.Border_Location = tbl_Border.Description)
LEFT JOIN tbl_LineTypes ON tbl_ReportFormat.Border_Style = tbl_LineTypes.Description
GROUP BY tbl_ReportFormat.LineNumber, tbl_ReportFormat.Print_Description, tbl_
ReportFormat.Excel_R1C1_Formula, tbl_ReportFormat.Excel_Number_Format, tbl_ReportFormat.
Font_Bold, tbl_Border.Excel_Border_Constant_Value, tbl_LineTypes.Excel_Line_Constant_
Value, tbl_ReportFormat.Font_Size
ORDER BY tbl_ReportFormat.LineNumber;
```

With the queries, we are ready to write the code in Access VBA to automate Excel. In this example, I have a variable for the type of store, and I fill in a value; you could easily run multiple types by using a recordset, as we did in the earlier examples. For simplicity, run only one, shown in Example 8-8.

Example 8-8. Building a report in Excel using a report format table

```
Public Sub ExcelReportFormat()
Dim xlapp As Excel.Application
Dim xlwb As Excel.Workbook
Dim xlws As Excel.Worksheet
Dim xlrng As Excel.Range

Dim db As DAO.Database
Dim qry As DAO.QueryDef
Dim rs As DAO.Recordset
Dim fld As DAO.Field

Dim LocationChoice As String
Dim w, x, y, z As Integer

LocationChoice = "Storefront Locations"

Set xlapp = New Excel.Application
xlapp.Visible = True
Set xlwb = xlapp.Workbooks.Add
Set xlws = xlwb.ActiveSheet

Set db = CurrentDb
Set qry = db.QueryDefs("qry_ReportStep2")
qry.Parameters(0).Value = LocationChoice
```

Example 8-8. Building a report in Excel using a report format table (continued)

```
Set rs = qry.OpenRecordset

xlws.Range("A1").Value = "Sales Report for " & LocationChoice
x = 1
For Each fld In rs.Fields
  xlws.Cells(3, x).Value = fld.Name
  x = x + 1
Next fld

Set xlrng = xlws.Range("A4")
xlrng.CopyFromRecordset rs
y = 4 + rs.RecordCount

For z = 4 To y
    ' We are assuming that there are only going to be two fields with
    ' values that need totaled.  You can also write it so that you get
    ' the count of fields -1 and assume that the result of that calculation
    ' minus 8 is the last x rows that need to have calculations
    For w = 3 To 8
      Set xlrng = xlws.Range(xlws.Cells(z, 9), xlws.Cells(z, 10))
      Select Case xlws.Cells(3, w).Value
        Case "Excel_R1C1_Formula"
          If xlws.Cells(z, w).Value <> "" Then
          xlrng.FormulaR1C1 = xlws.Cells(z, w).Value
          End If
        Case "Excel_Number_Format"
          If xlws.Cells(z, w).Value <> "" Then
          xlrng.NumberFormat = xlws.Cells(z, w).Value
          End If
        Case "Font_Bold"
          If xlws.Cells(z, w).Value = vbTrue Then
          Set xlrng = xlws.Rows(z)
          xlrng.Font.Bold = True
          End If
        Case "Excel_Border_Constant_Value"
          If xlws.Cells(z, w).Value <> "" Then
            With xlrng.Borders(xlws.Cells(z, w).Value)
               .LineStyle = xlws.Cells(z, w + 1).Value
            End With
            w = w + 1
          End If
         Case "Font_Size"
           If xlws.Cells(z, w).Value <> "" Then
             Set xlrng = xlws.Rows(z)
             xlrng.Font.Size = xlws.Cells(z, w).Value
           End If
      End Select
    Next w
 Next z

  Set xlrng = xlws.Range(xlws.Columns(3), xlws.Columns(8))
  xlrng.Delete
```

```
xlws.Columns.AutoFit
xlws.Columns(1).Font.Size = 10
xlws.Rows(1).Font.Size = 14
xlws.Range("A3").Value = "Line #"
xlws.Range("B3").Value = "Description"
Set xlrng = xlws.Range(xlws.Cells(1, 1), xlws.Cells(1, 4))
xlrng.HorizontalAlignment = Excel.xlCenterAcrossSelection
xlws.Columns.AutoFit

rs.Close
qry.Close
Set fld = Nothing
Set qry = Nothing
Set rs = Nothing
Set db = Nothing
Set xlrng = Nothing
Set xlws = Nothing
Set xlwb = Nothing
Set xlapp = Nothing

End Sub
```

Since this procedure does not take any parameters, press the Run button or F5 inside the procedure when you have finished typing it in. There are a few things to note. First, it uses Select...Case instead of additional nested IF statements to make the code more readable. Also, this procedure assumes that the line style of the border is the column to the right of the border location because the location and line style are set at the same time. Next, increment w by 1 to skip that column during the next cycle of the For loop. You could also store all of the options in variables during the loop. Once we are done using the information for the report format, I set a range equal to those columns and delete them.

In reality, I would not format a report like Figure 8-4. However, it demonstrates setting different font styles, font size, border styles, etc. Also, look at the formulas. Writing R1C1-style notation in a table makes it easy to count the rows above or below a row to set your formulas. You are essentially forced into using R1C1-style notation unless you can be certain that you will always use the same columns and rows. Also, if you make changes to the format using A1-style notation, you are in for much more difficult changes to the formulas. It might seem more difficult to use a table, but if you hardcode reports and later need to make changes, you quickly see the value of spending the time up front to create the reports with information in a table. You might need to work though this a few times before you see the value, but I encourage you to do that.

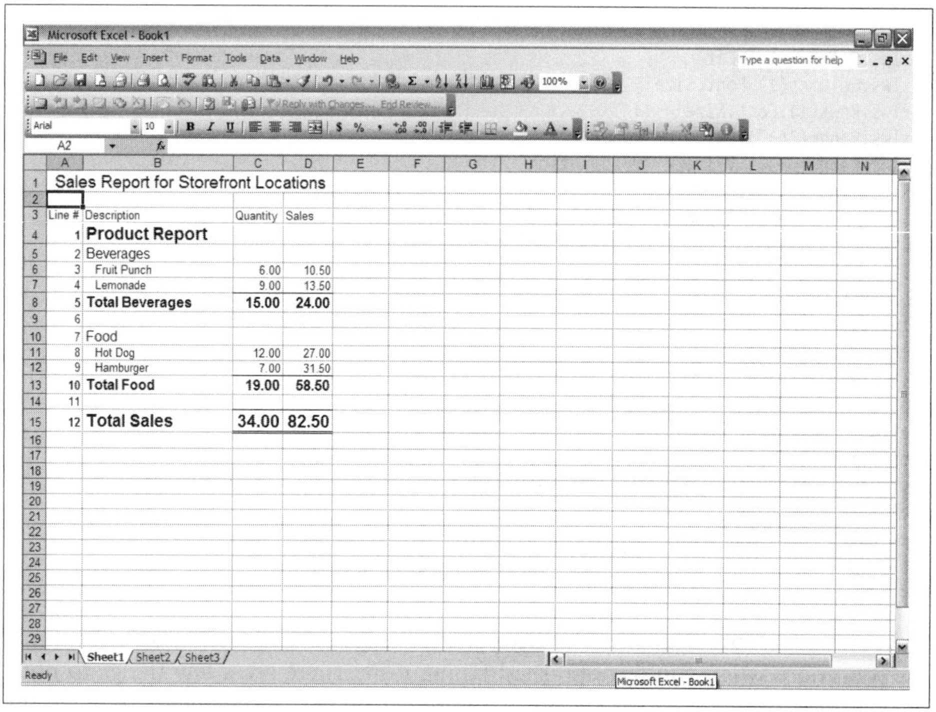

Figure 8-4. The resulting workbook from Example 8-8, formatted to demonstrate the options that you have

Putting It Together

The best choice for reporting automation depends on your situation. I have built single report formats for income statements that are used for actual versus budget reports, trend reports, crosstab reports, and comparison reports. If I had not used a report format, I would have had to rewrite the code for every report each time there were changes. By using a report format, I can respond to changes without making any changes to code. Having said that, if you do a simple report, just want to automate it, and it is unlikely that you will make significant changes, I suggest using a template or just building it from scratch with code.

Another good concept to keep in mind is that you can have two number formats and two formulas, and then use the report format in conjunction with the created crosstab query. So, you can have results in dollars/units as well as in ratios. It is unlikely that any one solution given in this book will fully solve a particular problem. For most, the expectation is that you combine different methods to create the solution. For a project that I recently completed for a client, I had to build a database that pulled data in from text files, multiple Excel workbooks, SQL Server, and a table in the Access database. When it was finished, it automated Word to send letters, built reports in Excel, and sent a specially formatted text file to a vendor via FTP. All of the steps were automated using the techniques used in this book.

In the next chapter, you will see how other applications can be automated from Access. There are a number of tasks (sending letters, for example) that are better handled in applications other than Access or Excel. Each time you add applications, you continue to increase the complexity of the code. However, to the extent that you can use the best tool for the job, the quality of the product you produce will be that much better.

CHAPTER 9

Using Access and Excel Data in Other Applications

There are many times when you want to use data in either Access or Excel for other purposes, including sending letters, drawing maps, creating PowerPoint presentations, and more. For the most part, you probably don't want to retype all of your data, and to the extent that you deal with a large volume of data, it probably isn't practical. Things like mail merge have been around for a long time, but this chapter focuses on automation of other applications. For example, a mail merge from Word creates all of the generated documents from the data source at the same time. In Example 9-1, you will see how to determine which letter to send based on information in a table and have the application process each one individually. The end user still ends up with your entire data set processed, but the approach is very different and more precise.

While there may be exceptions, in order to perform automation with another application you need an application object, and you generally need a second object referenced by the File → Open menu command in the application that you are automating. In some cases, you need a third object, an active document (consider Excel, in which the Workbook is a container for Worksheets, while in Word, you simply open a document with File → Open). There will be other application-specific objects, but as soon as you get an active reference to another application and some type of document, you can begin performing actions.

Automating Microsoft Word

Next to automating Excel, automating Word is one of the most useful things you can learn to do with VBA. There are many times when you need to print information that may not lend itself to an Access report. Even if it can be done with an Access report, you might want to give the end user complete control over the look of the document so that he can make changes without having to call you, the developer. There are a lot of ways to use automation to create documents users can later modify, but for these examples I focus on using Form Fields.

There are several form controls available in Microsoft Word. Access them by going to View → Toolbars → Forms from the top menu in Word. You end up with the toolbar that you see in Figure 9-1. To insert a Form Field, click on the button on the far left side of the toolbar. You get a gray box at the current cursor location. After you have the gray box, click the fourth button from the left of the toolbar to get to the field properties, where you have several options. Determine the type of entry being done (Text, Number, Date, etc.), or set it up to run a macro when you enter or exit the field. Set the field name by changing the bookmark description. You can also choose to have it as a calculated field.

Figure 9-1. The forms toolbar in Microsoft Word, which can be used to insert several form controls

If you want to perform calculations, there is something to keep in mind that for me was not intuitive. Assume that you have three form fields on a Word document called Price, Quantity, and Total. You set up Price and Quantity to be number fields, and Total to be a calculated number field (by selecting Calculation from the Type drop down menu). There is a checkbox at the bottom of the Form Fields Properties dialog that says "Calculate on Exit." I am always tempted to check this box on the calculated field, but in reality, you need to have the "Calculate on Exit" boxes checked on the fields used to calculate the total. The reason for this is that you will never be in the calculated field to have anything run on exit. Having said this, I rarely perform calculations in Word, but you can do it, and it might make sense for things such as a performance appraisal or a survey where you need to get a score at the end.

Here is a quick example that we will also use to automate from Access. Go into a blank Word document and set it up so that you have Form Fields for Name, Address, City, State, Zip, Phone, Days_Past_Due, and Amount_Past_Due (set the bookmark to these names). While in the properties dialog for each form field, set the number of characters, the data type, the number format, etc. Below the form fields, type in Letter #1 and save the file as Letter1.doc; then update it to Letter #2 and save it as Letter2.doc. Now, close Microsoft Word and go into Access.

You will create two tables in Access; the first is called tbl_CustomerData. In this table, create fields for CustomerDataID (Autonumber), Name, Address, City, State, Zip, Phone, Sales, Days_Past_Due, and Past_Due_Amount. Next, create a second table called tbl_MailInformation. In this table, create fields for MailID (Autonumber), CustomerDataID (Long), Date_Mailed, and Letter_Mailed. Now, we are ready to automate Word. I suggest always naming the bookmarks in Word with the exact same names as your Access field names because it becomes much easier to perform the automation. You can use the procedure in Example 9-1 with slight modifications for many purposes. Keep in mind that you need to set a reference to the Microsoft

Word Object Library by going to Tools → References while in design view of the module. Also, there are several file locations noted in the example that will be different on your computer.

Example 9-1. Word automation example

```
Public Sub SendLetters()
Dim wapp As Word.Application
Dim wdoc As Word.Document
Dim fld As Word.FormField

Dim db As DAO.Database
Dim rs As DAO.Recordset
Dim rs2 As DAO.Recordset

Dim filenm As String

Set db = CurrentDb
Set rs = db.OpenRecordset("tbl_CustomerData")
Set rs2 = db.OpenRecordset("tbl_MailInformation")

Set wapp = New Word.Application
wapp.Visible = True

rs.MoveFirst

While Not rs.EOF
  If rs.Fields("Days_Past_Due").Value <= 30 Then
    filenm = "C:\BookInformation\Chapter9\Letter1.doc"
  End If
  If rs.Fields("Days_Past_Due").Value > 30 Then
    filenm = "C:\BookInformation\Chapter9\Letter2.doc"
  End If

  Set wdoc = wapp.Documents.Open(filenm)

  For Each fld In wdoc.FormFields
    fld.Result = rs.Fields(fld.Name).Value
  Next fld

  wdoc.SaveAs "C:\BookInformation\Chapter9\" & _
      rs.Fields("Name").Value & ".doc"
  wdoc.Close

  rs2.AddNew
  rs2.Fields("CustomerDataID").Value = rs.Fields("CustomerDataID").Value
  rs2.Fields("DateMailed").Value = Now()
  rs2.Fields("LetterMailed").Value = filenm
  rs2.Update

  Set wdoc = Nothing
  rs.MoveNext
Wend
```

Example 9-1. Word automation example (continued)

```
Set fld = Nothing
wapp.Quit
Set wapp = Nothing
rs2.Close
rs.Close
Set rs2 = Nothing
Set rs = Nothing
Set db = Nothing

End Sub
```

The most critical thing to notice about using form fields is that the value of the form field is actually stored in a property called `Result`. What makes this code very easy to use is that the form fields are given the same names as the field names in the Access table. Since the table can have more fields than you might want in a document, the code cycles through the form fields in the Word document using a `For Each...Next` loop.

The second table stores the letter sent to each customer and the day it was sent. From a business perspective, this information can be very useful to know. This code saves the document as the customer name. If you have a large customer set, this probably isn't practical; save it as the `CustomerDataID` and then the customer name to avoid duplicate values. If you want to print the document, use a single line of code:

```
wdoc.PrintOut
```

While this example can be very useful, there are some limitations. For example, you can't have the customer's name in the header or footer because it is not possible to put a form field in the header or footer. Let's look at an example where you want to have the customer's name in the header and embed an Excel worksheet in the document.

Create a new Word document and go into the header by going to View → Header and Footer from the menu in Word. Next, go to Insert → Bookmark, call the bookmark CustomerName, and press the Add button. Get out of the Header/Footer by going to View → Header and Footer or by using the Close button on the Header and Footer toolbar. Type "Here is the Excel Document" in the body of the Word document, and press Enter. Next, go to Insert → Bookmark, call the bookmark ExcelDoc, and press the Add button. Save the document as WordExcelTest.doc.

Go into Excel and create an Excel workbook that looks like the Excel document shown in Figure 9-2. Select the cells that you want to show in Word, and go to File → Print Area → Set Print Area. This determines which cells are used when the Excel worksheet is embedded in the Word document. Save this workbook as *WordExcelTest.xls*. Next, find a way to access the bookmarks in Word and put in text or an Excel document. Look at Example 9-2. You need to reference both

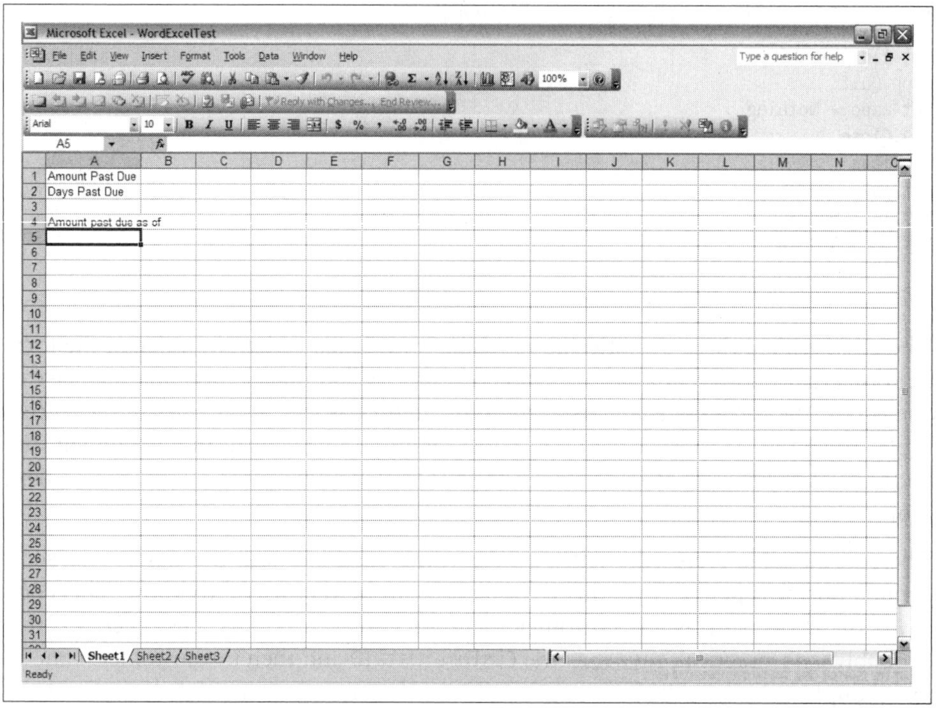

Figure 9-2. The Excel workbook used in Example 9-2

Word and Excel. This example uses the same table and Access database used in Example 9-1. Also, note that the filenames and paths used in this example will be different on your system.

Example 9-2. Example of Access automating Excel and Word

```
Public Sub WordExcelAutomation()
Dim xlapp As Excel.Application
Dim xlwb As Excel.Workbook
Dim xlws As Excel.Worksheet

Dim wapp As Word.Application
Dim wdoc As Word.Document

Dim db As DAO.Database
Dim rs As DAO.Recordset


Set xlapp = New Excel.Application
xlapp.Visible = True
Set wapp = New Word.Application
wapp.Visible = True

Set db = CurrentDb
Set rs = db.OpenRecordset("tbl_CustomerData")
```

Example 9-2. Example of Access automating Excel and Word (continued)

```
rs.MoveFirst

While Not rs.EOF
 Set xlwb = xlapp.Workbooks.Open _
      ("C:\BookInformation\Chapter9\WordExcelTest.xls")

 Set xlws = xlwb.ActiveSheet
 xlws.Range("B1").Value = rs.Fields("Amount_Past_Due").Value
 xlws.Range("B2").Value = rs.Fields("Days_Past_Due").Value
 xlws.Range("C4").Value = Now( )
 xlws.Columns.AutoFit

 xlwb.SaveAs "C:\BookInformation\Chapter9\temp.xls"
 xlwb.Close
 Set xlws = Nothing
 Set xlwb = Nothing

 Set wdoc = wapp.Documents.Open _
   ("C:\BookInformation\Chapter9\WordExcelTest.Doc")

 wdoc.Bookmarks.Item("CustomerName").Select
 wapp.Selection.TypeText Text:=rs.Fields("Name").Value
 wapp.Selection.TypeParagraph

 wdoc.Bookmarks.Item("ExcelDoc").Select
 wapp.Selection.InlineShapes.AddOLEObject _
      ClassType:="Excel.Sheet.8", FileName:= _
      "C:\BookInformation\Chapter9\temp.xls", LinkToFile:=False, _
      DisplayAsIcon:=False

 wdoc.SaveAs "C:\BookInformation\Chapter9\" & rs.Fields("Name").Value & ".doc"
 Kill "C:\BookInformation\Chapter9\temp.xls"
 wdoc.Close
 Set wdoc = Nothing
 rs.MoveNext
Wend

xlapp.Quit
wapp.Quit
Set xlapp = Nothing
Set wapp = Nothing
rs.Close
Set rs = Nothing
Set db = Nothing

End Sub
```

There are several important items in this code. Because the CustomerName bookmark
is in the header, you cannot use the GoTo method to access it. Instead, use the Select
method of the Bookmarks collection. You could use the GoTo method for the bookmark in the body of the document, but I use the same method for both. To enter text
at a bookmark location, use the TypeText method of the Word Selection class.

In this code, a temporary Excel workbook is created for each customer. For each customer record, the Excel document you created is opened, the current customer's information is filled in, and the workbook is saved as *temp.xls*. Then the Word document is opened, the CustomerName bookmark is selected, and the customer's name is typed beginning at the bookmark location. Next, the ExcelDoc bookmark is selected, and the temporary Excel file is embedded in the document. Because the Excel file is deleted after it is embedded, it is important that the LinktoFile property is set to False. Once the document is done, it is saved using the customer's name.

These Word examples should show you the possibilities available with Word automation. If you get stuck while using Word automation, record a macro and look at the code produced by Word automatically. The ability to automate two applications from Access and then integrate the documents is very useful for a number of business needs. For example, you want to embed a worksheet that shows sales results for each employee into a performance appraisal pre-filled in with each employee's information. Doing that manually would be very tedious, particularly if there are a large number of employees. This type of automation not only reduces the amount of time spent, but it also avoids errors.

Getting Information from Microsoft Word

If you need information from Word, there are many fill-in forms available for purchase, or you may have created one yourself. Say you have emailed a form to everyone in your organization, and they filled it in and emailed it back. Now you have a directory full of Microsoft Word documents, and you want to get that information into a database.

If you created the document, the form fields should have the same name as the database fields, but if you didn't, there is a possibility that you might not even know what the fields are called. When a document is protected, you can't view the properties of the fields by right-clicking on them, but there is an easy method to determine what the fields are called. Go into the protected document and type what you want the name to be into each field. Then go to File → Save As in Word and give it a new name.

Next, go into Microsoft Access and create a new database and a new table called tbl_ WordFields. In the table, you need two fields called FormFieldName and DatabaseFieldName set for a type of text. Set a reference to Microsoft Word by going to Tools → References in the Design View of the module in Access, and refer to Example 9-3.

Example 9-3. Code to document form fields in a protected Word document

```
Public Sub ProcessWordFields()
Dim wapp As Word.Application
Dim wdoc As Word.Document
Dim wfld As Word.FormField
```

Example 9-3. Code to document form fields in a protected Word document (continued)

```
Dim db As DAO.Database
Dim rs As DAO.Recordset

Set db = CurrentDb
Set rs = db.OpenRecordset("tbl_WordFields")

Set wapp = New Word.Application
wapp.Visible = True
Set wdoc = wapp.Documents.Open _
  ("C:\BookInformation\Chapter9\WordFilledIn.doc")

For Each wfld In wdoc.FormFields
  rs.AddNew
    rs.Fields("FormFieldName").Value = wfld.Name
    rs.Fields("DatabaseFieldName").Value = wfld.Result
  rs.Update
Next wfld
Set wfld = Nothing
wdoc.Close
Set wdoc = Nothing
wapp.Quit
Set wapp = Nothing
rs.Close
Set rs = Nothing
Set db = Nothing
End Sub
```

This code is actually a very simple iteration through the form fields in the Word document; it stores the name of the form field and the result (remember the value of a form field is stored in a property called result) in a database table. Depending on the Word document, you may have had to put numeric values in some of the fields because they did not have a type of text. In that case, you might have to edit this table by replacing the numeric value with the name of the database field. To make it easy on yourself, when entering the data into the Word document, put a value of 1 in the first numeric field, 2 in the second, etc., writing down what each number is as you go. Once you have entered the data into the Word document and run the procedure, you have a table in Access that includes all of the form fields. Once you have edited any of the numeric values in the Access table, use the table to process the Word documents that are filled in.

First, create a collection, fldcoll, which includes the database field name as the value and the form field name as the key. Then create a second collection that uses the form field name as the value. This serves as a collection of all of the keys. Next, open each Word document in a directory, pull in the information, and put it in a table. Assume you have a table in your database called tbl_ProcessedInformation that has all of the fields documented in the table called tbl_WordFields. Look at Example 9-4, keeping in mind that your filenames and paths may be different on your system.

Example 9-4. Example to process all Word documents in a folder

```
Public Sub GetWordInfo( )
Dim flname As String
Dim var As Variant

Dim wapp As Word.Application
Dim wdoc As Word.Document

Dim db As DAO.Database
Dim rs As DAO.Recordset

Dim fldcoll As Collection
Dim dbcoll As Collection

Set fldcoll = New Collection
Set dbcoll = New Collection
Set db = CurrentDb
Set rs = db.OpenRecordset("tbl_WordFields")
rs.MoveFirst
While Not rs.EOF
  dbcoll.Add rs.Fields("DatabaseFieldName").Value, _
      rs.Fields("FormFieldName").Value
  fldcoll.Add rs.Fields("FormFieldName").Value
  rs.MoveNext
Wend
rs.Close
Set rs = db.OpenRecordset("tbl_ProcessedInformation")

Set wapp = New Word.Application
wapp.Visible = True
flname = Dir("C:\BookInformation\Chapter9\WordProcess\*.doc")

While flname <> ""
  Set wdoc = wapp.Documents.Open _
    ("C:\BookInformation\Chapter9\WordProcess\" & flname)
  rs.AddNew
  For Each var In fldcoll
    rs.Fields(dbcoll.Item(var)).Value = _
      wdoc.FormFields(var).Result
  Next var
  rs.Update
  wdoc.Close
  flname = Dir
Wend

wapp.Quit
Set wdoc = Nothing
Set wapp = Nothing
Set dbcoll = Nothing
Set fldcoll = Nothing

rs.Close
Set rs = Nothing
Set db = Nothing
End Sub
```

Notice that I used the variable rs for both of the recordsets because I did not have to have both open at the same time. To go through all of the Word documents in a directory, I use the Dir function along with a While...Wend loop. Once the document is open, the code iterates through all of the values in the fldcoll collection, the collection of keys where the key value is the name of the form field in Word. So, for each value in that collection, the database field is the dbcoll collection's value where the key is the form field name from Word. The value of the database field is then set to the form field's result.

In a Word document where you might have five or six fields, it might make sense to use the information from your table to write code for each field name. However, if you are using a form with twenty or even hundreds of fields, this code saves you a lot of time, and once it is written, you can reuse it many times.

I should also mention that you can go to File → Save As in Word and then go to the Save Options dialog from the Tools drop-down menu in the Save As dialog. From there, you can check a box to save data only for forms. If you do that and save the document as text only, you could then import the text files into the database. I don't recommend it because it adds a lot of steps, but it is another option to get only the data from a form.

All of the examples from Word are generic enough that with minor tweaking they can be adapted for many purposes. When you have control over the Word document and the database, you can set it up to make it easy to process. When you don't have control, you can use the examples presented to document and process the Word document's fields.

Automating PowerPoint

While I really like PowerPoint for creating presentations, I do not particularly care for its object model. It is difficult to use for a number of reasons. First, the object model mixes constants from both the PowerPoint and Office object models. Also, when you add slides to the presentation, the objects are given names that do not identify them (such as Rectangle 2, Rectangle 5, etc.). However, once you have figured out the names for each slide, it is relatively straight forward to use them. Finally, you have to go through a number of steps for each object on the slide in order to be able to put in the text that you want.

Maybe it is because of the relative complexity or because heavy PowerPoint users might not be as versed in VBA as heavy Excel users, but, whatever the reason, I see a lot of requests for getting information like graphs, Excel worksheets, etc. into PowerPoint presentations automatically. So, the example that I present here puts each Excel chart from an Excel workbook on a new slide. For simplicity, I use the name of the chart as the title of the slide.

There is an important distinction in Excel between a Chart and a ChartObject. A chart is a type of sheet in Excel and is part of the Sheets collection, which contains both worksheets and charts. There are also collections for Worksheets and Charts. When you create a chart in Excel, it gives you an option at the end to create the chart as an object in the worksheet or as a separate sheet. For this example, assume that all of the charts are separate chart sheets.

You may wonder why I use Access to automate both Excel and PowerPoint but don't really do anything with Access; I could just as easily use Excel to perform the automation. I chose to use Access because most of the time when I do this, I create the charts in Excel through automation from Access data. So, in a real-world example, I would have a module that creates the charts in Excel, saves the workbook, and then either automates PowerPoint while the Excel workbook is already open or calls a procedure passing the Excel workbook's name as a parameter to perform the Power-Point automation.

Look at Example 9-5. To try this example, go into a new module in Access and set references to Excel, PowerPoint, and the Microsoft Office Object Libraries.

Example 9-5. Example of how to automate production of a PowerPoint presentation with Excel objects

```
Public Sub pptgraphs()
Dim xlapp As Excel.Application
Dim xlwb As Excel.Workbook
Dim xlchrtsht As Excel.Chart
Dim xlsht As Excel.Worksheet
Dim xlrng as Excel.Range
Dim pptapp As PowerPoint.Application
Dim pptpres As PowerPoint.Presentation
Dim pptslide As PowerPoint.Slide
Dim pptshapes As PowerPoint.Shape

Dim x As Integer

Set xlapp = New Excel.Application
xlapp.Visible = True

Set xlwb = xlapp.Workbooks.Open _
  ("C:\BookInformation\Chapter9\ExcelCharts.xls")

Set pptapp = New PowerPoint.Application
pptapp.Visible = Office.msoTrue
Set pptpres = pptapp.Presentations.Add
x = 1

For Each xlchrtsht In xlwb.Charts
  Set pptslide = pptpres.Slides.Add(x, PowerPoint.ppLayoutObject)
  pptapp.ActiveWindow.View.GotoSlide (pptslide.SlideIndex)
  Set pptshapes = pptslide.Shapes("Rectangle 3")
  xlchrtsht.Activate
  xlchrtsht.ChartArea.Copy
```

```
  pptshapes.Select
  pptapp.ActiveWindow.View.Paste

  Set pptshapes = pptslide.Shapes("Rectangle 2")
  pptshapes.TextFrame.TextRange.Text = xlchrtsht.Name
  x = x + 1
Next xlchrtsht

Set xlsht = xlwb.Sheets("Sheet1")
xlsht.Activate
Set xlrng = xlsht.Range(xlsht.Cells(1, 1), _
    xlsht.Cells.SpecialCells(Excel.xlCellTypeLastCell))
xlrng.Copy
Set pptslide = pptpres.Slides.Add(x, PowerPoint.ppLayoutObject)
pptapp.ActiveWindow.View.GotoSlide (pptslide.SlideIndex)
Set pptshapes = pptslide.Shapes("Rectangle 3")
pptshapes.Select
pptapp.ActiveWindow.View.PasteSpecial PowerPoint.ppPasteOLEObject, _
    Office.msoFalse
Set pptshapes = pptslide.Shapes("Rectangle 2")
pptshapes.TextFrame.TextRange.Text = "Excel Data"

xlwb.Close False
Set xlrng = Nothing
Set xlchrtsht = Nothing
Set xlsht = Nothing
xlapp.Quit
Set xlapp = Nothing
Set pptshapes = Nothing
Set pptpres = Nothing
Set pptapp = Nothing
End Sub
```

You may get an error message when referencing the PowerPoint shapes collections by specific names, which, in the previous example, are Rectangle 2 and Rectangle 3. Because you probably don't know what it defaults to on your PC and version of Microsoft Office, place the following three lines of code before the line with the error. The first value in your Immediate Window is the Title box, and the second is the Object box.

```
For Each pptshapes In pptapp.ActiveWindow.Selection.SlideRange.Shapes
    Debug.Print pptshapes.Name
Next
```

When I tested this code, on one machine it was Rectangle 3 for the Object box, and on another it was Rectangle 5. In any case, this error is relatively easy to fix. Also, since you know that the type of slide you are using has only two boxes, you can iterate through the slides collection, increment a variable by 1 each time, and have the code run that way, which would work regardless of how it was numbered.

There are some items of note in the code. First, when the graph is pasted into the PowerPoint, it is pasted as an embedded Excel workbook. You can also use the following line of code to paste it as a bitmap picture:

```
pptapp.ActiveWindow.View.PasteSpecial ppPasteBitmap
```

If you paste it as a bitmap, you can't edit the graph later by double-clicking on it and going into Excel. If you do not want or need that functionality, then pasting it as a picture is a good idea.

Also, notice that when you type in the code to make the Excel and PowerPoint applications visible, different options come up. The Excel application has only True and False, and they are the simply the Boolean values, but the options for the PowerPoint application to be visible are part of the Office Object's msoTriState enumeration. You'll also notice the same options when you do the PasteSpecial for the Excel range into the presentation.

In addition, take note that each time that I copy something, I make sure that the worksheet, chart, or slide is the object in the respective application. If you omit these lines, you might get errors (it will depend on whether, by chance, the object you copy happens to be the active object). Finally, as the code iterates through the Charts collection in Excel, it adds 1 to the variable x because as we add a new slide, we must tell PowerPoint where to place it. By incrementing a variable by 1 each time that a slide is created, we can easily do this. When you add the slide, you must choose a slide layout. The choices come up when you type the code. I suggest making your presentation the first time from scratch and using the Macro recorder to make sure that you are selecting the correct types.

This code is particularly useful if you keep an Excel workbook of key statistics for a company or department that is put into a presentation each month. Let's assume you have 20 graphs and put all of them into a presentation each month. Tunning this code could create your entire presentation in minutes. You could tweak the code to put the correct titles on the slides or even put on a title slide. If you run into trouble writing your code, say changing font size, you can also record a Macro in Power-Point and review the code.

Using Data in MapPoint

If you have never used Microsoft MapPoint, you may be in for a pleasant surprise. MapPoint software creates regular maps, puts data on maps, draws territories, shows demographic information, provides driving directions, plans a route, and more. If you do not own MapPoint, at the time of this writing you can get a 60-day trial from Microsoft for under $15 (price depends on whether you want the US version, the Europe version, or both). In addition to ordering the trial CD, you can explore many VBA samples available on the Microsoft MapPoint web site that show how to perform automation of MapPoint. What I show here are two things that are both frequently requested by clients and very straightforward to do.

This first example shows how to create a map of territories, a very common request in sales organizations. You have many options available, such as Zip Code, three digit Zip Code, census tract, county, state, and metropolitan area. For this example, I use Zip Codes. I got a list of all of the Zip Codes for Philadelphia, PA. I then took the list of Zip Codes, which were in numerical order, and called the first 20 Territory A, the next 23 Territory B, and the rest Territory C. I saved this information in an Access database table.

Next, I went into MapPoint and went to Data → Territories to use the Territory Wizard. When you go into the Territory Wizard, you see the screen in Figure 9-3. You can create the territories manually or from data. This example uses data in the Access database created from the Zip Code list.

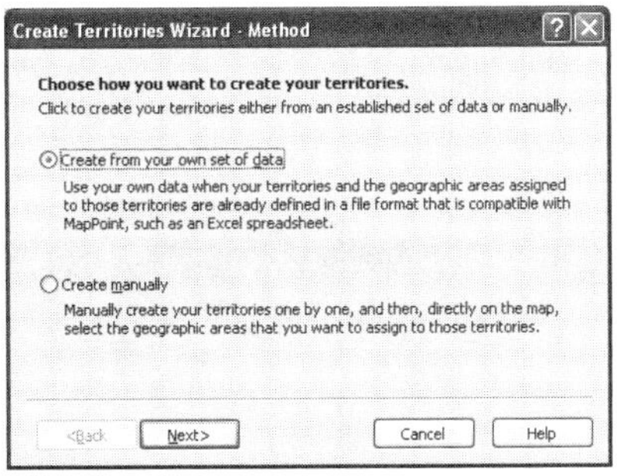

Figure 9-3. The first screen in the MapPoint territory wizard

The next screen gives you the option of importing or linking to the data. Because the data is in a database and would likely be updated there if this were a real application, I choose to link to the data. If you import the data from here, it will be more difficult to update the data in the future. This screen is shown in Figure 9-4.

A file dialog comes up asking you to browse to the datafile that you want to use. You can choose from Excel, Access, Text Files, or Microsoft Data Link. Then it asks you to choose the table or query that you want to link to. After you choose, MapPoint takes a shot determining what fields hold the data that it needs. In this case, because I called the fields Territory and ZipCode, MapPoint makes the correct determination. Notice the drop-down boxes in Figure 9-5. If you want to change the selection that MapPoint assigned to the field, you can do so with the drop-down box.

When you move to the next screen, it asks you to choose a primary key for your data source. In this case, the Zip Code is the primary key. It imports the data and lets you know which Zip Codes (or whatever field you are using) could not be found. It then gives you a list of possible matches to use, where you can skip only the matching record or all records that could not be found by pressing the Skip All Records button. After it lists the possible matches, you see the map shown in Figure 9-6.

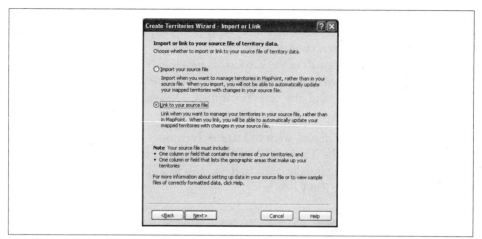

Figure 9-4. The second screen in the MapPoint territory wizard, which lets you choose to import or link to your data

Figure 9-5. The second screen in the MapPoint territory wizard, which lets you choose to import or link to your data

Notice on this map that the territories are not contiguous, which is the very reason that many people want to map data like this. Once this is done, you can take sales data by zip code, import or link to the data, and show it on the map.

To do the same thing from VBA, use Excel, Word, or Access. However, if you use an Access table and you try to do this from the same database, you get an error message that MapPoint cannot access the table. Look at Example 9-6. To use this example from any application, set a reference to the MapPoint Object Library.

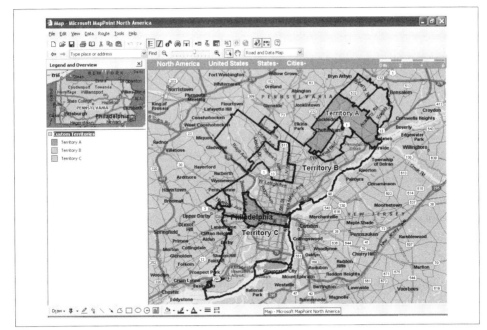

Figure 9-6. An example of a territory map created from data in Access

Example 9-6. Excel automation of a MapPointTerritory map using Access data

```
Public Sub mappointProg( )
Dim mpApp As MapPoint.Application
Dim mpMap As MapPoint.Map
Dim mpRslt As MapPoint.FindResults

Set mpApp = New MapPoint.Application
Set mpMap = mpApp.NewMap
mpApp.Visible = True

Dim xlwb As Excel.Workbook
Dim xlws As Excel.Worksheet
Dim acFile As String

Set xlwb = ActiveWorkbook
Set xlws = xlwb.ActiveSheet

acFile = "C:\BookInformation\Chapter9\Chapter9DBMappoint.MDB"
mpMap.MapStyle = MapPoint.geoMapStyleData
mpMap.DataSets.LinkTerritories _
  acFile & "!tbl_Territories", PrimaryKeyField:="ZipCode", _
  ImportFlags:=geoImportAccessTable
Set mpRslt = mpMap.FindAddressResults(, "Philadelphia, PA")
mpRslt.Item(1).Goto
```

```
mpMap.CopyMap
xlws.Paste
mpMap.SaveAs "C:\BookInformation\Chapter9\temp.ptm"
Set mpMap = mpApp.NewMap
mpApp.Quit

Set mpRslt = Nothing
Set mpMap = Nothing
Set mpApp = Nothing
Set xlwb = Nothing
Set xlws = Nothing
Kill "C:\BookInformation\Chapter9\temp.ptm"
End Sub
```

Automation of MapPoint is very similar to the other Office applications. First, set the application object to be equal to a new MapPoint application. While Excel has a workbook, Word has a document, and PowerPoint has a Presentation as the file, MapPoint has a map as its file or document. There is a NewMap method of the Map-Point application object used to set the reference to the map. Once that is done, become familiar with the MapPoint object model.

For this procedure, we use a data map (as opposed to a road and data map) by setting the MapStyle property of the map object. Next, there is a collection that holds all of the data for a given map called DataSets, which has a number of methods to bring in data, link to data, add demographics, or to add pushpins to the map. We use the method to link territories to an external data source. When you do this with the wizard in the MapPoint GUI, the map automatically zooms to the appropriate level so that you can see what you mapped. However, when you do it from VBA, you need to zoom the map yourself. Since I mapped Zip Codes in Philadelphia, all I had to do is find Philadelphia on the map. There is a collection called FindResults that holds all possible results of a search. Since I am looking for a very familiar place, I am confident that the first result will be the correct result. So, I tell the map to zoom to that location using the GoTo method of the first Item in the FindResults collection.

There is a CopyMap method of the Map object that places the graphic of the current map on the clipboard. Use the Paste method of any Office application to paste it.

The final MapPoint example, shown in Example 9-7, shows how to get directions between two points in MapPoint. With this example, you could pass the locations as parameters and make a more general-purpose procedure. The example shown calculates the directions from Philadelphia, PA to Baltimore, MD, and then pastes the directions to an Excel worksheet.

Other Techniques

Sometimes you'll want to move data from other applications into Office. There are a lot of ways that this can be accomplished: text file export, DDE, copy and paste, etc. I have built several applications that use DDE to bring in the data from a field in a different application. Normally, those decisions are driven from the other application. For example, if you have a Sales Force Automation (SFA) application, and you want to send a letter to certain customers that you speak with, you can set up a Word document to pull data from particular fields to fill in a letter anytime that it is opened. In most cases, DDE will be a very easy way to do this. There are many examples on how to do this with various applications on the Internet.

Another way to accomplish these tasks is if the other application has an Application Programming Interface (API). Depending on the application, you might need an additional license to use the API or have to sign up as a developer with the software publisher. As a general rule, using an API gives you more control over the application than DDE.

DDE and application-specific APIs are outside the scope of this book, but if you need to interact with another application, it is certainly something to consider. All of this can be done from within VBA. If you are in Excel, you can easily get data via DDE into a single cell using a formula. The formula is =Application|File Name!FieldName, so if you want to get data from a form field in Word named Text1, and the document is called Chapter9DDEDocument.DOC, type the following formula into Excel. When you try this, have the Word document open, or you have to go through a warning and Excel opens the Word document anyway.

```
=WinWord|'C:\Chapter9\Chapter9DDEDocument.doc'!Text1
```

This formula can also be used with other applications that allow you to communicate via DDE. Notice that you should use single quotes for the file name. For some applications, you use a topic name instead of a document name; this is common in SFA applications where you are not opening up documents, but rather structured customer records. In cases like this, there are often topics like Contact, Billing, Sales, etc. If you do this type of automation, I strongly suggest that you go to the vendor's documentation to ensure that you are pulling in the right information.

Example 9-7. Procedure to calculate the directions between locations

```
Public Sub mappointProg2()
Dim mpApp As MapPoint.Application
Dim mpMap As MapPoint.Map
Dim mpDir As MapPoint.Route

Set mpApp = New MapPoint.Application
Set mpMap = mpApp.NewMap
mpApp.Visible = True
Set mpDir = mpMap.ActiveRoute
```

Example 9-7. Procedure to calculate the directions between locations (continued)

```
Dim xlwb As Excel.Workbook
Dim xlws As Excel.Worksheet
Dim acFile As String

Set xlwb = ActiveWorkbook
Set xlws = xlwb.Sheets("Sheet2")
xlws.Activate

mpMap.MapStyle = MapPoint.geoMapStyleRoad
mpDir.Waypoints.Add mpMap.FindAddressResults(, "Philadelphia, PA").Item(1)
mpDir.Waypoints.Add mpMap.FindAddressResults(, "Baltimore, MD").Item(1)
mpDir.Calculate

While mpDir.IsCalculated = False
  Debug.Print "Waiting"
Wend
mpDir.Directions.Location.Goto

mpMap.CopyDirections
mpMap.SaveAs "C:\BookInformation\Chapter9\temp.ptm"
Set mpMap = mpApp.NewMap
mpApp.Quit

xlws.Paste

Set mpDir = Nothing
Set mpMap = Nothing
Set mpApp = Nothing
Set xlwb = Nothing
Set xlws = Nothing
Kill "C:\BookInformation\Chapter9\temp.ptm"
End Sub
```

The new object used in this procedure is the Route object, which also includes a Waypoints collection that holds the stops on the route. Once you have set the waypoints, calculate the route. Because you cannot access the Directions collection of the route until it has been calculated, I put in a while loop that makes sure the route is calculated before accessing the Directions collection. If the route has not finished calculating yet, it prints Waiting in the Immediate Window in Excel. In the previous example, we used the CopyMap method to copy the map to the clipboard. In this example, we use the CopyDirections method to copy the directions to the clipboard.

As you might imagine, there are a lot of uses for this. For example, you could send customers directions to your company personalized for their actual address. You might also want to show a map, and you could easily use the CopyMap method to do so. It is probably more likely that you would use Word for these applications of MapPoint and the code would be very similar.

Summary

At this point, I hope you can see how to use the data in Access and Excel in other applications that expose an object model. Because Microsoft Office is the dominant productivity suite, this type of automation can be put to use at most companies. There are only very small differences between the object models in Office versions 97 through Office 2003, so most of the code can be used in other versions of Office. The last point to make is that Microsoft provides very good documentation of the object models for the applications in the help file. This documentation often includes small code samples that show how to use the objects, methods, and properties.

CHAPTER 10

Creating Form Functionality in Excel

It may come as a surprise, but not everyone gets the full install of Microsoft Office on their desktop at work. Many companies put Microsoft Office for Small Business (or Office Standard) on the PCs of a large group of workers, meaning that these users don't have Microsoft Access on their PC. While these users will still have access to the data stored in Access databases through ADO or DAO, they won't be able to use the database frontend.

The features used in Figure 7-1 that placed a button on an Excel sheet and accepted parameters inside individual cells on a worksheet can be employed here. While they work, there may be times that you want to give a more polished frontend to the users, but a client (or your employer) does not want to purchase Access licenses for all users. You can accomplish some of the same Form functionality through an Excel feature called user forms. To see how this works, go to the Visual Basic Editor through Tools → Macro → Visual Basic Editor (or press Alt+F11). When you are in the Visual Basic Editor, go to the top menu and select Insert → UserForm. This brings up a blank UserForm as shown in Figure 10-1. Notice that to the left side of the blank form there is a toolbox, which shows the built-in controls.

While you don't get as many built-in controls or the same features that you get in Access, you can still build a nice frontend to an Access database with a UserForm, which lets you:

- Enter new records or edit records in a database
- Accept parameters to pull data from a database
- Provide buttons to open other UserForm objects
- Use the RefEdit control to easily accept the entry of an Excel Range
- Collect parameters to run an Excel Macro/VBA Code

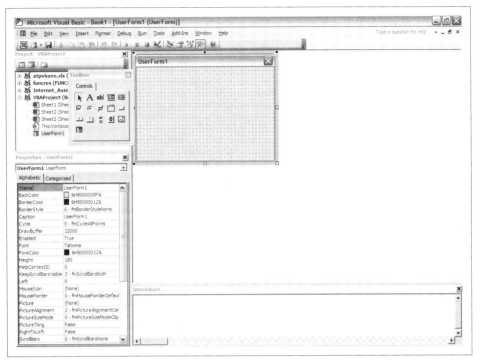

Figure 10-1. Adding a blank UserForm object to an Excel workbook in the Visual Basic Editor

Working with the UserForm

Now that you have a blank UserForm open, let's look at some of these examples. Assume that you have two Excel workbooks that your company uses to produce expense reports: one used by the end user with drop-down boxes, list boxes, etc. on the worksheet to give a nice look and feel, and one is used by people who maintain the database for things such as the list of cost centers, approvers, etc. It is relatively easy to give this type of user the ability to add or edit records in the database.

To support these needs, let's make this UserForm a form that looks up a cost center record in the database. If it is an existing record, it gives you the ability to edit the cost center name, and if the center number does not exist, it gives you the ability to add the record to the database. To accomplish this, you need a text box for the lookup field, a text box for the center number from the database, a text box for the center name from the database, a button to perform the lookup, a button to complete the Add/Edit, and a button to cancel. Add the controls by clicking on the appropriate control on the control toolbox and then clicking and dragging the object to the appropriate size. Figure 10-2 shows what the completed form could look like. (I have the same label, Center Number, for the lookup value and the result of the lookup, but you could certainly give these different names.)

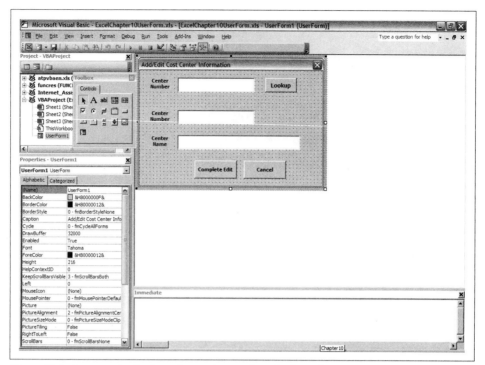

Figure 10-2. An example of a form that performs a basic lookup of a record and allows the user to edit a record or add a new record

Now that you have a form to use as the GUI, let's look at the code. The first button to look at is the Lookup button. If you double-click on the button, it brings up the code for the button. We need code (shown in Example 10-1) that checks whether the center number in the text box exists in the database. If the center number exists, bring the center number and center name across and fill in the boxes. If the number does not exist, prompt the user for a Yes/No, asking them whether they want to add the record. We need an ADO Connection, an ADO Recordset, an integer, and string variables to accomplish this. Go to Tools → References to create a reference to the ADO Library. In this example, I use ADO 2.1, since it is likely that all users have that on their PC. Keep in mind that this is being built for the majority of users who may or may not have Access on their PC and may or may not be current with the latest versions of Microsoft updates. Also, note that the path and filenames used in this example will be different on your system.

Example 10-1. Lookup and add center code

```
Private Sub CommandButton1_Click( )
Dim adoconn As ADODB.Connection
Dim adors As ADODB.Recordset
Dim criteria As String
Dim center As Long
```

Example 10-1. Lookup and add center code (continued)

```
Dim centername As String
Dim createchoice As Long

Set adoconn = New ADODB.Connection
adoconn.ConnectionString = "PROVIDER=Microsoft.Jet.OLEDB.4.0;Data Source=" & _
          "C:\BookInformation\Chapter10\Chapter10DB.MDB;"
adoconn.Open
Set adors = New ADODB.Recordset


' The text boxes are named LocalCenter for the number being entered
' by the user, DatabaseCenter for the center number being pulled from
' the database, and DatabaseCenterName for the center name being pulled
' from the database.  You could have just as easily left them as
' TextBox1, TextBox2, and TextBox3, but this makes it easier to understand
' what each box represents.

If IsNumeric(Me.LocalCenter.Value) Then
  center = CLng(Me.LocalCenter.Value)
End If
If Not IsNumeric(Me.LocalCenter.Value) Then
  MsgBox "You must enter a number for the Center Number to Lookup.", vbInformation
  GoTo closeout
  End If

tryagain:
adors.Open "Select CostCenter, CenterName from " & _
  "tbl_CostCenters Where CostCenter = " & center, adoconn, adOpenStatic

If adors.EOF And adors.BOF Then
  createchoice = MsgBox("Center does not exist, do you want to create " & _
        "this center?", vbYesNo, "CreateCenter?")
  If createchoice = vbYes Then
    centername = InputBox("What Name would you like to give this center?", _
        "Center Name", "")
    adors.Close
    adors.Open "tbl_CostCenters", adoconn, adOpenDynamic, adLockOptimistic
    adors.AddNew
      adors.Fields("CostCenter").Value = center
      adors.Fields("CenterName").Value = centername
    adors.Update
    adors.Close
    GoTo tryagain
  End If
End If

If Not adors.EOF Then
  adors.MoveFirst
  Me.DatabaseCenter.Value = adors.Fields("CostCenter").Value
  Me.DatabaseCenterName.Value = adors.Fields("CenterName").Value
  adors.Close
End If
```

Example 10-1. Lookup and add center code (continued)

```
closeout:

adoconn.Close
Set adors = Nothing
Set adoconn = Nothing

End Sub
```

There are a couple of items that should be very familiar to you by now, such as creating the connection to the database and opening the recordset. Notice the two lines that say tryagain: and closeout:, which allow you to direct the flow of the code execution to those lines. For example, once the new record is added to the database, rather than having code that pulls the data again in that section, add the line that says GoTo tryagain to re-run the code it tried to pull from the database earlier. Provided that the add method worked, this should fill in the form with the data from the database. The other line that might be new to you is the IsNumeric function. Keeping in mind that the CenterNumber in the database is a long integer, we want to avoid errors of a user entering in anything other than a number. By checking that the field is a number, we also eliminate the possibility that the user leaves that field blank. To jazz up this code a little more, you could have it clear out that text box and move the focus to the center number entry by adding the following two lines prior to the GoTo closeout line:

```
Me.LocalCenter.Value = ""
Me.LocalCenter.SetFocus
```

This shows the user exactly where she needs to enter the center number. This type of request normally doesn't come up during the design phase, but is often requested later. Keep your eye out for opportunities like this during programming.

Now that you see how to lookup and add a record, let's look at the other button that will update a record. In this button's code, first, make sure that the center exists. The user could have just typed in a center number and the center name and clicked Complete Edit. If the user knows which center he wants to update, you might want to allow this, so to avoid errors, make sure that it does exist first. You could also change the Enabled property of the DatabaseCenter textbox to False so that the user is forced to do a lookup. Either way works, so for Example 10-2, we test to make sure that the center number exists.

Example 10-2. Code for the complete edit button

```
Private Sub CommandButton2_Click()
Dim adoconn As ADODB.Connection
Dim adors As ADODB.Recordset
Dim criteria As String
Dim center As Long
Dim centername As String
Dim createchoice As Long
```

Example 10-2. Code for the complete edit button (continued)

```
Set adoconn = New ADODB.Connection
adoconn.ConnectionString = "PROVIDER=Microsoft.Jet.OLEDB.4.0;Data Source=" & _
            "C:\BookInformation\Chapter10\Chapter10DB.MDB;"
adoconn.Open
Set adors = New ADODB.Recordset

If IsNumeric(Me.DatabaseCenter.Value) Then
  center = CLng(Me.DatabaseCenter.Value)
End If
If Not IsNumeric(Me.DatabaseCenter.Value) Then
  MsgBox "Center must be a number, please use Lookup", vbInformation
  Me.LocalCenter.Value = ""
  Me.LocalCenter.SetFocus
  GoTo closeout
End If

adors.Open "tbl_CostCenters", adoconn, adOpenDynamic, adLockOptimistic
adors.MoveFirst
adors.Find "CostCenter = " & center, 0, adSearchForward
If Not adors.EOF Then
adors.Fields("CenterName").Value = Me.DatabaseCenterName.Value
adors.Update
End If
If adors.EOF Then
  MsgBox "Center does not exist, please use Lookup", vbInformation
  Me.LocalCenter.Value = ""
  Me.LocalCenter.SetFocus
  GoTo closeout
End If

adors.Close

closeout:
adoconn.Close
Set adors = Nothing
Set adoconn = Nothing

End Sub
```

There are really two things going on in this code: first, the code checks to ensure that the center number is, in fact, a number, and second, the code determines whether the center number exists. Since we have the add method as part of the lookup, the user is directed to look up the center if it does not exist. It is worth noting that you could force the user to look up the record first by locking out cells, but by doing it this way, you allow the user to update the centers where they know what they want to edit and avoid the lookup step. In real production code, you might want to trap other errors, such as the size of the center name field, etc.

The other piece of code that is necessary is the code for the Cancel button. In this example, the name of that button is CommandButton3 and its code is one line, shown in Example 10-3.

Example 10-3. Cancel button example

```
Private Sub CommandButton3_Click()
Unload Me
End Sub
```

If you have done some programming in Visual Basic, the Unload method should be familiar to you. You can also Unload other forms and objects. So, if you have multiple user forms open, you might have some code that runs at the very end to unload any forms left open. The Me keyword simply refers to the current open form (actually, to the current Class that is executing code, but in our examples it would only be referring to user forms). We have been using the Me keyword to refer to the names of the text boxes on the current form in the first two examples in this chapter.

Accepting Parameters

If you look back to Chapter 7, where we had an Excel workbook take the username and password from two cells in the worksheet to connect to the database, this is a good place to use a user form instead. Open the workbook and use Alt + F11 to go to the Visual Basic Editor. Right-click on the name of the project and go to Insert → UserForm. Now you have a blank user form. You need two labels, two textboxes, and two buttons, and it could look similar to Figure 10-3.

There are a couple items that make this form a little more useful. First, in the properties of the password box, you can choose a character to display so that someone cannot see what is being typed. Generally, I use the "*" character to do that. However, you can use any character that you want. The code then changes slightly from the original. First, the code on the worksheet's button needs to change to what you see in Example 10-4.

Example 10-4. Worksheet button code

```
Private Sub CommandButton1_Click()
UserForm1.Show
End Sub
```

This code shows the form created in Figure 10-3. The codes for the Connect and Cancel buttons are shown in Example 10-5 and Example 10-6.

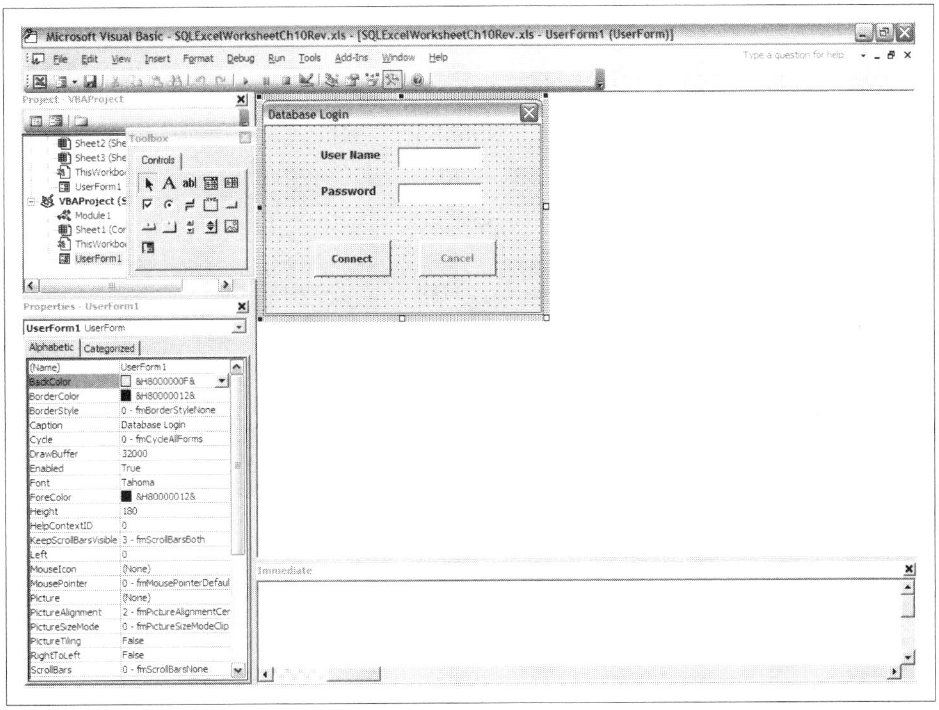

Figure 10-3. Example of a database login form

Example 10-5. Connect button code

```
Private Sub CommandButton1_Click( )
Call Module1.OpenSQLWriteExcel(Me.TextBox1.Value, Me.TextBox2.Value)
End Sub
```

Example 10-6. Cancel button code

```
Private Sub CommandButton2_Click( )
Unload Me
End Sub
```

The last piece of this is to update the original code to take the parameters from the form instead of taking them from the worksheet. This is shown in Example 10-7.

Example 10-7. Chapter 7's code modified to use a user form

```
Public Sub OpenSQLWriteExcel(usn As String, pwd As String)
Dim adocn As ADODB.Connection
Dim adoconnrs As ADODB.Recordset
Dim adors As ADODB.Recordset
Dim adofld As ADODB.Field
Dim ConnString As String
Dim xlwb As Excel.Workbook
Dim xlws As Excel.Worksheet
```

Example 10-7. Chapter 7's code modified to use a user form (continued)

```
Dim xlrng As Excel.Range
Dim x As Integer
Dim UserName As String
Dim Password As String

UserName = usn
Password = pwd

Set adoconnrs = New ADODB.Recordset
adoconnrs.Open "C:\Documents and Settings\All Users\" & _
            "Documents\SQLConn.XML"

adoconnrs.MoveFirst
While Not adoconnrs.EOF
  ConnString = ConnString & _
      adoconnrs.Fields(0).Value & " = '" & adoconnrs.Fields(1).Value & "';"
  adoconnrs.MoveNext
Wend

adoconnrs.Close

ConnString = ConnString & "User ID = '" & UserName & "';"
ConnString = ConnString & "Password = '" & Password & "';"

Set adocn = New ADODB.Connection
adocn.ConnectionString = ConnString
adocn.Open

Set adors = New ADODB.Recordset

adors.Open "pubs.dbo.Authors", adocn
adors.MoveFirst

Set xlwb = ActiveWorkbook
Set xlws = xlwb.Worksheets.Add
xlws.Name = "Data"
x = 1
For Each adofld In adors.Fields
  xlws.Cells(1, x).Value = adofld.Name
  x = x + 1
Next adofld
Set xlrng = xlws.Range("A2")
xlrng.CopyFromRecordset adors
xlws.Columns.AutoFit

adors.Close
adocn.Close

Set xlrng = Nothing
Set xlws = Nothing
Set xlwb = Nothing
Set adoconnrs = Nothing
```

Example 10-7. Chapter 7's code modified to use a user form (continued)

```
Set adocn = Nothing
Set adors = Nothing
End Sub
```

The only changes made to this code were to use the variables usn and pwd to pass the username and password instead of pulling the information from the worksheet. If you look back to Chapter 7, we used the following lines of code to pull in the username and password:

```
UserName = Sheets("Connection Info").Range("B1").Value
Password = Sheets("Connection Info").Range("B2").Value
```

In this example, we needed to refer to the variables we created. You could also have simply removed the variable declaration for UserName and Password and just used UserName and Password in place of usn and pwd. Either way works, and I wanted to use as much of the original code as possible.

While it might not matter to you whether you use a user form or cells on a worksheet, using a user form certainly does make your mini-application look better. In addition, you are not limited to having things set up in rows and columns when you use a user form, and your ability to force data validation is much better when using a user form.

Other Useful Items

There are a few other useful things that you can do when designing a user form. You might notice that the text boxes are aligned with the labels, and the left and right margins of each are also aligned. If you attempt to do this using only your eyes, you may have some difficulty. The easiest way to do this is to make the sizes the same using the properties dialog's height and width properties. You can drag one text box or label to the right size, look at the height and width properties, and set the properties of the other text boxes to be the same. Then, when you want to align the text boxes or labels, click and drag to select the text boxes or labels that you want to align, go to the top menu and select Format → Align, and choose whether you want Lefts, Right, Tops, Bottoms, Centers, or Middles. This automatically lines up your controls.

If you need the user to enter a range, there is an object that you can put on a user form that makes it very easy to do. It is called the RefEdit control and is on the bottom left of the control toolbox. When you put it on the user form, the user clicks on it and selects a range which is stored as a text value A1-style reference and can be retrieved using the Value property.

The other control that I use quite a bit is the MultiPage control. This lets you use one form while allowing you to gather a lot more information. It also makes it nice when you want to break up the data entry into pieces. I have used this control in cases when I allow the user to select multiple parameters to search records, as well as when retrieving information from a database. For example, have one page that displays contact information, and have another page that displays sales information, etc. You can probably come up with a lot of examples. It is a very nice control to use, particularly because most users are used to seeing multi-page forms when they edit properties in many Windows programs.

Next Steps

By this point, the information that needs to be covered to integrate Access and Excel has been covered. This chapter showed you some ways to add some additional functionality around how your applications work without changing the nuts and bolts of what happens in the code. The next chapter builds on this and offers some additional tips for GUI design as it relates to Microsoft Access.

If you have not done so already, it is a good idea to familiarize yourself with the properties available for each control on the Excel user forms. In Excel, anytime you click on a control on a UserForm, on the left side of the Visual Basic Editor, you see the available properties. (If the properties window is not visible, press F4 when you are in the Visual Basic Editor to show it.) Also, don't forget to click on the form to see the form-specific properties.

CHAPTER 11

Building Graphical User Interfaces

Regardless of how good your code is, a user generally judges the application by the look and feel of the user interface. This doesn't mean that your code doesn't have to work correctly, but it does mean that you should put some thought into the best ways to gather information from your users about how they will navigate the application. This chapter focuses on Microsoft Access, as it has the richest GUI development possibilities.

The first thing you can do in Access is set the startup properties for your database. This lets you have a form open when the application opens, put a title on the application, and set some other options around menus and special keys. You get to the startup options by going to the top menu under Tools → Startup in the database windows. You might have to expand the menu to see that option if you have not used it before (press the double arrow at the bottom of the menu or keep it open without selecting anything for a few seconds). The startup options are shown in Figure 11-1.

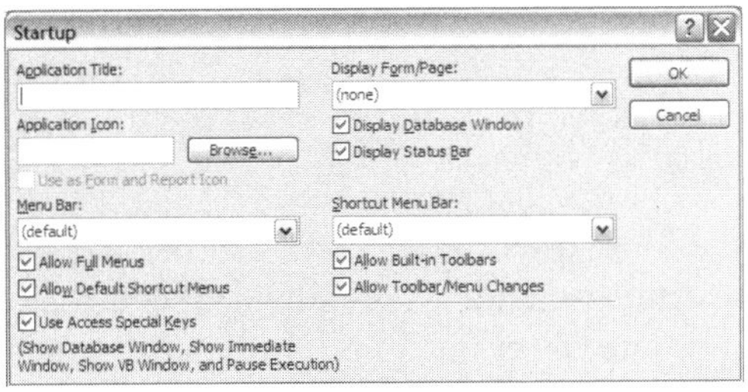

Figure 11-1. Startup options available for Microsoft Access databases

I generally don't like to restrict the user's menus unless it's required for security or some other important reason. Generally, I uncheck the box for the Database Window and have a main menu form open. In addition, I put a title on the application so that it is easy to identify the application even if the user changes the actual filename.

If you make changes and want to see the database window after you open the application, press F11 (anytime you use F11 in Access it takes you back to the database window, provided you have not disabled this feature by unchecking the box for Use Access Special Keys).

Setting Up a Form

When I set up a new form, there are a couple things that I do to make the form a little easier to use. First, I put on a form header and footer to hold the title of the form and add any basic form buttons like Close, Search, etc. Next, I try to determine what the form will be used for to get the best look. For example, by default, Microsoft Access puts on record selectors and record navigation buttons. These may or may not be useful for your application in some places, but generally will not be useful on a main menu form or on a form where you collect information to send parameters to a procedure. The other item that I change for almost any form except data entry forms is the Border Style. The Border Style, by default, is set to Sizable. Because I normally don't want the user to resize the main menu, I change this setting to Dialog to keep them from changing it. Also, for a main menu form, I normally disable the ability for the user to "X-Out" of the form by setting the Close Button property to No. You can also change the setting for Min Max Buttons or eliminate the Control Toolbox altogether (Close, Min, and Max buttons). In addition to these, I generally set AutoCenter and Auto-Resize to Yes.

The properties for a form are categorized in a tabbed dialog under Format, Data, Event, Other, and All. I suggest getting familiar with the options that you have available to you under these properties. Microsoft has made it very easy for you to figure out what each property does by putting a short description in the status bar. Additionally, press F1 in any of the value boxes for a property for help to come up and describe what the property does.

Using Events

Events are some of the most useful things you can use to control a user interface. Events happen at the form level and at the individual control level. At the form and control levels, there are some key events I find very useful, which I outline here.

OnCurrent

The OnCurrent event runs each time the focus moves between records. There are several reasons to use this. First, based on values in a record, you might want to enable certain buttons and disable others. You can control this by setting the Enabled property of the command buttons based on If...Then statements or Select...Case statements. You might also want to perform some type of calculation or pull some data from another table based on what is in a current record. All of this can be done automatically using the OnCurrent event.

BeforeUpdate/AfterUpdate

The BeforeUpdate and AfterUpdate events are best used on text boxes, combo boxes, etc. The main difference between them is that BeforeUpdate fires prior to making the change to the field, and AfterUpdate fires after the change has been made to the field. Use BeforeUpdate when performing data validation. If the data is not what you expected, take actions to ensure proper data. Depending on what you are trying to do, you might want to test both to make sure that you use the correct one. If you use these events on a control connected to data (and the name of the field is different from the name of the control), when the BeforeUpdate event fires, the text box holds the current value shown on the form, and the field name holds the old value. When the AfterUpdate event fires, they will have the same value.

OnChange

The OnChange event fires when a control's value changes. Since it fires as you type each character in a control, it is often more appropriate to use the AfterUpdate event. However, for situations when you perform data validation, using the OnChange event can be the right choice if you need to know when a value changes.

OnDirty

The OnDirty event fires any time the contents of a form or text box change (depending on the object where you have the event set). It is useful if you want to set a global variable when a change happens. Essentially, the OnDirty event lets you know that something happened that will change the data in your application. Since you will find out prior to a change happening, you can write code to handle changes, which is useful if you need to perform time consuming data validation and only want to do it when something has changed.

OnEnter/OnExit

The OnEnter and OnExit events run when you enter or exit a control. They redirect the flow of the application but give you more control than you get by just setting the tab order of the controls on the form.

OnClick/OnDoubleClick

These events run when a control is clicked or double-clicked. Although I rarely use the OnClick event except for command buttons, I often use the OnDoubleClick event to allow users to add records on the fly to a combo box. Assume you have a combo box that displays values from a table and a form called frm_Table that allows you to add records to the table. Put the code shown in Example 11-1 in the OnDoubleClick event of the combo box.

Example 11-1. OnDoubleClick event example

```
Private Sub Combo2_DblClick(Cancel As Integer)
DoCmd.OpenForm "frm_Table"
Me.Text0.SetFocus
End Sub
```

Now, if a user needs to add records to the combo box, she can just double-click on the combo box, and the double-click event opens the form to add records and move the focus to a different text box (so that the requery event, shown next, works). You know that the user has completed entering information in the form when the focus returns to the original form. Use the code in Example 11-2 for the form's GotFocus event.

Example 11-2. GotFocus example

```
Private Sub Form_GotFocus( )
Me.Combo2.Requery
End Sub
```

While you might be tempted to put the Requery method in the OnDoubleClick event, Access opens the form and requeries immediately, which results in the data not being updated for what was just entered. I have also worked with applications that have requery or refresh buttons beside combo and list boxes, allowing the user to control when they are refreshed. I think that using the GotFocus event is a more elegant solution than making the user press extra buttons to perform a refresh.

In addition to using buttons to perform a refresh of data, I have also worked with applications that use buttons to add values to combo boxes. In my opinion, using the OnDoubleClick event to add records is a better solution and leads to less clutter on the form.

OnOpen

The OnOpen event fires when the form is first opened. Because the user may have maximized other forms, if I have a form that I do not want shown maximized, I use the OnOpen event to execute the `DoCmd.Restore` command. This is the equivalent of pressing the button in the command bar between the minimize and close buttons when a form is maximized. You can also put in code to perform other actions that you want to take place when a form is opened.

OnTimer

The OnTimer event works along with the Timer Interval property of the form that is set in milliseconds and is very useful for a number of functions. For example, you can have a database application that processes files in a directory. You can have a form open to check for new files in a directory every 15 minutes by setting the Timer Interval property to 900,000 (15 minutes×60 seconds×1000 to convert seconds to milliseconds).

Using Data

Because many times combo boxes and list boxes are filled in by data from tables or queries, instead of hardcoded values, you sometimes might want to change the underlying query for a control. A good example of this is if you have a form asking you to choose a store location. When the form first opens, all locations are available. Let's assume that there are combo boxes for state and location. It wouldn't be uncommon for a client to ask you to show only locations for a particular state when a user selects state. It also might not be a stretch for the client to ask that the combo box for location not be activated until the user chooses a state. Here are the steps you would follow to accomplish these two tasks.

First, using the form's OnOpen event (or OnCurrent event if this is a data entry form), set the `Enabled` property of the Location combo box to `FALSE`. Next, put code in the AfterUpdate event of the State combo box to change the underlying query of the Location combo box by changing the Row Source property via VBA. You can see what is currently in the Row Source property by looking at the Data tab of the combo box properties. Example 11-3 includes code for both of these events.

Example 11-3. Code to restrict locations to particular states

```
Private Sub Form_Open(Cancel As Integer)
Me.LocationCombo.Enabled = False
End Sub

Private Sub StateCombo_AfterUpdate()
Me.LocationCombo.Enabled = True
Me.LocationCombo.RowSource = "SELECT [tbl_Locations].[Location] " & _
```

Example 11-3. Code to restrict locations to particular states (continued)

```
   "FROM [tbl_Locations] Where " & _
   "[tbl_Locations].[State] = """ & Me.StateCombo.Value & """;"
Me.LocationCombo.Requery
Me.LocationCombo.SetFocus
End Sub
```

If you need help writing the query, go to the Query Designer in the Access GUI to write the query, and then switch to SQL view. Also, notice that I put the value of the state in double quotes. I could have just as easily used single quotes because I can be certain that a state will not have a single quote in its string, but I think it is a good practice to put all of the string in queries in double quotes to avoid the issue. If you use single quotes, whenever an apostrophe is used in text, you get errors in your application. This can be very frustrating for you and users because you might not test for this error when you build the application.

To make this even more user friendly, add code that changes the value of the location box to an empty string whenever the state value changes. Users might also ask to have all locations available by default (instead of having the Location combo box not enabled) with restrictions by state when a state is selected. Eliminate the Where clause from the query string in the properties tab of the Location combo box and get rid of the lines of code setting the enabled property.

These same techniques apply to list boxes. An interesting way to perform them with list boxes is to have a group of radio buttons that make your selection and set the SQL for the list box based on it. For example, let's say you are building a form to search for a car. You have radio buttons that let you choose whether to search by color, engine, or body style. Do this by adding an option group to the form. When you create the option group, Access assigns a numeric value to each selection. Next, have code for the option group's OnChange event to change the SQL of the list box.

In addition, you might want to give the user the ability to choose more than one item from the list box, by setting the Multi-Select property of the list box on the Other tab of the properties dialog to Extended. See Example 11-4. for the code for the option group.

Example 11-4. Code example to change queries based on a selection

```
Private Sub Frame6_AfterUpdate( )
Select Case Me.Frame6.Value
Case 1
  ' This is the value for Color
  Me.SearchList.RowSource = "Select Color from tbl_Colors"
  Me.SearchList_Label.Caption = "Color"
Case 2
  ' This is the value for Engine
  Me.SearchList.RowSource = "Select Engine from tbl_Engines"
  Me.SearchList_Label.Caption = "Engine"
Case 3
```

Example 11-4. Code example to change queries based on a selection (continued)

```
    ' This is the value for Style
    Me.SearchList.RowSource = "Select Style from tbl_Styles"
    Me.SearchList_Label.Caption = "Style"
End Select
Me.SearchList.Requery
End Sub
```

There are a couple things to take note of in the example. First, I change the caption for the label of the list box based on the selection. That certainly doesn't do anything for functionality, but it does add a nice touch. Second, it is unnecessary to have the Requery event in each condition of the Select Case because you can set the SQL for the source in the Select Case statement and requery at the end.

If you allow your users to make multiple selections, you need a way to get the selected values. The list box has a collection called ItemsSelected that is a collection of Variants. You can iterate through this collection with a For Each...Next loop to get the values. In Example 11-5, I show how to create a button that brings up a message box for each value selected in a multi-select list box.

Example 11-5. Code to cycle through a multi-select list box

```
Private Sub Command19_Click()
Dim itm As Variant

For Each itm In Me.SearchList.ItemsSelected
    MsgBox Me.SearchList.ItemData(itm), vbOKOnly
Next itm

End Sub
```

This is a very simplistic example of how to cycle through this collection. I often store the values in a string that I use in conjunction with an IN clause in SQL to perform a search. Once you understand how to cycle through the collection, you can use this technique to perform a number of tasks.

Adding Buttons

One of the nice features of Microsoft Access is that there is often a preprogrammed button to add basic functionality to your application. See Figure 11-2 to see the categories of preprogrammed buttons.

You should become familiar with the features in this dialog. Tasks such as opening a form, saving a record, or navigating through the records on a form can all be done just by dropping a button onto the form and selecting the appropriate action. If you want to customize, Access can write the code for you to open a form, and you can edit the code to take the value from a combo box to pick which form to open.

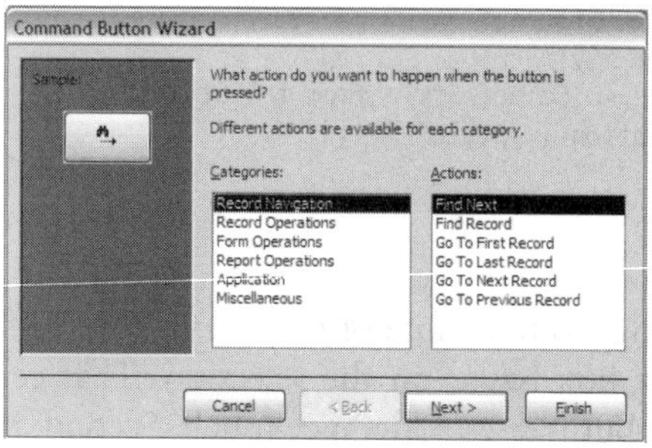

Figure 11-2. Preprogrammed buttons available for Microsoft Access databases

While it is unlikely that you can write an entire application using only the wizards, you can significantly reduce the amount of code that you have to write. In addition, since this code is written for you, testing is much less time-consuming, allowing you to focus on the aspects of your application that truly add value.

Tab Order

This is probably the item that gets skipped more than any other when developing an Access form. If you right-click on the header of the form, you see a drop-down of available options, one of which is the tab order for the form. When you bring up the tab order dialog, shown in Figure 11-3, you have the option of allowing Access to Auto Order the tab. This is usually a good starting point, but after you have done that, I suggest tabbing through the form to make sure that it is in the proper order. If it isn't, you can switch back to design view and click and drag the names of the controls into the proper order.

You can also set it up so that Access will not allow tabbing into a control. On the properties dialog, there is an option called Tab Stop on the Other tab. If you set this option to No, Access skips the control when the user tabs through the form. Although the control still shows up on the tab order dialog, moving it does not have the same effect as setting the Tab Stop option to "No."

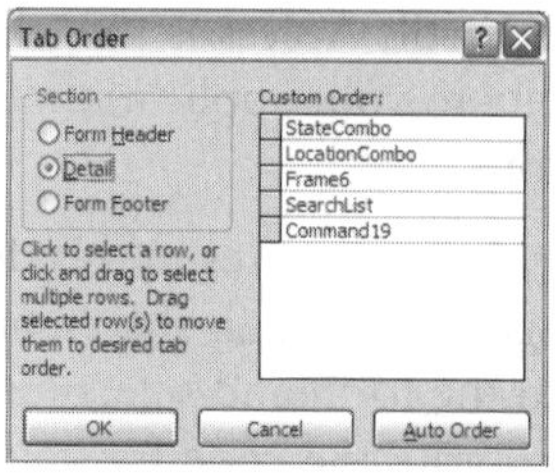

Figure 11-3. The Tab Order dialog, which allows you to set the tab order of a form's controls

Next Steps

The next chapter is a project. In the chapter, I describe an application to you that requests specific features involving both the user interface and integrating Excel and Access. This project is one that you would likely come across on a project web site where people search for someone to complete a short project.

Many times when you deal with project requests like this, the specifications will not be as detailed. However, it is still important to think through the things that the user likely wants so that you can adequately determine the amount of time required to complete the application.

In addition, the planning phase of the project is the most important. I see more projects fail because the requestor and the developer skips the planning phase thinking that they know what they want. Often when you begin to ask questions about the functionality required, additional items come up. If you don't address this up front, you might be in a situation where you want to be paid for an application that meets the specifications requested but doesn't perform the intended task, which is not a situation you want to be in.

Finally, I suggest spending a lot of time with form design in Access. There are a lot of things that can be done there that add a lot of value to the application. In addition, there are several books available from O'Reilly that are helpful when developing Access applications. *Access Cookbook* and *Access Hacks* show you how to solve specific programming problems that come up when developing Access applications.

CHAPTER 12

Tackling an Integration Project

This chapter describes a project that you should be able to tackle using the information presented in this book. If you have ever read project descriptions on the web sites that allow independent developers to bid on projects, you are probably aware that often they do not go into great detail as to what is required. For this project, I try to explain all of the needed functionality without specifying precisely how to complete the project. Following the project description, I will describe a potential solution to each piece of functionality. As with most programming items, there are many solutions to each.

In addition to performing integration tasks in the project, it will be necessary to build a graphical user interface (GUI). The project specifies that Access is the preferred tool for the GUI, but you can probably accomplish it using user forms in Excel. For a real-world example, consider creating a Windows application with Visual Basic that uses an Access database to store the data and automates Excel. This type of setup is sometimes required when not all of the users have Microsoft Access installed on their computers. The completed project is available on the O'Reilly web site implemented with Microsoft Access as the GUI. If you are not interested in working on the project from scratch, you can download the project and see how the features were implemented. As a reminder, if you want to open a database and skip the startup options, hold down the shift key while opening the database.

The Project Description

Create an application that will be used to run a small service business. The application needs to store customer information, standard service charges, monthly expenses, billing information, payment information, and a history of customer contact. In addition, the application needs to produce invoices and income statements, and generate marketing letters and letters for past due accounts.

The following screens are required:

- Main Menu
- Customer Information
- Billing Information
- Payment Information
- Contact History
- Services and Charges
- Expense Entry
- Invoices
- Letters
- Income Statements

The application should be flexible enough to allow a non-programmer to create additional letters. In addition, it is important to maintain a history of contact information for customers. It is also a requirement that the standard service charges can be overridden. It is preferred that the standard invoice be in Excel.

Main Menu

For the main menu, I suggest starting with an Access form in Design View that is not connected to a table or query. This menu should open automatically when the database opens, and I suggest setting the startup options to not show the database window.

If you look at the screens being requested, there are generally three categories. The first category is customer information, in which you have the customer contact information, billing information, payment information, and contact history. The second category is company-specific information on services, charges, and expense entry. The expense entry posts to general ledger accounts for expenses, and the customer payments posts to general ledger accounts for income. The third category is for production, including invoices, letters, and income statements.

To divide the main menu into these categories, I suggest using a tab control from the Access control toolbox and having a page for each category. Figure 12-1 shows how this would look. To create the blank form, go to the forms tab in Access, select "Create Form in Design View," and once the form is open, go to View → Form Header/Footer to put a header and footer on the form. Click on the tab control on the control toolbox and click and drag the control onto the form. If the control toolbox is not visible, go to View → Toolbox to see it.

Depending on the defaults on your computer, you might not see three pages on your tab control. If that is the case, you can add pages by right-clicking on a tab and selecting Insert Page from the menu. If you have too many pages, delete some by right-clicking on a tab and selecting Delete Page from the menu.

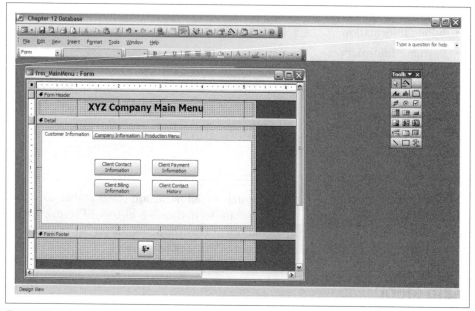

Figure 12-1. An example of using a tab control to break up a main menu into functional areas

To update the name on the tab, right-click on the tab and select Properties from the menu. You change the name shown by updating the caption property. If the caption property is blank, it shows the name of the tab. The caption property is on the Format tab and the name property is on the Other tab.

Put a title on the menu by clicking and dragging a label from the toolbox onto the header. You can also use the command button wizard to put a close button on the footer. When you click and drag a command button onto the form, the wizard comes up automatically. For the main menu, I suggest having the close button actually close the application, rather than just the form. For all other forms, I would have the exit button close only the form.

An additional suggestion that I will make is to get rid of the navigation buttons, dividing lines, and record selectors by going to the Properties dialog for the form and selecting No for each property.

Customer Information

The customer information form is probably most easily created by first creating the table to hold the necessary information and then using the Form Wizard from Access. Without complicating matters too much, your first decision is whether to hold all of the customer information in one table or having it in multiple tables. For example, you can have a table that holds only customer names, along with a unique identifier for the customer. You would also have address information, phone information, and company contacts in separate tables.

That approach is preferable for a number of reasons. First, many companies (and even people) have a number of phone numbers. If you designed a database in the mid-1980s, you would probably have only one phone number. When fax machines became popular, if you did not have a separate table, you would have needed to add a field to your original table to hold a fax number. Now, think about pagers, cell phones, conference call numbers, etc., and you can see how this would cause a lot of design work. If you have a separate table to hold phone information, you can add new phone numbers and new types of phone numbers with no programming. Some programmers disagree with this approach, saying that it makes it difficult to do a mail merge, print information on reports, etc. However, I solve this problem by simply having a checkbox on each phone record to signify whether it is the default phone number. You can do the same thing for addresses and company contacts.

It is rather easy to implement a form that links the separate tables of customer information. First, create simple forms that hold phone numbers, addresses, etc., making sure that you have a field with the ID number from the main customer table in each of the other tables. Next, create your form for the customer information and drag one of the other forms onto the customer information form. Go to the properties of this subform and set the child and master fields to be the ID field from the customer table. This tells Access to show only records related to the current customer.

Here is a tip: if you don't want to show all of the information forms at the same time, have the default show one of them, and have buttons for each subform. For the OnClick event for each button, change the SourceObject property of the subform to be the name of the form that relates to the button. For example, if you have a button to show addresses, and the address form is called frm_Address, your OnClick event would be the following code. The subform on this form is called multiSubForm so that you realize it is designed to show multiple forms. Also, it is best if you keep the size of these forms the same so that it looks clean.

```
Private Sub Command5_Click()
Me.multiSubForm.SourceObject = "frm_Address"
Me.multiSubForm.LinkChildFields = "CustomerID"
Me.multiSubForm.LinkMasterFields = "CustomerID"
End Sub
```

This method lets you use one form to put in all the information. You could also use a tab control and have a subform on each tab, but I like this method better. In the end, you need to decide what works best for you and the end user.

Billing and Payment Information

For billing and payment information, I suggest having a subform for billing information on the customer information form. However, I would make it a separate form, rather than including it with the address, phone, etc. subforms. When a customer pays a bill, have a button on the bill record that, when pressed, opens a form to enter the payment information and links it to the bill record. You could also set up a button on the customer record that allows you to enter a payment not linked to a bill.

Contact History

This functionality would also be best implemented as a subform on a customer information form. The fields on the form would be driven by end user needs, although you probably want to put in the phone number that is called (you would probably get extra points by having a drop-down box that links to the phone numbers for the client), a notes field, a field to hold the name of the person who was called, a field to hold the name of the person making the call, and a field for the date and time of the call. This allows you to create a report showing all calls made to a customer, all calls made on a particular day, or all calls made by a particular employee.

Once you make a few subforms, you see how many uses you have for them. The thing that makes them very nice is that by having the child and master fields, Access automatically put in the ID that links the records. This makes it less likely that you will end up with orphan records (phone records without a customer record, for example).

Services and Charges

How you build this form really depends on how you build the billing form. It is probably best to have a master bill record with a billing ID, customer ID, and date, along with a subform that holds each item, quantity, and default price. Also, have a field to override the price, to meet the requirements requested by the client. If you have that setup on the billing records, the services and charges table is relatively simple. For each type of service provided, have an ID field, the name of the service, the general ledger account that this revenue is booked to, and a default price.

Expense Entry

Because one of the requirements from the client is to produce income statements, you need to track expenses and put them in general ledger accounts. This means that you need a table to hold general ledger accounts; it would also hold the income accounts used in the services and charges table. Have a form that allows you to put in an effective date, a general ledger account, a description, and an amount. Depending on what the client wants, you might also create asset and liability accounts if they use double-entry accounting. For this project, I would just use income and expense. This section obviously requires some accounting knowledge; look at how this is implemented in the sample database if this section is confusing.

Invoices

Generally, you have two options for invoices. The first method has a field on the master bill record that says whether or not an invoice was created. If it was not created, you could add/change items in the bill detail. If it was created, it would be a good idea to lock those fields. I suggest either using a calculated field to show the bill amount, or having a field on the master bill record showing the amount actually billed for the detail. Because you probably want to know what was actually billed, it is best to store that information with a calculated field that lets you see easily whether changes happened to the bill information since the invoice was generated. The invoice form would be relatively simple; have one button to generate an individual invoice by going to a master bill record (you could also have this button on the bill record for the billing information form) and a second button to generate invoices for all unbilled master bill records.

The second method would be to have a bill cycle for customers and have the invoices generate on the bill cycle. This setup works well for something like lawn service, where the service comes three times per month and sends a bill out at the end of the month. You could enter a record in for each time the lawn was serviced, and at the end of the customer's bill cycle, an invoice could be created.

Whichever method you choose, whether you come up with a combination of those methods or one of your own, the general idea is to have an invoice created in Excel. This gives you the option of either creating the entire invoice from scratch or using an Excel workbook as a template. That choice is up to you. From the client's perspective, it is probably best to use a template because this allows them to make changes without additional programming.

Letters

If you remember the Word automation example, it is relatively easy to automate the production of a Word document with data from a database. The best way to implement this is with Form Fields, using the same name for the form field (by setting the bookmark property) as you use in the database. To make your application the most flexible, it is better to use the For Each...Next loop to loop through the form fields on the Word document, rather than all of the fields in the table or query that you use. The reason for this is that you can have fields in the database that you do not want in the letter. Rather than having to creating a procedure for each letter, you can use one procedure for all of them.

The easiest way to implement this is to have a form with two fields and a button. The first field asks for a table or query name (you could also put the names of the tables and/or queries in a combo box), and the second field holds the filename and path of the Word document. When you press the button, the application opens the Word document and a recordset with the table or query selected.

Next, fill in each form field, save the document, and move to the next method to start over again. You could use the same form to send marketing letters, collection letters, service reminders, etc. Create a query that gives you the information you want, and create a Word document with form fields for the data you want to pull in. This is easy to program and also meets the client's need to be able to change the Word document without programming.

Income Statements

This is the most complex of the client's requirements, and requires some understanding of accounting as well as Access and Excel. First, set up a report format, preferably in a table. Next, link the general ledger accounts to lines on your report. Have a query that calculates the net income, a query for a detailed income statement (by general ledger account), and a rolled-up income statement (by summary line). Finally, automate Excel to produce the income statements, and have an Access report show net income. Look at the example database to see how it was implemented. Again, this is one of the more complex requirements, but it is not impossible to follow.

The complexity of producing an income statement is that you need to take into account timing of the general ledger entries, build the tables to produce the income statement while ensuring that every general ledger account is used, and have checks in place to make sure that the net income ties out.

There was a basic income statement example in Chapter 8 that you can refer to while attempting to build this. For this income statement, I suggest putting in ratios to show margin percentage, variance from last month/year/etc., and a separate column to show each expense as a percentage of total expense and each revenue line as a percentage of total revenue. You could also show each as a percentage of net income. Put in number formats, colors, borders, etc. How you go about this affects how you program it.

Probably the easiest way would be to have a form with a begin month/year and an end month/year. Have an option to show the total of the months or a trend on the report and an option as to whether you want a detailed or rolled-up income statement. For both of these options, your best bet is to use an option group with radio buttons for each.

Project Summary

By design, there was not much detail of how to code this project, except for the part about using the tab control that was first introduced here. As stated previously, the completed project is available on the O'Reilly web site with the rest of the code samples. I suggest attempting it first by yourself and comparing how each item is done in the code sample. As long as your application works, there are no right answers for how to accomplish each task. I just think it would be useful for you to see how your solution differs from my recommended solution.

You can learn a lot by looking at how other people solve programming problems. Even if you don't use the same method, often you see something that you can use in other situations. Sometimes when you are confronted with a problem, you create a solution that works, and you later find that someone else was confronted with the same problem and solved it very differently. By seeing how others have solved the problem, you often gain insight into the thought process used in the solution. For example, one person uses an array, while another uses a collection. Both may have very good reasons for their decisions, but understanding how to do both and thinking through the pros and cons of each method allows you to really develop your programming skills.

The last thought to keep in mind is any time you can make your solution table-driven to enable changes without programming, the amount of maintenance required drops, and ultimately customer satisfaction goes up. As you develop your solutions, you should continually ask yourself, "What happens if this changes?" and figure out the best way to allow the change without requiring additional programming. Also, as you develop code that uses tables and code together to solve problems, I suggest that you keep the code and the empty table in an easily accessible place so that you can use it in other applications.

If you built this project from scratch, the best way to determine how you did is to have another person try to use it. See what questions she asks and find out whether you can accomplish it. I've probably learned as much about programming from trying to figure out how to meet a client requirement as I have from learning specific programming concepts in books or classes. Depending on the amount of time that you want to spend working on this, you could also attempt to answer business questions with queries such as past due customers, customers with single purchases, or expenses by month. With those queries, you could create automated form letters, produce graphs, etc.

Now that you have put some of these skills to use, you will likely find many other opportunities to integrate Excel and Access in a work setting. I suggest that each time you do this, you keep the used code in an accessible location so that you can reuse it in the future. Not only will this save you time, it will also give you access to code that has presumably already been tested, so you will know that it works.

Excel Object Model

For most of the programming tasks that you will do while integrating Excel and Access, Access VBA will automate Microsoft Excel. This makes understanding the Excel object model very important. I have broken down the key parts of the Excel object model that have been most useful to me in automation projects. This is not an all-inclusive list of properties and methods, but understanding this core will make the work much easier. See the Excel VBA help file to get more information on all the properties and methods.

Application Object

The Application object contains many properties and methods that can be very useful. In some cases, the collections of objects contained under the Application object also appear in the Workbook and Worksheet objects. When that is relevant, I'll note it in the text. In the examples shown, assume that the following code has already been entered in the VBA module from Access:

```
Dim xlapp as Excel.Application
Set xlapp = New Excel.Application
```

By doing this, the variable xlapp can be used to get the properties and methods discussed below.

Application Object Properties

The Application object's properties include a number of key pieces that provide your automation with a perspective on Excel, similar to the perspective users get through a GUI.

ActiveCell

This property is a range object that references the active cell in the application. If you have multiple workbooks open, and each has multiple worksheets, it refers to the active cell in the active workbook on the active sheet. If you have a range selected on the active worksheet, it refers to the cell in the range currently showing in the Name Box on the formula bar. The property returns a Range object and is read-only.

ActiveChart

This property returns the active embedded chart or chart sheet. If there are no active charts, this property returns Nothing. This property is read-only.

ActivePrinter

The ActivePrinter property returns the name of the active printer; this is the printer that comes up when you go to File → Print on the menu. This is a property that you can read and write. Programming this property is very useful if you know the names of the printers available and you want to print a workbook or worksheet to a specific printer. This could come in handy if you automate Excel reports through Access and want to print reports to different printers. For example, if you work in an organization that has network printers in different locations, you can set code to automatically print different worksheets to each printer. Your best bet to get the exact names of your printers is to print something to the printer, go into the Immediate Window in Excel, and type in:

```
? Application.ActivePrinter
```

This formula gives you the exact name of your printer. The following code sets the current printer to the Microsoft Document Image Writer, if it is an installed printer in the same location.

```
xlapp.ActivePrinter = "Microsoft Office Document Image Writer on Ne00:"
```

ActiveSheet

The ActiveSheet property returns a Sheet object that represents the current active sheet for the application. There is also an ActiveSheet property available as part of the Workbook object that returns the active sheet for that particular workbook. This property is useful to set a variable equal to the active sheet to work with it. If you have a variable called xlws and want it to refer to the active sheet for the application, the following code shows how. The ActiveSheet property is read-only.

```
Set xlws = xlapp.ActiveSheet
```

ActiveWorkbook

The ActiveWorkbook property returns a Workbook object that represents the currently active workbook in Excel. While you will generally work on a specific workbook, this can be useful when you have code working on multiple workbooks. You can set your variable to refer to the currently active workbook; note that if the active workbook changes after you set your variable, the variable still refers to the workbook that was active when it was set. If you have a variable called xlwb and you want to refer to the active workbook, see the following line of code. The `ActiveWorkbook` property is read-only.

```
Set xlwb = xlapp.ActiveWorkbook
```

AddIns

The `AddIns` property is a collection of all of the Add-Ins available to Microsoft Excel. To see all of the Add-Ins available, use an `AddIn` object and a `For Each...Next` loop to cycle through all of them. That may be useful from Excel, but from Access your use for this generally revolves around seeing whether a particular Add-In is installed. For example, the following `If...Then` statement only runs if the Analysis ToolPak is installed.

```
On Error Resume Next
If xlapp.AddIns("Analysis ToolPak").Installed = True Then
  MsgBox xlapp.AddIns("Analysis ToolPak").Name & _
    " is installed", vbInformation
End If
```

You need to have the On Error Resume Next line as the first line because if the particular Add-In is not available on the computer (versus being on the Add-Ins list but not installed), referring to it by title generates an error. It is important that the string needed to bring up the `AddIn` object is in the `Title` Property, which is not the same as the `Name` property. The `Title` property of the `AddIn` object is not documented in Excel or on the object browser, but it is available. Since Add-Ins are referred to by an Index, you can loop through the Add-Ins by going from 1 to the count of the number of Add-Ins. The following code gives you a message box with the title of each `AddIn` object. You need an integer variable called x to use this code.

```
For x = 1 To xlapp.AddIns.Count
MsgBox xlapp.AddIns(x).Title, vbInformation
Next x
```

CalculateBeforeSave

This is a property that you can read and write. Generally, you want this property to be `TRUE`. However, there may be times when you don't want workbooks recalculated before they are saved. In those cases, you can set this property to `FALSE` using the following line of code:

```
xlapp.CalculateBeforeSave = False
```

If you change this property for a particular purpose, be sure to change it back at the end of the code.

CalculateState

This property is a read-only property that tells whether Excel is currently performing calculations. This is useful if you want to wait until all calculations are done before running a portion of code. There are three constants that can be returned (the integer value of the constant is in parenthesis): xlDone (0), xlCalculating (1), and xlPending (2). Generally, you will check that the property is equal to 0, which means that there are no calculations being performed.

Caption

This is a property that you can read and write, which gives you the name on the Title Bar of Excel. You might want to set this if you build an application that you want to show up differently.

DisplayAlerts

This is a property that you can read or write, which returns a Boolean value. If you set it to FALSE, while your VBA code runs, alerts are automatically given the default response.

DisplayFullScreen

This is a property that you can read and write, which returns a Boolean value. Generally, this property is set to TRUE if you need more space to display a report, chart, etc. You also want to have an event programmed that returns the screen back to normal by setting this property to FALSE.

EnableEvents

This is a property that you can read and write, which returns a Boolean value. It is useful if you want to write values into an Excel workbook without worksheet and workbook events firing, such as Change, BeforeSave, etc. I generally use it more from Excel VBA within Excel, but when I use an existing workbook that has code behind events, this is something that I sometimes have to change in Excel.

FileSearch

This property returns a FileSearch object. (Note that the FileSearch object is not an Excel object, but rather an object in the Microsoft Office Object Library. If you automate from Access, make sure that you have the Microsoft Office Object Library selected in Tools → References in the VBA Editor.) Performing a file search is useful if you want to open files meeting certain criteria and perform actions on them. For example, you might want to open and print all Excel files that have a particular string in their name. The following piece of code looks for all Excel files on the C drive with the word "Product" in the filename. You could also search particular directories instead of an entire drive. The FileSearch object returns a FoundFiles Object (also an object in the Microsoft Office Object Library) that you can loop through. In this example, I have a message box come up for each file that was found. However, you can use the filename to open the file or perform any other action you want where the filename and path are needed. As in the previous examples, assume you have a variable named xlapp, which is the Excel Application object.

```
Dim found As Office.FoundFiles
With xlapp.FileSearch
  .NewSearch
  .LookIn = "C:\"
  .SearchSubFolders = True
  .FileType = Office.msoFileTypeExcelWorkbooks
  .Filename = "Product"
  .MatchTextExactly = False
  .Execute
  Set found = .FoundFiles
End With
For x = 1 To found.Count
  MsgBox found.Item(x)
Next x
```

FileDialog

This property returns a FileDialog object that lets the user select files or folders. This example opens a file dialog where you can select more than one file at a time and shows a message box of each file that the user selected. Generally, you will do some type of file operation with each file selected. For this example, you need a reference to the Microsoft Office Object Library.

```
With xlapp.FileDialog(Office.msoFileDialogFilePicker)
  .AllowMultiSelect = True
  .Show
  For x = 1 To .SelectedItems.Count
    MsgBox .SelectedItems(x), vbInformation
  Next x
End With
```

Here is the same example, except that you select a folder. It is important to note that with the folder picker you cannot select multiple folders. So, I could have simply used the number 1 for SelectedItems, but I wanted to use the same code to show you that it works. Using the same code enables you to potentially use a variable for the FileDialog type and use the same code regardless of which type of file dialog you need.

```
With xlapp.FileDialog(Office.msoFileDialogFolderPicker)
  .Show
  For x = 1 To .SelectedItems.Count
    MsgBox .SelectedItems(x), vbInformation
  Next x
End With
```

Here is the same example, except that you select an Excel file, and the `Execute` method is called to actually open the file.

```
With xlapp.FileDialog(msoFileDialogOpen)
  .Filters.Add "Microsoft Excel Files (*.xls)", "*.xls", 1
  .Show
  .Execute
End With
```

Selection

This property returns an object, depending on the object currently selected and is read-only. For example, if a single cell or multiple cells are selected, it will return a Range object. Generally, I use this along with the `Select` method so that I know what is selected. Normally, you set an object equal to `xlapp.Selection` to use the object.

Sheets

This property returns the collection of all sheets in the active workbook. If you want to get a collection of all the sheets in a specific workbook, use this property along with the Workbook object instead. This collection contains Chart Sheets and Worksheets. There are also collections specifically for Charts and Worksheets if you only want to see one type. The following code brings up a message box with the name of each worksheet in the active workbook:

```
For x = 1 To xlapp.Sheets.Count
  MsgBox xlapp.Sheets(x).Name, vbInformation
Next x
```

Generally, use either the Charts or Worksheets collection. However, there are times when you will want to take certain actions on all sheets. You can also use a single line such as `xlapp.Sheets.PrintOut` to print all of the sheets in the active workbook.

ShowWindowsInTaskbar

This is a property that you can read and write, which returns a Boolean value. If you set it to FALSE, it does not show the name of each open Excel document in the task bar. Instead, you access the open files through the Windows menu option. If you set this property to TRUE, you have each open file separately in the taskbar. Setting this property to FALSE is useful if you will have several files open at the same time and don't want to clutter the user interface.

UserName

This property gives you the current username and is read-only. If you have certain options that you want to show to particular users, you can use a `Select...Case` statement on the value of the UserName property to do that. However, I don't suggest using this if security is the primary concern. It would be more something to show user preferences. Anyone can create a username, which would be shown by this property, making it easy to defeat this method if it were used for security.

Visible

This is a property that you can read and write, which returns a Boolean value. Use this property to hide the Excel application from the user. This is sometimes nice if you are just automating Excel and saving files and don't need the user to see the result. When doing that, set this property to FALSE after the Excel application object is set to New Excel.Application. However, use this with caution because when errors occur and you exit out of the module, the Excel application is still open but not visible. You can close these instances of Excel by going into the Processes tab on the Task List in Windows and selecting End Process for each Excel instance that you did not want open. I suggest always setting this to visible when in testing mode and having error traps that close the Excel application when errors occur in production mode.

Workbooks

This returns a collection with all of the workbooks currently open. With this collection, you can call methods that Add workbooks, Close workbooks, and Open workbooks among other options. When you automate Excel and want to create a new workbook, set the variable for the workbook equal to xlapp.Workbooks.Add. To open a workbook where you want to hold a reference to the workbook in a variable, use:

```
Dim xlwb As Excel.Workbook
Set xlwb = xlapp.Workbooks.Open("filename.xls")
```

If you just want to open a workbook, you should not put in the parenthesis. That line of code would look like this:

```
xlapp.Workbooks.Open "filename.xls"
```

WorksheetFunction

This property returns a WorksheetFunction object, which allows you to perform a worksheet function on arguments such as variables, individual numbers, ranges, etc. If you set a cell equal to a WorksheetFunction statement, only the value is stored in Excel. If you want to keep the formula in the cell in Excel, use one of the formula properties of the Worksheet object.

Worksheets

This property returns a collection of all the Worksheet objects in the active workbook. This collection exists for each workbook. See the Sheets property for additional information on how to use this property.

Application Object Methods

While there are many methods available in the `Application` object, there are fewer methods as compared to properties that I find useful when automating Excel. However, if you use VBA in Excel directly, there are many methods that I encourage you to evaluate, such as `AddCustomList`, `Goto`, `OnTime`, `OnKey`, `OnUndo`, `Volatile`, and `Wait`. While these methods can be useful, they are less likely to be useful when automating Excel. The following methods are the ones I find most useful.

Calculate, CalculateFull, CalculateFullRebuild

These methods are very similar; they are all used to force a recalculation. The `Calculate` method can be called from the `Application`, `Worksheet`, and `Range` objects. The `CalculateFull` method performs a full calculation of all open workbooks. The `CalculateFullRebuild` method also performs a full calculation of all open workbooks, and it also rebuilds all of the dependencies. The `CalculateFullRebuild` method simulates entering all of the formulas in the workbooks again. The code example below assumes that you have a variable called `xlapp`, which is the Excel `Application` object, does a full calculation, and rebuilds all dependencies.

```
xlapp.CalculateFullRebuild
```

The `CalculateFullRebuild` method is useful if you have custom functions that are not set to be volatile, so you need to force the calculation. By simply calling the `Calculate` method, you do not get the same result. I found that out the hard way when I first began writing custom functions that were called from the worksheet in a formula.

ConvertFormula

There are times when you have a range or a formula that is in one format, and you need to have it in another because a method needs it that way. This method makes those formatting changes. The first code example shows how to change an A1-style range to an R1C1-style range and puts it into a string variable called `formulastr`.

```
Formulastr = xlapp.ConvertFormula("$A$1:$A$6",Excel.xlA1,Excel.xlR1C1)
```

The result of this formula is `R1C1:R6C1`. The next example changes a `Sum` formula in A1-style to a `Sum` formula in R1C1-style.

```
formulastr = xlapp.ConvertFormula("=Sum($A$1:$A$6)", Excel.xlA1, Excel.xlR1C1)
```

The result of this formula is `=SUM(R1C1:R6C1)`.

InchesToPoints

The `InchesToPoints` method is useful when you have properties that need to be set in points (such as margins in page setup) but you know what you want in inches. This method returns a number representing the number of points. The following code example prints the number of points that are equivalent to two inches in the immediate window.

```
Debug.Print xlapp.InchesToPoints(2)
```

The result of this method is 144.

Quit

This method is used to close down the Excel application instance. The code would look like the following code example:

```
xlapp.Quit
```

Workbook and Worksheet Objects

The majority of the properties and methods that you use will be part of the workbook and worksheet objects. For these properties and methods, I group together related items.

Workbook and Worksheet Properties

Range Objects

There are several properties that return Range objects, and they are part of the Worksheet object. The ones that you use most often are Cells, Columns, Range, and Rows. You saw many of these used in the main text of the book. The code example that I show iterates through all of the cells in a range, one cell at a time, and prints the cell's formula in the Immediate Window.

```
Dim xlapp As Excel.Application
Set xlapp = Application

Dim xlws As Excel.Worksheet
Dim xlrng As Excel.Range
Dim xlcell As Excel.Range
Set xlws = xlapp.ActiveWorkbook.ActiveSheet
Set xlrng = xlws.Range("A1:A10")
For Each xlcell In xlrng.Cells
  Debug.Print xlcell.Formula
Next xlcell
```

Sheet Objects

The Sheet objects are part of the Workbook object. All of the following properties are Sheet object collections: Sheets, Worksheets, and Charts. Use a For Each...Next loop to cycle through the objects. The sheets collection is described in the section on Application objects earlier in this appendix.

QueryTables Property

The QueryTables property is a collection of QueryTable objects in the worksheet. If you remember from the main text, a QueryTable is a table of data on a worksheet that comes from an external data source. The following code cycles through all of the QueryTable objects on a worksheet and refreshes the data.

```
Dim xlapp As Excel.Application
Set xlapp = Application
Dim qry As Excel.QueryTable
Dim xlws As Excel.Worksheet
Set xlws = xlapp.ActiveWorkbook.ActiveSheet
For Each qry In xlws.QueryTables
   qry.Refresh
Next qry
```

Name Property

The Name property refers to the name of the Worksheet and Workbook objects. You can read and write this property when dealing with a worksheet, but it is read-only when dealing with a workbook. When you change the name of the worksheet, it changes what is shown on the tab for the worksheet in the workbook. The Name property of the Workbook object returns the filename without the path.

Names Property

The Names property is the same as the Name property. The Names property is a collection of all the Name objects in a workbook or worksheet. You create names in Excel by going to Insert → Name → Define. The following code prints each of the name objects in the active workbook to the Immediate Window. Use this code when you need to know the actual range that relates to a named range:

```
Dim xlapp As Excel.Application
Set xlapp = Application
Dim xlwb As Excel.Workbook
Dim xlnm As Excel.Name
Set xlwb = xlapp.ActiveWorkbook
For Each xlnm In xlwb.Names
   Debug.Print xlnm.Name & " - " & xlnm.RefersTo
Next xlnm
```

There is also a property called RefersToR1C1 of the Name object that is used if you need to know the range address in R1C1-style notation.

Workbook and Worksheet Methods

PrintOut Method

The PrintOut method refers to the Worksheet and Workbook objects. If you call the method from a Workbook object, it prints the entire workbook. If you call the method from a Worksheet object, it prints only the worksheet.

Copy, Delete, Paste, and PasteSpecial Methods

These methods are part of the Worksheet object. The Copy and Delete methods are also available on many other objects in Excel.

Protect Method

The Protect method applies to both Workbook and Worksheet objects. Call this method to protect an object from changes. The nice part about the Protect method is that when you call it from code, you can protect the object for only the user interface. This enables you to make changes to the object through code without having to unprotect the object.

Excel Object Model Summary

There are many objects, properties, collections, and methods available in the Excel object model that were not covered here. It is probably worth several hours of time just to peruse the Excel Object Model through Microsoft Visual Basic Help or the Object Browser. Search for keywords to determine where the particular property, method, object, or collection is located. Based on where it is located, determine how to access the item. Also, in the help window, you are often given a small snippet of code that demonstrates how to use the item.

I often find very neat ways to code functionality into Excel by finding a method that I didn't know about. Keep in mind that each of the objects, properties, and collections in the Application, Workbook, Worksheet, etc. objects have their own objects, properties, collections, and methods. I also encourage you to check out many of the online resources offered by Microsoft; in Office 2003, the help window can be set to search the online content. Often, you can download examples that you can learn a lot by going into the code. Finally, in the main text of the book, I let you know that by using the Macro Recorder, you can see how to program many items. I just want to reiterate that here because if you know how to do something via the Excel User Interface, you are just the Macro Recorder away from learning how to code the same task.

VBA Basics

This appendix provides a short tutorial on some basic VBA programming structures. Clearly, this isn't designed to teach you everything, and you should be familiar with basic programming concepts, such as variables and objects, but it should give you some information to help you get through the tasks in this book.

Dim and Set Statements

The Dim statement is used to declare a variable and assign it to a particular type. If the variable is an object, use the Set statement to assign an object to the variable. If the variable is not an object, use the variable, an equal sign, and the value. The following code example shows how to declare a variable called xlapp and set it to a new Excel application:

```
Dim xlapp as Excel.Application
Set xlapp = New Excel.Application
```

Loops

There are several types of loops that you can use in VBA. Here are three that I use most often.

For...Next Loop

The For...Next loop is used to go through a set of numbers and execute a block of code through each iteration. By default, VBA increments by 1 each time it comes to a Next statement. However, you can use Step to change the increment. The following example goes from 0 to 10 in increments of 2 and writes the value of the number to the Immediate Window:

```
Dim x As Integer
For x = 0 To 10 Step 2
  Debug.Print x
Next x
```

For Each...Next Loop

This loop cycles through an array or collection. To use this loop, the variable that you use either has to be a type Variant, Object, or a specific type of object (such as Excel.Worksheet). Following is an example of cycling through each item in a collection using a Variant:

```
Dim xColl As Collection
Dim xItm As Variant

Set xColl = New Collection

xColl.Add 2
xColl.Add 10
xColl.Add 15

For Each xItm In xColl
  Debug.Print xItm
Next

Set xColl = Nothing
```

There were several examples in the book of cycling through a collection of objects. Here is an example that you can use in Excel that puts the name of each worksheet and chart sheet in the active workbook into the Immediate Window.

```
Dim xlWs As Excel.Worksheet
Dim xlCs As Excel.Chart

For Each xlWs In ActiveWorkbook.Worksheets
  Debug.Print xlWs.Name & " - Worksheet"
Next xlWs
For Each xlCs In ActiveWorkbook.Charts
  Debug.Print xlCs.Name & " - Chart Sheet"
Next xlCs

Set xlWs = Nothing
Set xlCs = Nothing
```

While Loop

The While loop continues to run a block of code until a condition is met. In the book, you saw this type of loop with a recordset where the code ran until it reached the end of the recordset. I find it interesting to learn more than one way to do something. Here is an example of using a While loop, which performs the same function as the previous For...Next loop above. Also, note that you end a While loop with Wend.

```
Dim x As Integer
x = 0
While x <= 10
  Debug.Print x
  x = x + 2
WendAddIns
```

Loops are one of the most basic features of VBA, and they are critical to performing many automation tasks. There are many examples of loops in the VBA help that comes with Microsoft Office.

With Statement

I find myself using the With statement more and more. Anytime you refer to properties and methods of an object in multiple lines, you can save a lot of effort by using a With statement. The following example uses the With statement on a Worksheet object to change the Name of the worksheet, change the color of the tab for the worksheet, and then select cell A10. When you type this, notice that when you type . at the beginning of each line within the With statement, you get the same type of help that you get if you type . after the variable name. This example should be run in Excel.

```
Dim xlWs As Excel.Worksheet
Set xlWs = Excel.ActiveSheet
With xlWs
   .Name = "Test Sheet"
   .Tab.ColorIndex = 33
   .Range("A10").Select
End With
Set xlWs = Nothing
```

Goto Statement

Generally, avoid the Goto statement when you can. However, there are times when a condition is met and you want to skip down to a line of code. I find the best way to do this is to use a line label, which you create by using a string of characters that begins with a letter and end with a colon. Here is an example that takes input from a user, notifying him and exiting the procedure if a number is entered out of range. Notice that you have to use Exit Sub prior to the line label in this example, or the user would get both messages. However, that is not necessarily the case in all situations. In this example, a simple If statement would work, but I hope that you can see where the Goto statement would be helpful in other situations. As a final note, the code goes to the line label called errln if there is an error or if the number entered is out of range.

```
Dim x As Integer
Dim inpstr As String
On Error GoTo errln
inpstr = InputBox("Enter a number between 1 and 10", "Input Required")
x = CLng(inpstr)

If x < 1 Or x > 10 Then GoTo errln

MsgBox "You entered " & x & " which is between 1 and 10", vbInformation
Exit Sub
errln:
   MsgBox "You entered a number out of range or entered text.", vbInformation
```

Select Case Statement

The Select Case statement is one of the most important in VBA, in my opinion. If you have ever had multiple If conditions that were difficult to write and even more difficult to read in code, it is likely that you could have benefited from a Select Case statement. This statement bascially evaluates a condition once, determines which cases meet the condition, and runs only that code assigned to the first case. Here is an example that takes input from a user and goes through two Select Case statements to give feedback to her.

```
Dim x As String
Dim y As Double
x = InputBox("Enter characters in the box", "Input Required")
Select Case IsNumeric(x)
  Case True
     y = CDbl(x)
     Select Case y
       Case 1 To 10
         MsgBox "Your number was between 1 and 10", vbInformation
       Case 20, 40, 60
         MsgBox "Your number was 20, 40, or 60", vbInformation
       Case Is > 10
         MsgBox "Your number was greater than 10", vbInformation
       Case Else
         MsgBox "Your number was less than 1", vbInformation
     End Select
  Case False
     MsgBox "You did not enter a number", vbInformation
End Select
```

When your run this code, notice that once a condition is met in a Case statement, it exits the statement. You can test this by typing in 20. You get only the message about the number being 20, 40, or 60. Even though that number is also greater than 10, you won't see that message. If you put the Case 20, 40, 60 line after the Case Is > 10 line, it would never run.

If Statements

The If statement is probably one of the most widely used statements. It checks a Boolean value or the value of a Boolean comparison and if it is TRUE, code runs. You can have a single line If statement or a code block ended by End If. One thing I notice is that some people have a Boolean value but they still put a test in to see whether it is TRUE, which is unnecessary. For example, the IsNumeric statement returns a Boolean. Putting in IsNumeric(x) = TRUE is the same as putting in IsNumeric(x). Putting in IsNumeric(x) = False is the same as putting in Not IsNumeric(x). See the following example.

```
Dim x As String
Dim y As Double
x = InputBox("Enter a number", "Input Required")
If IsNumeric(x) Then
    y = CDbl(x)
    If y / 2 = Int(y / 2) Then MsgBox "Number is Even", vbInformation
    If y / 2 <> Int(y / 2) Then MsgBox "Number is Odd", vbInformation
End If
If Not IsNumeric(x) Then MsgBox "You did not enter a number", vbInformation
```

If you are in Excel, you can use the worksheet functions IsEven and IsOdd. However, testing whether a number divided by two is equal to the integer of that result is another way to test whether a number is even.

VBA Summary

There are entire books dedicated to VBA, many of them very good. This appendix has only covered some very basic items that might be helpful to someone who has not had much experience with VBA. Most VBA books focus only on the core language and don't give you much help dealing with objects. Having stated that, mastering the VBA language makes your job of performing automation of other applications much easier.

I strongly suggest that when you use VBA, you use Option Explicit at the top of all your modules. This forces you to declare all variables. While some people consider this to be a pain, it ensures that you get an error message if you misspell a variable. I have helped people find errors that took hours to find that would have been found instantly if variable declaration had been required.

The most important thing to keep in mind is that your main goal is to get a job done with VBA. In most cases, inefficient code outperforms efficient work done by people. In the grand scheme of things, as long as your code works, you are ahead of the game. Other than that, you might get some style points from other people if you do something a certain way.

If you are interested in learning more about the VBA language, I recommend *VB and VBA in a Nutshell: The Language* by Paul Lomax (O'Reilly). The book covers the VBA language very well and is very easy to read.

Index

We'd like to hear your suggestions for improving our indexes. Send email to *index@oreilly.com*.

W

While loop (VBA), 207
wildcards, 107
With statement, 208
Word
    automation, 146–152
        Excel worksheets, embedding in
           documents, 149
    database population from
        forms, 152–155
    form controls, 147
    protected documents, accessing form
        fields in, 152
Workbook and Worksheet objects
    (Excel), 203–205
    methods, 205
        Copy, Delete, Paste, and
           PasteSpecial, 205

        PrintOut, 205
        Protect, 205
    Name property, 204
    Names property, 204
    QueryTables property, 204
    Range objects, 203
    Sheet objects, 203
    Workbooks object, 59–61
    Worksheet object, 2, 61
        column reference, 31

X

XML files
    opening, 110
    saving recordsets as, 108

About the Author

Michael Schmalz works in the financial services industry and also provides consulting services to a variety of industries. He specializes in Microsoft products, particularly the Microsoft Office Suite. Michael graduated with a B.S. in finance from Penn State and lives with his family in Pennsylvania.

Colophon

Our look is the result of reader comments, our own experimentation, and feedback from distribution channels. Distinctive covers complement our distinctive approach to technical topics, breathing personality and life into potentially dry subjects.

The animals on the cover of *Integrating Excel and Access* are common partridges (*perdix cinerea* or *perdix perdix*), one of several species known collectively as the gray partridge. A non-migratory game bird native to Europe, the gray partridge was introduced to North America when its numbers in Europe began to decline, and it is now common in the northern United States and southern Canada. The decline of the gray partridge in Europe is thought to be due to changes in European agricultural practices, such as the use of herbicides, rather than to overenthusiastic hunters.

The gray partridge is a round, plump bird usually between a foot and a foot and a half long. The male has a mottled plumage of gray and brown, highlighted by a cinnamon-red face and throat and a distinctive horeshoe-shaped, chestnut-colored mark on his belly. The female looks similar but is duller in color, and her horseshoe patch may be lighter or smaller than the male's, or it may not show up at all. Once known simply as "the partridge," their name changed when the red-legged partridge became common—the "gray" was then added due to the color of their legs.

Gray partridges live mainly on farmland and feed on grass and seeds, although chicks eat insects for the first few weeks of life. Their breeding season lasts from mid-April to early September, when the female may lay up to 20 eggs in her nest, also known as a clutch, which is usually hidden in a depression in the ground at the base of a hedge or a group of plants. The eggs hatch after almost a month, and both parents tend the chicks together. After the breeding season, they form larger groups called coveys.

Despite the impression given in the holiday song "The Twelve Days of Christmas," gray partridges generally fly close to the ground and do not nest in trees. However, the male red-legged partridge apparently sat in pear trees and was commonly known in folklore to be lascivious, not unlike the way we think of rabbits today. Pear trees were involved in traditional celebrations of Twelfth Night, including wassailing of fruit trees and even fertility rituals, in which a maiden circled a pear tree backward to reveal her future husband's face within its branches. Perhaps these associations eventually helped "the partridge in the pear tree" work his way into the song.

Reba Libby was the production editor and copyeditor for *Integrating Excel and Access*. Ann Atalla proofread the book. Colleen Gorman and Claire Cloutier provided quality control. John Bickelhaupt wrote the index.

Karen Montgomery designed the cover of this book, based on a series design by Edie Freedman. The cover image is a 19th-century engraving from *Cassel's Natural History*. Karen Montgomery also produced the cover layout with Adobe InDesign CS using Adobe's ITC Garamond font.

David Futato designed the interior layout. This book was converted by Keith Fahlgren to FrameMaker 5.5.6 with a format conversion tool created by Erik Ray, Jason McIntosh, Neil Walls, and Mike Sierra that uses Perl and XML technologies. The text font is Linotype Birka; the heading font is Adobe Myriad Condensed; and the code font is LucasFont's TheSans Mono Condensed. The illustrations that appear in the book were produced by Robert Romano, Jessamyn Read, and Lesley Borash using Macromedia FreeHand MX and Adobe Photoshop CS. The tip and warning icons were drawn by Christopher Bing. This colophon was written by Reba Libby.

Better than e-books

Buy *Integrating Excel and Access* and access
the digital edition FREE on Safari for 45 days.

Go to www.oreilly.com/go/safarienabled
and type in coupon code 56J3-KEPK-NFSL-CFKE-JFPJ

Search
thousands of
top tech books

Download
whole chapters

Cut and Paste
code examples

Find
answers fast

Search Safari! The premier electronic reference
library for programmers and IT professionals.

Related Titles from O'Reilly

Windows Users

Access Cookbook, *2nd Edition*

Access 2003 Personal Trainer

Access Database Design & Programming, *3rd Edition*

Excel Annoyances

Excel Hacks

Excel Pocket Guide

Excel 2003 Personal Trainer

Excel: The Missing Manual

Outlook 2000 in a Nutshell

Outlook Pocket Guide

PC Annoyances, *2nd Edition*

PowerPoint 2003 Personal Trainer

QuickBooks 2005: The Missing Manual

Windows XP Annoyances For Geeks

Windows XP Cookbook

Windows XP Hacks, *2nd Edition*

Windows XP Home Edition: The Missing Manual, *2nd Edition*

Windows XP in a Nutshell, *2nd Edition*

Windows XP Personal Trainer

Windows XP Pocket Guide

Windows XP Power Hound

Windows XP Pro: The Missing Manual, *2nd Edition*

Windows XP Unwired

Word Annoyances

Word Hacks

Word Pocket Guide, *2nd Edition*

Word 2003 Personal Trainer

O'REILLY®

Our books are available at most retail and online bookstores.

To order direct: 1-800-998-9938 • *order@oreilly.com* • *www.oreilly.com*

Online editions of most O'Reilly titles are available by subscription at *safari.oreilly.com*

Keep in touch with O'Reilly

Download examples from our books

To find example files from a book, go to: *www.oreilly.com/catalog* select the book, and follow the "Examples" link.

Register your O'Reilly books

Register your book at *register.oreilly.com* Why register your books? Once you've registered your O'Reilly books you can:

- Win O'Reilly books, T-shirts or discount coupons in our monthly drawing.
- Get special offers available only to registered O'Reilly customers.
- Get catalogs announcing new books (US and UK only).
- Get email notification of new editions of the O'Reilly books you own.

Join our email lists

Sign up to get topic-specific email announcements of new books and conferences, special offers, and O'Reilly Network technology newsletters at:

elists.oreilly.com

It's easy to customize your free elists subscription so you'll get exactly the O'Reilly news you want.

Get the latest news, tips, and tools

www.oreilly.com

- "Top 100 Sites on the Web"—PC Magazine
- CIO Magazine's Web Business 50 Awards

Our web site contains a library of comprehensive product information (including book excerpts and tables of contents), downloadable software, background articles, interviews with technology leaders, links to relevant sites, book cover art, and more.

Work for O'Reilly

Check out our web site for current employment opportunities:

jobs.oreilly.com

Contact us

O'Reilly Media, Inc.
1005 Gravenstein Hwy North
Sebastopol, CA 95472 USA
Tel: 707-827-7000 or 800-998-9938
    (6am to 5pm PST)
Fax: 707-829-0104

Contact us by email

For answers to problems regarding your order or our products:
order@oreilly.com

To request a copy of our latest catalog:
catalog@oreilly.com

For book content technical questions or corrections: **booktech@oreilly.com**

For educational, library, government, and corporate sales: **corporate@oreilly.com**

To submit new book proposals to our editors and product managers:
proposals@oreilly.com

For information about our international distributors or translation queries:
international@oreilly.com

For information about academic use of O'Reilly books:
adoption@oreilly.com
or visit:
academic.oreilly.com

For a list of our distributors outside of North America check out:
international.oreilly.com/distributors.html

Order a book online

www.oreilly.com/order_new

Our books are available at most retail and online bookstores.
To order direct: 1-800-998-9938 • *order@oreilly.com* • *www.oreilly.com*
Online editions of most O'Reilly titles are available by subscription at *safari.oreilly.com*